CSS Master, 2nd Edition

Copyright © 2018 SitePoint Pty. Ltd.

Product Manager: Simon Mackie
Technical Editor: Rachel Andrew
English Editor: Ralph Mason
Cover Designer: Alex Walker

Notice of Rights

Notice of Liability

Trademark Notice

Published by SitePoint Pty. Ltd.
48 Cambridge Street Collingwood
VIC Australia 3066
Web: www.sitepoint.com
Email: books@sitepoint.com
ISBN 978-0-6483315-0-6 (print)
ISBN 978-1-925836-16-5 (ebook)
Printed and bound in the United States of America

About Tiffany B. Brown

Tiffany B. Brown is a freelance web developer based in Los Angeles, California. She has worked on the web for nearly two decades with a career that includes media companies, marketing agencies, and government.

Brown was also part of the Digital Service Team at the United States Department of Veterans Affairs, the United States Digital Service, and the Opera Software Developer Relations team.

Brown is also a co-author of SitePoint's *Jump Start: HTML 5,* and has contributed to Dev.Opera, A List Apart, SitePoint.com, and Smashing Magazine.

About SitePoint

SitePoint specializes in publishing fun, practical, and easy-to-understand content for web professionals. Visit http://www.sitepoint.com/ to access our blogs, books, newsletters, articles, and community forums. You'll find a stack of information on JavaScript, PHP, Ruby, mobile development, design, and more.

Table of Contents

Preface

CSS has grown from a language for formatting documents into a robust language for designing web applications. Its syntax is easy to learn, making CSS a great entry point for those new to programming. Indeed, it's often the second language that developers learn, right behind HTML.

However, the simplicity of CSS syntax is deceptive. It belies the complexity of the box model, stacking contexts, specificity, and the cascade. It's tough to develop interfaces that work across a variety of screen sizes and with an assortment of input mechanisms. CSS mastery lies in understanding these concepts and how to mitigate them.

Mastering CSS development also means learning how to work with new tools such as linters and optimizers. Linters inspect your code for potential trouble spots. Optimizers improve CSS quality, and reduce the number of bytes delivered to the browser. And of course, there's the question of CSS architecture: which selectors to use, how to modularize files, and how to prevent selector creep.

CSS has also grown in its capabilities. Until recently, we had to use clunky methods such as float, or weighty JavaScript libraries, to create the kinds of layouts that are now possible with the Flexbox, multicolumn, and Grid layout modules. Three-dimensional effects were impossible—or required images—before the rise of CSS transforms. Now we even have support for variables.

What's Changed in This Edition?

The second edition of a book may be tougher to write than a first edition. You have to determine what to keep, what to remove, and what to update. Much has changed in the three years since *CSS Master* was first published.

Preprocessors and post-processors are less relevant today. Browser vendors have abandoned vendor prefixes. Variables can be replaced by custom properties. As a result, we won't discuss them in this edition.

CSS Grid layout, on the other hand, was considered leading edge in the last edition. It's now widely supported and fully included in this one. This edition also includes introductions to writing modes, and box alignment—two CSS modules that interact with and affect Grid, multicolumn, and Flexbox layouts.

Something else that's changed: web users receive browser updates far more frequently, and there are more flavors of WebKit than before. Trying to keep up with each of these versions is a special kind of folly. So you'll notice there are no browser support charts in this edition.

It's still a fascinating time to be a front-end developer. My hope is that you'll come away from this book with a better sense of how CSS works and how to write it well.

Who Should Read This Book?

This book is for intermediate-level CSS developers, as it assumes a fair amount of experience with HTML and CSS. No time is spent covering the basics of CSS syntax. Coverage of CSS concepts such as the box model and positioning are included to illuminate tricky concepts for the experienced developer, but this coverage is not meant as an introduction for beginners. Experience with JavaScript is helpful, but not necessary.

Conventions Used

You'll notice that we've used certain typographic and layout styles throughout this book to signify different types of information. Look out for the following items.

Code Samples

Code in this book is displayed using a fixed-width font, like so:

```
<h1>A Perfect Summer's Day</h1>
<p>It was a lovely day for a walk in the park.
The birds were singing and the kids were all back at school.</p>
```

Where existing code is required for context, rather than repeat all of it, ⋮ will be displayed:

```
function animate() {
    ⋮
new_variable = "Hello";
}
```

Some lines of code should be entered on one line, but we've had to wrap them because of page constraints. An ↪ indicates a line break that exists for formatting purposes only, and should be ignored:

```
URL.open("http://www.sitepoint.com/responsive-web-
↪design-real-user-testing/?responsive1");
```

Tips, Notes, and Warnings

Hey, You!

Tips provide helpful little pointers.

Ahem, Excuse Me ...

Notes are useful asides that are related—but not critical—to the topic at hand. Think of them as extra tidbits of information.

Make Sure You Always ...

... pay attention to these important points.

Watch Out!

Warnings highlight any gotchas that are likely to trip you up along the way.

Supplementary Materials

- https://github.com/spbooks/csspro2 is the book's code archive, which contains code examples found in the book, plus game library that we'll build in the book.
- https://www.sitepoint.com/community/ are SitePoint's forums, for help on any tricky problems.
- **books@sitepoint.com** is our email address, should you need to contact us to report a problem, or for any other reason.

CSS Architecture and Organization

Chapter

1

If you've ever worked on a CSS codebase of any size—or even a small codebase with multiple developers—you'll have realized how difficult it is to create CSS that's predictable, reusable, and maintainable without being bloated. With added developers often comes added complexity: longer selectors, colliding selectors, and larger CSS files.

In this chapter, we'll explore CSS architecture and organization. First up: file organization. We'll take a look at strategies for managing CSS across projects, or as part of your own CSS framework.

Then we'll look at *specificity*. It's a frequent pain point for CSS development, especially for teams. **Specificity** is the means by which browsers decide which declarations to apply. If you've ever wondered why all of the buttons on your site are green when you wanted some of them to be orange, this section is for you. We'll discuss how to calculate selector specificity, and choose selectors that maximize reusability while minimizing the number of characters you'll need.

Finally, we'll discuss some guidelines and methodologies for writing CSS. These rules make it easier to avoid selector-naming collisions and overly specific selectors—the kinds of issues that arise when working within teams.

File Organization

Part of a good CSS architecture is file organization. A monolithic file is fine for solo developers or very small projects. For large projects—sites with multiple layouts and content types, or multiple brands under the same design umbrella—it's smarter to use a modular approach and split your CSS across multiple files.

Splitting your CSS across files makes it easier to parcel tasks out to teams. One developer can work on typography-related styles, while another can focus on developing grid components. Teams can split work sensibly and increase overall productivity.

So what might a good file structure that splits the CSS across files look like? Here's a structure that's similar to one that I've used in projects:

- *typography.css* : font faces, weights, line heights, sizes, and styles for headings and body text
- *forms.css* : styles for form controls and labels
- *lists.css* : list-specific styles
- *tables.css* : table-specific styles
- *accordion.css* : styles for the accordion component
- *cards.css* : styles for the card component

CSS frameworks such as <u>Foundation</u>[1] and <u>Bootstrap</u>[2] use a similar approach. Both become quite granular, with separate files for progress bars, range inputs, close buttons, and tooltips. That granularity allows developers to include only the components they need for a project.

The details of how you split your CSS will depend on your own preferences and practices. If your workflow includes a pre-processor such as Sass or Less, these would be partials with a `.scss` or `.less` extension. You may also add a `_config.scss` or `_config.less` file that contains color and font variables.

Or perhaps you have a more component-centric workflow, as with the pattern-library tool <u>Fractal</u>[3], or JavaScript frameworks like <u>React</u>[4] and <u>Vue.js</u>[5]. You might instead opt for a single `base.css` or `global.css` file that smooths out browser differences, and use a separate CSS file for each pattern or component.

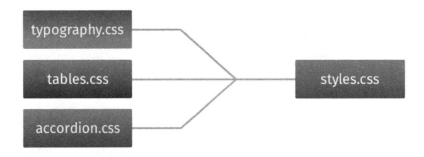

1-1. In many cases, you'll want to combine these smaller files into one larger bundle

Something to avoid: organizing your CSS by page or view. Page-centric approaches encourage repetitious code and design inconsistencies; you probably don't need both `.contact-page label` and `.home-page label` rulesets. Instead, try to find common patterns or components in your site's design, and build your CSS around them.

Using multiple files during site development doesn't necessarily mean you'll use multiple files in production. In most cases, you'll want to optimize CSS delivery by concatenating files, and separating critical from non-critical CSS. We discuss optimization techniques in the chapter _Debugging and Optimization_.

---

[1] https://foundation.zurb.com/
[2] https://getbootstrap.com/
[3] https://fractal.build/
[4] https://reactjs.org/
[5] https://vuejs.org/

File organization is just one aspect of CSS architecture. Despite its position in this chapter, it's actually the least important aspect. In my experience, most CSS architecture problems arise from selector choice and specificity. We'll discuss how to avoid these issues in the next section.

Specificity

A common observation, particularly from developers who are coming to CSS from more traditional programming languages, is this: *CSS has a global scope.* In other words, using `button` as a selector applies those declarations to every `<button>` element, whether that was intended or not.

Where this begins to go awry is when we try to solve the "global" problem by using longer selectors—for example, changing `button` to `form button` or `a` to `#content a`. As your site or application adds more patterns and features, however, you may find yourself in a selectors arms race. You may add a `form.location-search button` selector to override `form button` or `#content .sidebar a` to override `#content a`.

The "global" nature of CSS is really an issue of *specificity* and the cascade in *Cascading* Style Sheets. Although it may seem arbitrary at first, CSS has well-defined rules for determining what declarations to apply. Understanding specificity may be what separates good CSS developers from CSS masters.

Think of specificity as a score or rank that determines which style declarations are applied to an element. The universal selector (`*`) has a low degree of specificity. ID selectors have a high degree. Descendant selectors such as `p img` and child selectors such as `.panel > h2` are more specific than type selectors such as `p` , `img` , or `h1` . Class names fall somewhere in the middle.

Higher-specificity selectors are higher priority selectors. Declarations attached to high specificity selectors are the what the browser ultimately applies.

Calculating exact specificity values seems tricky at first. As explained in the <u>Selectors Level 3</u>[6] specification, you need to:

- count the number of ID selectors in the selector (= A)
- count the number of class selectors, attribute selectors, and pseudo-classes in the selector (= B)

[6.] https://drafts.csswg.org/selectors-3/#specificity

count the number of type selectors and pseudo-elements in the selector (= C)

ignore the universal selector

If you're like me, you may have to stare at these rules for a while before they make sense.

A, B, and C combine to form a final specificity value. ID selectors such as `#foo` have a specificity of 1,0,0—that's one ID selector, and no class or type selectors. Attribute selectors, such as `[type=email]` and class selectors such as `.story` have a specificity of 0,1,0. Adding a pseudo-class such as `:first-child` (for example, `.story:first-child`) gives us a specificity of 0,2,0. But using a simple type or element selector such has `h1` or `p` only gives us a specificity of 0,0,1. Pseudo-elements such as `::before` and `::after` are as specific as type selectors (0,0,1).

 Learning More About Specificity

Keegan Street's <u>Specificity Calculator</u>[7] and Joshua Peek's <u>CSS Explain</u>[8] are helpful for learning about and calculating selector specificity.

When two selectors are equally specific, the cascade kicks in, and the last rule wins. Here's an example:

```
a:link {
    color: #369;
}
a.external {
    color: #f60;
}
```

Both `a:link` and `a.external` have a specificity value of 0,1,1—zero ID selectors, one class or pseudo-class, and one type (or element) selector. However, the `a.external` ruleset follows the `a:link` ruleset. As a result, `a.external` will take precedence. In this case, most of our links will be cadet blue. But those with `class="external"` will be orange.

Complex and combinator selectors, of course, give us higher specificity values. Consider the following CSS:

---

7. http://specificity.keegan.st/
8. http://josh.github.io/css-explain/

```
ul#story-list > .book-review {
    color: #0c0;
}
#story-list > .book-review {
    color: #f60;
}
```

Although these rulesets look similar, they aren't the same. The first selector, `ul#story-list > .bookreview`, contains a type selector (`ul`), an ID selector, (`#story-list`), and a class selector (`.bookreview`). It has a specificity value of 1,1,1. The second selector, `#story-list > .book-review` only contains an ID and a class selector. Its specificity value is 1,1,0. Even though our `#story-list > .book-review` rule follows `ul#story-list > .bookreview`, the higher specificity of the former means that those elements with a `.book-review` class will be green rather than orange.

Choose Low-specificity Selectors

Err on the side of using low-specificity selectors. They make it easier to reuse your CSS, and they extend patterns in new ways.

Consider the following:

```
button[type=button] {
    background: #333;
    border: 3px solid #333;
    border-radius: 100px;
    color: white;
    line-height: 1;
    font-size: 2rem;
    padding: .5rem 1rem;
}
```

This gives us a charcoal gray button with white text, and rounded ends, as shown in the following image:

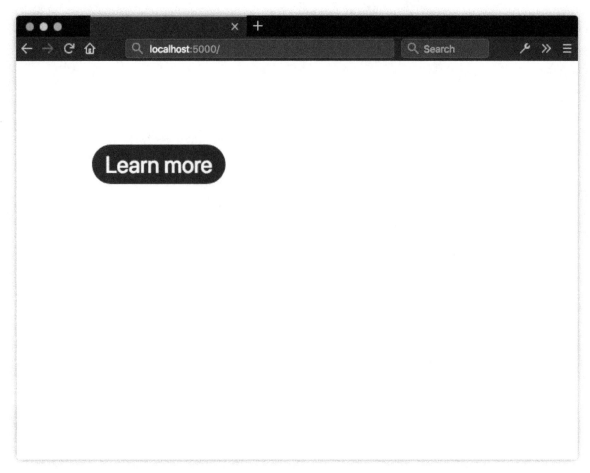

1-2. A charcoal gray button with white text, styled using the CSS above

Let's add some styles for a close button. We'll use a `.close` class, as shown below:

```css
button[type=button] {
    background: #333;
    border: 3px solid #333;
    border-radius: 100px;
    color: white;
    line-height: 1;
    font-size: 2rem;
    padding: .5rem;
}
.close {
    width: 3rem;
    height: 3rem;
    background: #c00;
    border: 0;
    border-bottom: 5px solid #c00;
    font-size: 3rem;
```

```
    line-height: 0;
    padding: 0;
}
```

Now we have two charcoal gray buttons with white text and rounded ends:

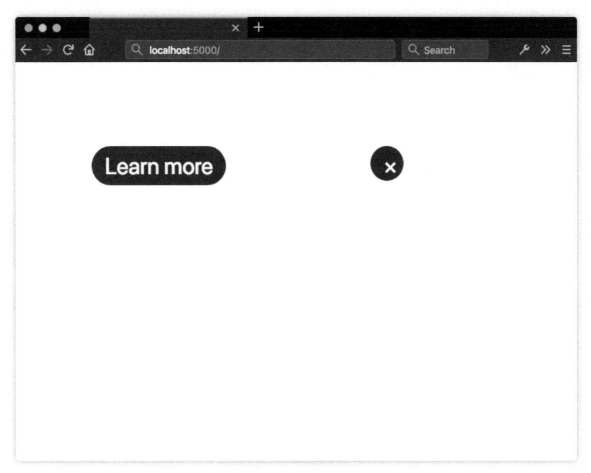

1-3. Our second button inherits unintended styles from button[type=button]

What's happening? Our `button[type=button]` selector has a specificity of 0,1,1. However, `.close` is a class selector. Its specificity is only 0,1,0. As a result, most of our `.close` rules do not get applied to `<button type="button" class="close">` .

We can ensure that our `.close` styles are applied by either:

- changing `.close` to `button[type=button].close`
- making `button[type=button]` less specific

The second option adds fewer bytes, so that's what we'll use:

```css
[type=button] {
    background: #333;
    border: 3px solid #333;
    border-radius: 100px;
    color: white;
    line-height: 1;
    font-size: 2rem;
    padding: .5rem;
}
.close {
    width: 3rem;
    height: 3rem;
    background: #c00;
    border: 0;
    border-bottom: 5px solid #c00;
    font-size: 3rem;
    line-height: 0;
}
```

Changing the specificity of our selector leaves us with our intended result:

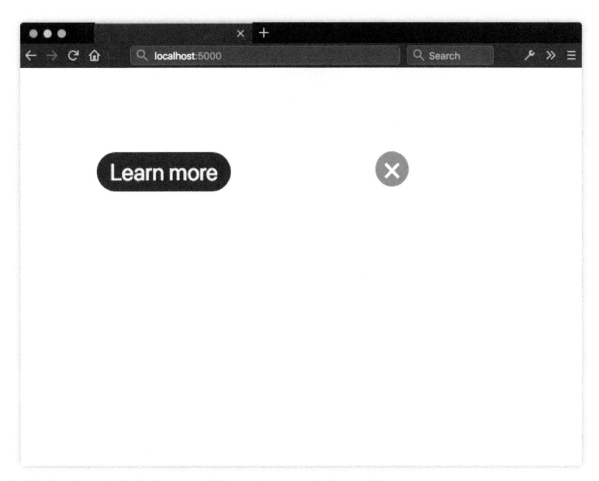

1-4. Declarations attached to lower-specificity selectors are easier to override

Avoid Chaining Class Selectors

Another way to minimize specificity is to avoid chaining class selectors. Selectors such as
.message.warning have a specificity of 0,2,0. Higher specificity means they're hard to override.
What's more, chaining classes may cause side effects. Here's an example:

```
.message {
    background: #eee;
    border: 2px solid #333;
    border-radius: 1em;
    padding: 1em;
}
.message.error {
    background: #f30;
    color: #fff;
}
.error {
```

```
    background: #ff0;
    border-color: #fc0;
}
```

Using `<p class="message">` with this CSS gives us a nice gray box with a dark gray border:

> A message.

1-5. The visual effect of our .message selector.

Using `<p class="message error">`, however, gives us the background of `.message.error` and the border of `.error` shown below.

> An error occurred.

1-6. The visual effect of using .message.error as a selector.

The only way to override a chained class selector is to use an even more specific selector. To be rid of the yellow border, we'd need to add a class name or type selector to the chain: `.message.warning.exception` or `div.message.warning`. It's more expedient to create a new class instead.

If you do find yourself chaining selectors, go back to the drawing board. Either the design has inconsistencies, or you're chaining prematurely in an attempt to prevent problems you don't have. The maintenance headaches you'll prevent and the reusability you'll gain are worth it.

Avoid Using `id` Selectors

HTML only allows each identifier (that is, an `id` attribute) to be used once per document. As a result, rulesets that use `id` selectors are hard to repurpose. Doing so typically involves using a list of `id` selectors—for example, `#sidebar-feature, #sidebar-sports`, and so on.

Identifiers also have a high degree of specificity, so we'll need longer selectors to override declarations. In the CSS that follows, we need to use `#sidebar.sports` and `#sidebar.local` to override the background color of `#sidebar`:

```
#sidebar {
    float: right;
    width: 25%;
    background: #eee;
```

```
}
#sidebar.sports  {
    background: #d5e3ff;
}
#sidebar.local {
    background: #ffcccc;
}
```

Switching to a class selector, such as `.sidebar`, lets us simplify our selector:

```
.sidebar {
    float: right;
    width: 25%;
    background: #eee;
}
.sports  {
    background: #d5e3ff;
}
.local {
    background: #ffcccc;
}
```

As well as saving us a few bytes, our `.sports` and `.local` rulesets can now be added to other elements.

Using an attribute selector such as `[id=sidebar]` lets us get around the higher specificity of an identifier. Though it lacks the reusability of a class selector, the low specificity means that we can avoid selector chaining.

 When You Want Higher Specificity

> In some circumstances, you might *want* the higher specificity of an `id` selector. For example, a network of media sites might wish to use the same navigation bar across all of its web properties. This component must be consistent across sites in the network, and should be hard to restyle. Using an `id` selector reduces the chances of those styles being accidentally overridden.

Let's discuss a selector such as `#main article.sports table#stats tr:nth-child(even) td:last-child`. Not only is it absurdly long, but with a specificity of 2,3,4, it's also not reusable. How many *possible* instances of this selector can there be in your markup?

Let's make this better. We can immediately trim our selector to `#stats tr:nth-child(even)` `td:last-child` . It's specific enough to do the job. An even simpler approach: use a class name such as `.total` . It's a much shorter selector, and those styles aren't limited to `#stats` tables.

Minimize Nesting When Using a Preprocessor

Overly long, highly specific selectors are often caused by nested rulesets. Both Sass and Less support nested ruleset syntax, which is useful for grouping related styles and saving keystrokes. Take, for example, the following CSS:

```
article {
    margin: 2em auto;
}
article p {
    margin: 0 0 1em;
    font-family: 'Droid Serif','Liberation Serif',serif;
}
```

In both Less and Sass, we can rewrite this to take advantage of nesting:

```
article {
    margin: 2em auto;
    p {
        margin: 0 0 1em;
        font-family: 'Droid Serif','Liberation Serif',serif;
    }
}
```

This gives us a descendant selector, and the output will match the standard CSS above.

It's also possible to nest a ruleset inside a nested ruleset. Take a look at this example:

```
nav {
    > ul {
        height: 1em;
        overflow: hidden;
        position: relative;

        &::after {
            content: ' ';
            display: block;
            clear: both;
        }
    }
}
```

Here we've nested styles for `::after` inside a declaration block for `ul`, which itself is nested inside a `nav` declaration block. When compiled, we end up with the following CSS:

```css
nav > ul {
    height: 1em;
    overflow: hidden;
    position: relative;
}
nav > ul::after {
    content: ' ';
    display: block;
    clear: both;
}
```

So far, so good. Our selectors aren't terribly long or specific. Now let's look at a more complex example of nesting:

```css
article {
    color: #222;
    margin: 1em auto;
    width: 80%;

    &.news {
        h1 {
            color: #369;
            font-size: 2em;

            [lang]{
                font-style: italic;
            }
        }
    }
}
```

That doesn't seem too egregious, right? Our `[lang]` selector is only four levels deep. Well, take a look at our compiled CSS output:

```css
article {
    color: #222;
    margin: 1em auto;
    width: 80%;
}
```

```
article.news h1 {
    color: #369;
    font-size: 2em;
}
article.news h1 [lang] {
    font-style: italic;
}
```

Uh-oh! Now we have a couple of high-specificity selectors: `article.news h1` and `article.news h1[lang]`. They use more characters than necessary, and require longer and more specific selectors to override them. Mistakes like this can swell the size of our CSS when repeated across a codebase.

Neither Less nor Sass has a hard limit on how deeply rulesets can be nested. A good rule of thumb: avoid nesting your rulesets by more than three levels. Less nesting results in lower specificity and CSS that's easier to maintain.

Use Type and Attribute Selectors with Caution

It's good to keep specificity low, but be careful about the selectors you use to accomplish that. Type and attribute selectors can be the most bothersome.

Type selectors are element selectors such as `p`, `button`, and `h1`. Attribute selectors include those such as `[type=checkbox]`. Again, style declarations applied to these selectors will be applied to every such element across the site. Here's an example:

```
button {
    background: #FFC107;
    border: 1px outset #FF9800;
    display: block;
    font: bold 16px / 1.5 sans-serif;
    margin: 1rem auto;
    width: 50%;
    padding: .5rem;
}
```

This seems innocuous enough. But what if we want to create a button that's styled differently? Let's style a `.close` button that will be used to close dialog modules:

```
<section class="dialog">
    <button type="button" class="close">Close</button>
</section>
```

Markup Choices

We're using *section* here instead of the *dialog* element, because support for *dialog* is largely limited to Chromium-based browsers. Firefox's support is incomplete, and only available when the user has changed their configuration settings.

Now we need to write CSS to override every line that we don't want to inherit from the *button* ruleset:

```css
.close {
    background: #e00;
    border: 2px solid #fff;
    color: #fff;
    display: inline-block;
    margin: 0;
    font-size: 12px;
    font-weight: normal;
    line-height: 1;
    padding: 5px;
    border-radius: 100px;
    width: auto;
}
```

We'd still need many of these declarations to override browser defaults, but what if we scope our *button* styles to a *.default* class instead? We can then drop the *display*, *font-weight*, *line-height*, *margin*, *padding*, and *width* declarations from our *.close* ruleset. That's a 23% reduction in size:

```css
.default {
    background: #FFC107;
    border: 1px outset #FF9800;
    display: block;
    font: bold 16px / 1.5 sans-serif;
    margin: 1rem auto;
    width: 50%;
    padding: .5rem;
}
.close {
    background: #e00;
    border: 2px solid #fff;
    color: #fff;
    font-size: 12px;
    padding: 5px;
    border-radius: 100px;
}
```

```
}
```

Just as importantly, avoiding type and attribute selectors reduces the risk of styling conflicts. A developer working on one module or document won't inadvertently add a rule that creates a side effect in another module or document.

These selectors are perfectly okay for resetting and normalizing default browser styles. It's best to avoid them otherwise. Class-name selectors will help you avoid many of these problems.

Choosing What to Name Things

When choosing class-name selectors, use *semantic* class names.

When we use the word **semantic**, we mean *meaningful*. Class names should describe what the rule does or the type of content it affects. Ideally, we want names that will endure changes in the design requirements. Naming things is harder than it looks.

Here are examples of what not to do: `.red-text`, `.blue-button`, `.border-4px`, `.margin10px`. What's wrong with these? They're too tightly coupled to the existing design choices. Using `class="red-text"` to mark up an error message does work. But what happens if the design changes and error messages become black text inside orange boxes? Now your class name is inaccurate, making it tougher for you and your colleagues to understand what's happening in the code.

A better choice in this case is to use a class name such as `.alert`, `.error`, or `.message-error`. These names indicate how the class should be used and the kind of content (error messages) that they affect.

 More on Architecture

> Philip Walton discusses these and other rules in his article "CSS Architecture[9]". I also recommend Harry Roberts' site CSS Guidelines[10] and Nicolas Gallagher's post "About HTML Semantics and Front-end Architecture"[11] for more thoughts on CSS architecture.

We'll now look at two methodologies for naming things in CSS. Both methods were created to

---

[9]. https://philipwalton.com/articles/css-architecture/
[10]. https://cssguidelin.es/
[11]. http://nicolasgallagher.com/about-html-semantics-front-end-architecture/

improve the development process for large sites and large teams, but they work just as well for teams of one. Whether you choose one or the other, neither, or a mix of both is up to you. The point of introducing them is to help you to think through approaches for writing your own CSS.

Block-Element-Modifier (BEM)

BEM[12], or Block-Element-Modifier, is a methodology, a naming system, and a suite of related tools. Created at Yandex[13], BEM was designed for rapid development by sizable development teams. In this section, we'll focus on the concept and the naming system.

BEM methodology encourages designers and developers to think of a website as a collection of reusable component *blocks* that can be mixed and matched to create interfaces. A **block** is simply a section of a document, such as a header, footer, or sidebar, illustrated below. Perhaps confusingly, "block" here refers to the segments of HTML that make up a page or application.

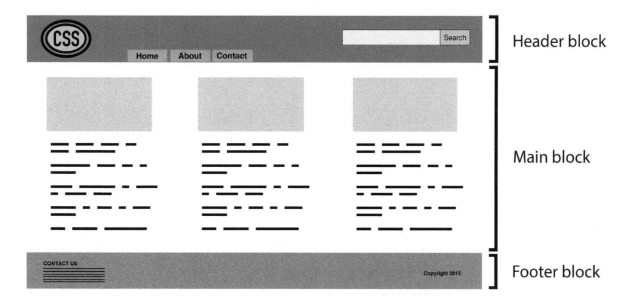

1-7. A home page might have header, main, and footer blocks

Blocks can contain other blocks. For example, a header block might also contain logo, navigation, and search form blocks, as seen below. A footer block might contain a site map block.

[12.] https://en.bem.info/
[13.] https://www.yandex.com/

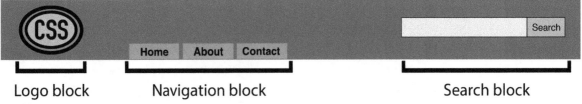

1-8. A header block that contains logo, navigation, and search blocks

More granular than a block is an **element**. As the <u>BEM documentation explains</u>[14]:

> *An element is a part of a block that performs a certain function. Elements are context-dependent: they only make sense in the context of the block they belong to.*

A search form block, for example, contains a text input element and a submit button element, as evident below. (To clarify, we're using "element" in the design element sense rather than the HTML element sense.)

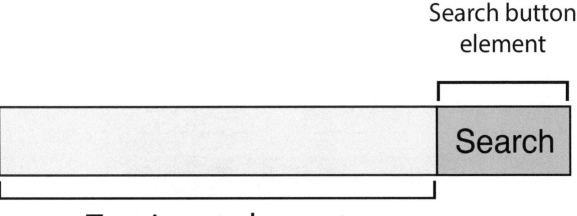

1-9. A search block with text input and submit button elements

A main content block, on the other hand, might have an article-list block. This article-list block might contain a series of article promo blocks. And each article promo block might contain image, excerpt, and "Read more" elements, as presented below.

---

14. https://en.bem.info/methodology/key-concepts/#element

Excerpt element

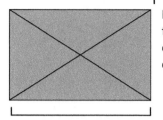

Lorem ipsum dolor sit amet, consectetur adipisicing elit, sed do eiusmod tempor incididunt ut labore et dolore magna aliqua. Ut enim ad minim veniam, quis nostrud exercitation ullamco laboris nisi ut aliquip ex ea commodo consequat.

Read more ▶] Read more element

Image element

1-10. A promotional block for a website article

Together, blocks and elements form the basis of the BEM naming convention. According to the rules of BEM:

- block names must be unique within a project
- element names must be unique within a block
- variations of a block—say, a search box with a dark background—should add a modifier to the class name

Block names and element names are usually separated by a double underscore (`.block__element`). Block and element names are typically separated from modifier names by a double hyphen (for example, `.block--modifier` or `.block__element--modifier`).

Here's what BEM looks like using a search form example:

```
<form class="search">
    <div class="search__wrapper">
        <label for="s" class="search__label">Search for: </label>
        <input type="text" id="s" class="search__input">
        <button type="submit" class="search__submit">Search</button>
    </div>
</form>
```

A variation of this form with a dark background might use the following markup:

```
<form class="search search--inverse">
    <div class="search__wrapper search__wrapper--inverse">
        <label for="s" class="search__label search_label--inverse">Search for: </label>
        <input type="text"  id="s" class="search__input search__input--inverse">
        <button type="submit" class="search__submit search__submit--inverse">Search</button>
    </div>
</form>
```

Our CSS might look like this:

```
.search {
    color: #333;
}
.search--inverse {
    color: #fff;
    background: #333;
}
.search__submit {
    background: #333;
    border: 0;
    color: #fff;
    height: 2rem;
    display: inline-block;
}
.search__submit--inverse {
    color: #333;
    background: #ccc;
}
```

In both our markup and CSS, *search--inverse* and *search__label--inverse* are *additional* class names. They're not replacements for *search* and *search__label* . Class names are the only type of selector used in a BEM system. Child and descendant selectors may be used, but descendants should also be class names. Element and ID selectors are verboten. Enforcing block and element name uniqueness also prevents naming collisions, which can become a problem among teams.

There are several advantages to this approach:

- it's easy for new team members to read the markup and CSS, and understand its behavior
- adding more developers increases team productivity
- consistent naming reduces the possibility of class-name collisions and side effects
- CSS is independent of markup
- CSS is highly reusable

There's a lot more to BEM than can comfortably fit in a section of a chapter. The BEM site describes this methodology in much greater detail, and also features tools and tutorials to get you started. To learn more about the naming convention aspect of BEM, another fantastic resource is Get BEM[15].

---

15. http://getbem.com/introduction/

Atomic CSS

If BEM is the industry darling, Atomic CSS is its rebellious maverick. Named and explained by Thierry Koblentz of Yahoo in his 2013 piece, "<u>Challenging CSS Best Practices[16]</u>," Atomic CSS uses a tight library of class names. These class names are often abbreviated and divorced from the content they affect. In an Atomic CSS system, you can tell what the class name does—but there's no relationship between class names (at least, not those used in the stylesheet) and content types.

Let's illustrate with an example. Below is a set of rules in what we might call a conventional CSS architecture. These rulesets use class names that describe the content to which they apply—a global message box, and styles for "success," "warning," and "error" message boxes:

```css
.msg {
    background-color: #a6d5fa;
    border: 2px solid #2196f3;
    border-radius: 10px;
    font-family: sans-serif;
    padding: 10px;
}
.msg-success {
    background-color: #aedbaf;
    border: 2px solid #4caf50;
}
.msg-warning {
    background-color: #ffe8a5;
    border-color:  #ffc107;
}
.msg-error {
    background-color: #faaaa4;
    border-color: #f44336;
}
```

To create an error message box, we'd need to add both the `msg` and `msg-error` class names to the element's `class` attribute:

```html
<p class="msg msg-error">An error occurred.</p>
```

Let's contrast this with an atomic system, where each declaration becomes its own class:

```css
.bg-a {
    background-color: #a6d5fa;
```

```css
}
.bg-b {
    background-color: #aedbaf;
}
.bg-c {
    background-color: #ffe8a5;
}
.bg-d {
    background-color: #faaaa4;
}
.bc-a{
    border-color: #2196f3;
}
.bc-b {
    border-color: #4caf50;
}
.bc-c {
    border-color:  #ffc107;
}
.bc-d {
    border-color:  #f44336;
}
.br-1x {
    border-radius: 10px;
}
.bw-2x {
    border-width: 2px;
}
.bss {
    border-style: solid;
}
.sans {
    font-style: sans-serif;
}
.p-1x {
    padding: 10px;
}
```

That's a lot more CSS. Let's now recreate our error message component. Using Atomic CSS, our markup becomes:

```html
<p class="bw-2 bss p-1x sans br-1x bg-d bc-d">
    An error occurred.
</p>
```

Our markup is also more verbose. But what happens when we create a warning message component?

```
<p class="bw-2 bss p-1x sans br-1x bg-c bc-c">
    Warning: The price for that item has changed.
</p>
```

Two class names changed: *bg-d* and *bc-d* were replaced with *bg-c* and *bc-c*. We've reused five rulesets. Now, let's create a button:

```
<button type="button" class="p-1x sans bg-a br-1x">Save</button>
```

Hey now! Here we've reused four rulesets and avoided adding any more rules to our stylesheet. In a robust atomic CSS architecture, adding a new HTML component such as an article sidebar won't require adding more CSS (though, in reality, it might require adding a bit more).

Atomic CSS is a bit like using utility classes in your CSS, but taken to the extreme. Specifically, it:

- keeps CSS trim by creating highly granular, highly reusable styles, instead of a ruleset for every component
- greatly reduces specificity conflicts by using a system of low-specificity selectors
- allows for rapid HTML component development once the initial rulesets are defined

However, Atomic CSS is not without controversy.

The Case Against Atomic CSS

Atomic CSS runs counter to just about everything we've been taught on writing CSS. It feels almost as wrong as sticking *style* attributes everywhere. Indeed, one of the major criticisms of the Atomic CSS methodology is that it blurs the line between content and presentation. If *class="fl m-1x"* floats an element to the left and adds a 10px margin, what do we do when we no longer want that element to float left?

One answer, of course, is to remove the *fl* class from our element. But now we're changing HTML. The whole reason behind using CSS is so that markup is unaffected by presentation and vice versa. (We can also solve this problem by removing the *.fl {float: left;}* rule from our stylesheet, although that would affect every element with a class name of *fl*.) Still, updating the HTML may be a small price to pay for trimmer CSS.

In Koblentz's original post, he used class names such as *.M-10* for *margin: 10px* and *.P-10* for *padding: 10px*. The problem with such a naming convention should be obvious. Changing to a margin of 5px or 20px means we'd need to update our CSS *and* our HTML, or risk having class names that fail to accurately describe their effect.

Using class names such as `p-1x`, as done in this section, resolves that issue. The `1x` part of the class name indicates a ratio rather than a defined number of pixels. If the base padding is 5px (that is, `.p-1x { padding: 5px; }`), then `.p-2x` would set 10px of padding. Yes, that's less descriptive of what the class name does, but it also means that we can change our CSS without updating our HTML, and without creating a misleading class name.

An atomic CSS architecture doesn't prevent us from using class names that describe the content *in our markup*. You can still add `.button-close` or `.accordion-trigger` to your code. Such class names are actually preferable for JavaScript and DOM manipulation.

BEM versus Atomic CSS

BEM works best when you have a large number of developers building CSS and HTML modules in parallel. It helps to prevent the kind of mistakes and bugs that are created by sizable teams. It scales well, in part, because the naming convention is descriptive and predictable. BEM isn't *only* for large teams, but it works *really well* for large teams.

Atomic CSS works better when there's a small team or a single engineer responsible for developing a set of CSS rules, with full HTML components built by a larger team. With Atomic CSS, developers can just look at a style guide—or the CSS source—to determine which set of class names they'll need for a particular module.

Know when to go your own way

In practice, your CSS may include a mix of approaches. You may have class names that describe content or components in addition to utility class names that affect layout. If you don't have full control over the markup, as with a CMS, then neither of these approaches may be useful. You may even need to use long and specific selectors to achieve what you want.

Conclusion

After reading this chapter, you should now know:

- how to organize your CSS for easier development and maintenance
- how browsers determine which CSS rules to use
- why class selectors are the most flexible selector for writing scalable, maintainable CSS
- the basics of BEM and Atomic CSS, and the pros and cons of each

In the next chapter, you'll learn what to do when you notice a bug in your CSS. We'll also discuss several tools for making your CSS files smaller.

Debugging and Optimization

Chapter

2

On your road to becoming a CSS master, you'll need to know how to troubleshoot and optimize your CSS. How do you diagnose and fix rendering problems? How do you ensure that your CSS creates no performance lags for end users?

It's also important to ensure code quality. Were you a little too verbose with your comments? Are there too many unused selectors? Are your selectors overly specific in a way that could affect performance?

Knowing which tools to use will help you ensure that your front end works well. In this chapter, we'll look at tools to help you analyze and troubleshoot your CSS. They fall into three categories:

1. debugging tools, such as browser-based developer tools and remote debugging services

2. minification tools

3. code-quality tools

In this chapter, we'll delve into the browser-based developer tools for Chrome, Safari, Firefox, and Microsoft Edge. We'll also explore a few command-line, Node.js-based tools to help you streamline the CSS you put into production.

We'll also look at how to concatenate files, using tools that are available with your computer's operating system.

Browser-based Developer Tools

Most desktop browsers include an element inspector feature that you can use to troubleshoot your CSS. Start using this feature by right-clicking and selecting **Inspect Element** from the menu. Mac users can also inspect an element by clicking the element while pressing the **Ctrl** key. The image below indicates what you can expect to see in Firefox Developer Edition.

2-1. The developer tools of Firefox Developer Edition

In Firefox, Chrome and Safari you can also press **Ctrl** + **Shift** + I (Windows/Linux) or **Cmd** + **Option** + I (macOS) to open the developer tools panel. The screenshot below shows the Chrome developer tools.

2-2. Chrome Developer Tools

While in Microsoft Edge, open developer tools by pressing the **F12** key, as shown in figure 2-3.

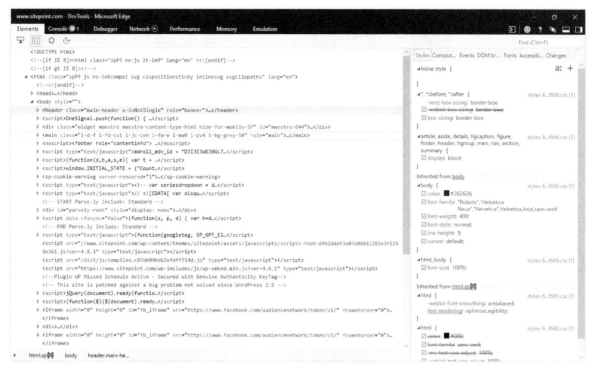

2-3. Microsoft Edge Developer Tools

You can also open each browser's developer tools using the application's menu:

- Microsoft Edge: **Tools > Developer Tools**
- Firefox: **Tools > Web Developer**
- Chrome: **View > Developer**
- Safari: **Develop > Show Web Inspector**

In Safari, you may have to enable the **Develop** menu first by going to **Safari > Preferences… > Advanced** and checking the box next to **Show Develop menu in menu bar**. The view for Safari developer tools is illustrated below.

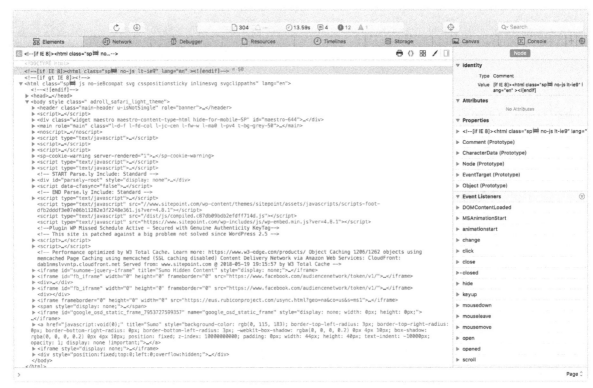

2-4. Safari 11 developer tools

After opening the developer tools interface, you may then need to select the correct panel:

- Microsoft Edge: **DOM Explorer**
- Firefox: **Inspector**
- Chrome: **Elements**
- Safari: **Elements**

You'll know you're in the right place when you see HTML on one side of the panel, and CSS rules on the other.

 Generated Markup

> The markup you'll see in the HTML panel is a representation of the DOM. It's generated when the browser finishes parsing the document and may differ from your original markup. Using **View Source** reveals the original markup, but keep in mind that for JavaScript applications there may not be any markup to view.

Using the Styles Panel

Sometimes an element isn't styled as expected. Maybe a typographical change failed to take, or there's less padding around a paragraph than you wanted. You can determine which rules are affecting an element by using the **Styles** panel of the Web Inspector.

Browsers are fairly consistent in how they organize the **Styles** panel. Inline styles, if any, are typically listed first. These are styles set using the `style` attribute of HTML, whether by the CSS author or programmatically via scripting.

Inline styles are followed by a list of style rules applied via author stylesheets—those written by you or your colleagues. Styles in this list are grouped by media query and/or filename.

Authored style rules precede user agent styles. User agent styles are the browser's default styles. They too have an impact on your site's look and feel.[1]

Properties and values are grouped by selector. A checkbox sits next to each property, letting you toggle specific rules on and off. Clicking on a property or value allows you to change it, so you can avoid having to edit, save and reload.

Identifying Cascade and Inheritance Problems

As you inspect styles, you may notice that some properties appear crossed out. These properties have been overridden either by a cascading rule, a conflicting rule, or a more specific selector, as depicted below.

---

[1] In Firefox, you may have to select the **Show Browser Styles** option in order to view user agent styles. You can find this setting in the **Toolbox Options** panel.

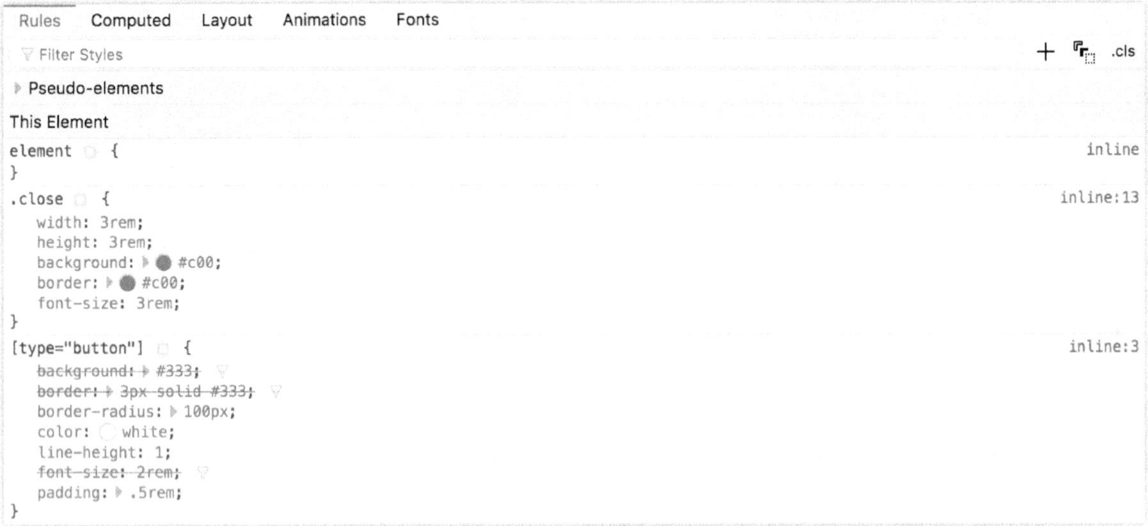

2-5. Identifying property and value pairs that have been superseded by another declaration

In the image above, the *background*, *border*, and *font-size* declarations of the *[type=button]* block are displayed with a line through them. These declarations were overridden by those in the *.close* block, which succeeds the *[type=button]* in our CSS.

Spotting Invalid Properties and Values

You can also use the element inspector to spot invalid or unsupported properties and property values. In Chromium-based browsers, invalid CSS rules both have a line through them and an adjacent warning icon, which can be seen below.

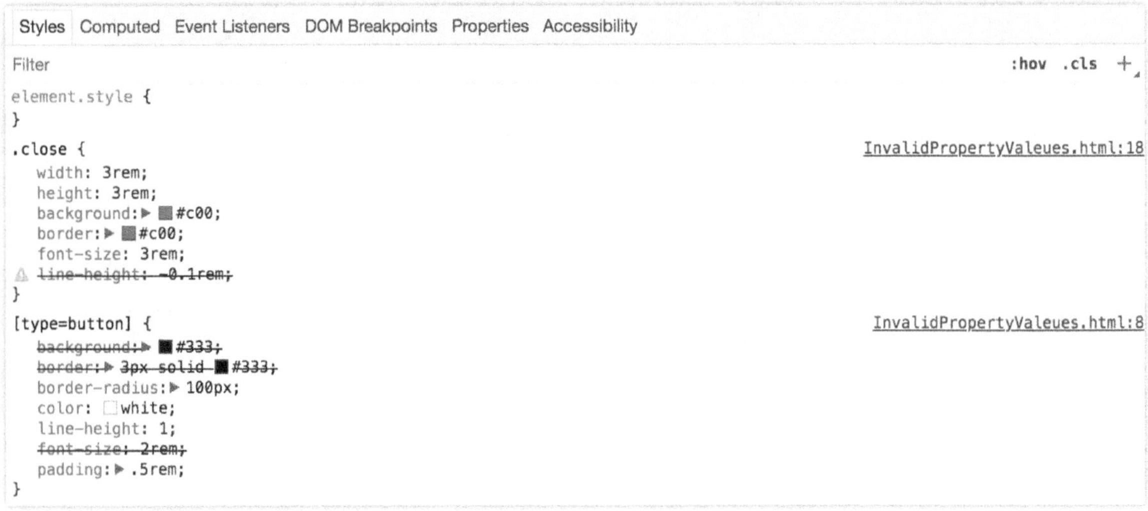

2-6. Spotting an invalid CSS property value using Chrome

Firefox also strikes through invalid or unsupported properties and values. Firefox Developer Edition also uses a warning icon, as shown below. Standard Firefox displays errors similarly, but doesn't include the warning icon.

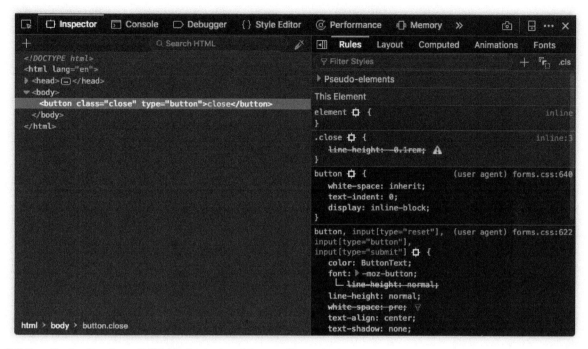

2-7. How Firefox Developer Edition indicates invalid properties and values

In the screenshot below, Safari strikes through unsupported rules with a red line, and highlights them with a yellow background and warning icon.

2-8. An invalid CSS property value in Safari

Microsoft Edge instead uses a wavy underline to indicate unsupported properties or values.

```
Styles    Computed    Events    DOM breakpoints    Fonts    Accessibility    Changes

◢Inline style  {                                                                    a:  +

}
◢ins  {                                                                   10.0.1.103:5000 (33)
    ☑ background:   ▷☐rgba(255, 205, 0, .25);
    ☑ padding:   ▷2px;
       text-decoration-style:  wavy;
}
Inherited from body
◢body  {                                                                  10.0.1.103:5000 (7)
    ☑ font:   ▷16px / 1.5 sans-serif;
}
```

2-9. An unsupported CSS property value in Microsoft Edge

When it comes to basic debugging and inheritance conflicts, whichever browser you choose doesn't matter. Familiarize yourself with all of them, however, for those rare occasions when you need to diagnose a browser-specific issue.

Debugging Responsive Layouts

On-device testing is always best. During development, however, it's helpful to simulate mobile devices with your desktop browser. All major desktop browsers include a mode for responsive debugging.

Chrome

Chrome offers a device toolbar feature as part of its developer toolkit. To use it, click the device icon (pictured below) in the upper-left corner, next to the **Select an element** icon.

2-10. Chrome's Responsive Design Mode icon

Device mode lets you mimic several kinds of Android and iOS devices, including older devices such as the iPhone 5 and Galaxy S5. Device mode also includes a network throttling feature for approximating different network speeds, and the ability to simulate being offline.

Firefox

In Firefox, the equivalent mode is known as **Responsive Design Mode**. Its icon resembles early iPods. You'll find it on the right side of the screen, in the developer tools panel, as shown below.

2-11. Firefox's Responsive Design Mode icon

In responsive mode, you can toggle between portrait and landscape orientations, simulate touch events, and capture screenshots. Like Chrome, Firefox also allows developers to simulate slow connections via throttling.

Microsoft Edge

Microsoft Edge makes it possible to mimic Windows mobile devices—such as the Surface—with its **Emulation** tab. Select **Windows Phone** from the **Browser profile** menu, as shown below.

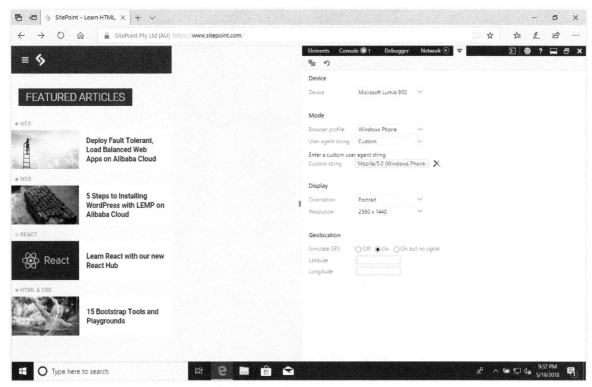

2-12. SitePoint.com using Microsoft Edge's device emulation mode

In addition to mimicking orientation and resolution, emulation mode enables you to test geolocation features. However, you can't use its emulation mode to simulate network conditions.

Safari

Safari's Responsive Design Mode is in its developer toolkit. It's similar to Emulation Mode in Firefox, but adds the ability to mimic iOS devices, as illustrated below.

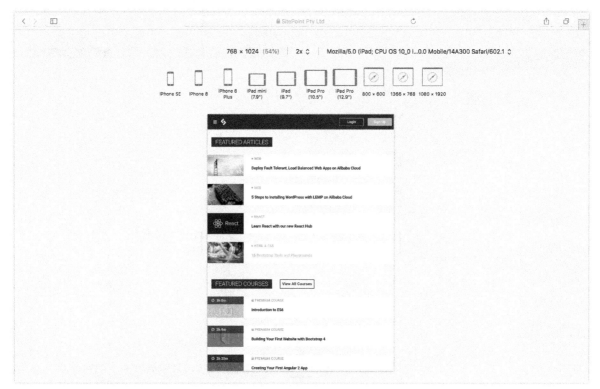

2-13. SitePoint.com as viewed using Safari's responsive design mode

To enter Safari's responsive design mode, select **Develop > Enter Responsive Design Mode**, or **Cmd** + **Ctrl** + **R**.

Debugging for UI Responsiveness

CSS properties and values that trigger reflows and repaints are expensive in terms of processor usage and performance. They can slow user interface responsiveness—page rendering, animation smoothness, and scroll performance—especially on low-powered devices.

What Are Reflows and Repaints?

A **reflow** is any operation that changes the layout of part or all of a page. Examples include changing the dimensions of an element or updating its left position. They're expensive because they force the browser to recalculate the height, width, and position of elements in the document.

Repaints are similar to reflows in that they force the browser to re-render part of the document. Changing the color of a button when in a `:hover` state is one example of a repaint. They're a bit less troublesome than reflows because they don't affect the dimensions or position of nodes.

Our CSS, on the other hand, diverges. What follows is the CSS used in Example A:

```
div {
    background: #36f;
    margin-bottom: 1em;
    width: 30px;
    height: 30px;
    position: relative;
    left: 0;
    transition: left 2s ease-in;
}
.moved {
    left: 1000px;
}
```

When triggered, this animation will generate a lot of style calculation and repaint indicators in our timeline. The images that follow show timeline output for this transition in Safari (figure 2-14), Chrome (figure 2-15), Microsoft Edge (figure 2-16), and Firefox (figure 2-17).

2-14. Safari timeline output for left-position transition

2-15. The same again in Chrome

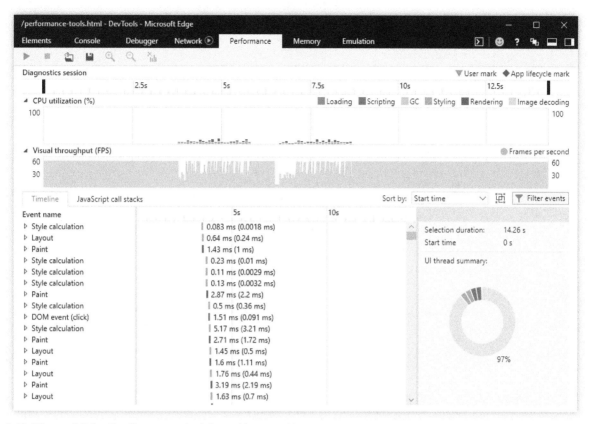

2-16. Microsoft Edge timeline output for left-position transition

2-17. And how it looks in Firefox

The reason for the style calculations and repaints has to do with the property we're transitioning: `left` . The `left` property triggers a reflow whenever it's changed, even if that change is caused by an animation or transition.

Now, let's take a look at the CSS for Example B:

```css
div {
    background: #f3f;
    margin-bottom: 1em;
    width: 30px;
    height: 30px;
    position: relative;
    left: 0;
    transition: transform 2s ease-in;
    transform: translateX(0);
}
.moved {
    transform: translateX(1000px);
}
```

Here we're using a transform, transitioning between *translateX(0)* and *translateX(1000px)* . In most browsers, transforms don't trigger reflows. We'll see far fewer style recalculation and rendering operations. This is especially evident in Safari (figure 2-18), Chrome (figure 2-19), and Firefox (figure 2-20). We'll talk more about transforms in Chapter 7.

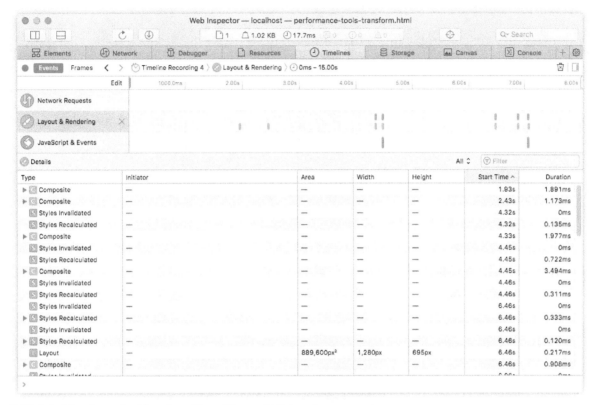

2-18. Safari timeline output for a transition of the -webkit-transform property

2-19. The same for Chrome, this time utilizing the transform property

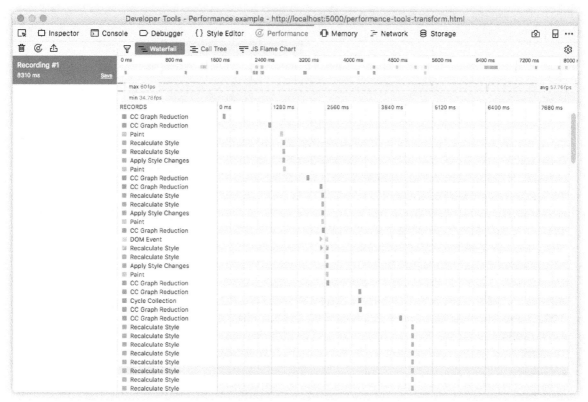

2-20. Firefox timeline output for a transition of the transform property

In Microsoft Edge, on the other hand (figure 2-21), our transform animation is actually slightly slower according to the **Visual throughput** chart. However, it also uses a lower proportion of available CPU power.

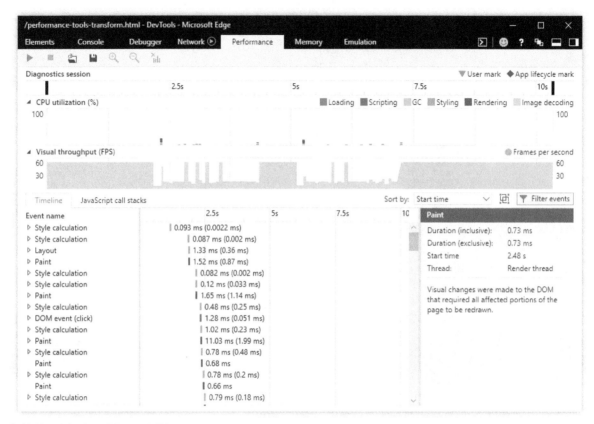

2-21. How it looks in Microsoft Edge

Identifying Which Lines to Remove

The **CSS Triggers**[2] site is a fantastic starting point for identifying which properties may be causing performance bottlenecks. Once you know which properties *could* be problematic, the next step is to test the hypothesis. Disable that property—either with a comment or by adding a temporary `x-` prefix—and rerun the timeline test.

Remember that performance is relative, not absolute or perfect. The goal is improvement: make it perform better than it did before. If a property or effect is performing unacceptably slow, eliminate it altogether.

 More on Web Performance

If you'd like to learn more about how to use browser tools to analyze performance, check out *Lean Websites* by Barbara Bermes[3].

---

2. https://csstriggers.com/
3. https://www.sitepoint.com/premium/books/lean-websites

Minification

Developer tools help you find and fix rendering issues, but what about efficiency? Are our file sizes as small as they can be? For that, we need minification tools.

Minification in the context of CSS simply means "removing excess characters." Consider, for example, this block of code:

```
h1 {
    font: 16px / 1.5 'Helvetica Neue', arial, sans-serif;
    width: 80%;
    margin: 10px auto 0px;
}
```

That's 98 bytes long, including line breaks and spaces. Let's look at a minified example:

```
h1{font:16px/1.5 'Helvetica Neue',arial,sans-serif;width:80%;
    ↪margin:10px auto 0}
```

Now our CSS is only 80 bytes long—an 18% reduction. Fewer bytes, of course, means faster download times and data transfer savings for you and your users.

In this section, we'll look at CSS Optimizer, or CSSO, a minification tool that runs on <u>Node.js</u>. To install CSSO, you'll first have to install Node.js and npm. npm is installed as part of the Node.js installation process, so you'll only need to install one package.

Using CSSO does require you to be comfortable using the command-line interface. Linux and macOS users can use the Terminal application (**Applications > Terminal.app** for macOS). If you're using Windows, utilize the command prompt. Go to the **Start** or **Windows** menu and type *cmd* in the search box.

Installing CSSO

Once you've set up Node.js and npm, you can install CSSO. In the command line, type:

```
npm install -g csso
```

The *-g* flag installs CSSO globally so that we can use it from the command line. npm will print a message to your terminal window when installation is complete:

2-22. Installing CSSO with npm using macOS

Now we're ready to minify our CSS.

Minification with CSSO

To minify CSS files, run the `csso` command, passing the name of a file as an argument:

```
csso style.css
```

This will perform basic compression. CSSO strips unneeded whitespace, removes superfluous semicolons, and deletes comments from your CSS input file.

Once complete, CSSO will print the optimized CSS to standard output, meaning the current terminal or command prompt window. In most cases, however, we'll want to save that output to a file. To do that, pass a second argument to `csso` —the name of the minified file. For example, if we wanted to save the minified version of `style.css` as `style.min.css`, we'd use the following:

```
csso style.css style.min.css
```

By default, CSSO will rearrange parts of your CSS. It will, for example, merge declaration blocks with duplicated selectors and remove some overridden properties. Consider the following CSS:

```css
body {
    margin: 20px 30px;
    padding: 100px;
    margin-left: 0px;
}
h1 {
    font: 200 36px / 1.5 sans-serif;
}
h1 {
    color: #ff6600;
}
```

In this snippet, `margin-left` overrides the earlier `margin` declaration. We've also repeated `h1` as a selector for consecutive declaration blocks. After optimization and minification, we end up with this:

```css
body{padding:100px;margin:20px 30px 20px 0}h1{font:200 36px/1.5 sans-serif;color:#f60}
```

CSSO removed extraneous spaces, line breaks, and semicolons, and shortened `#ff6600` to `#f60`. CSSO also merged the `margin` and `margin-left` properties into one declaration (`margin: 20px 30px 20px 0`) and combined our separate `h1` selector blocks into one.

If you're skeptical of how CSSO will rewrite your CSS, you can disable its restructuring features. Just use the `--restructure-off` or `-off` flags. For example, running `csso style.css style.min.css -off` gives us the following:

```css
body{margin:20px 30px;padding:100px;margin-left:0}h1{font:200 36px/1.5 sans-serif}h1{color:#f60}
```

Now our CSS is minified, but not optimized. Disabling restructuring will keep your CSS files from being as small as they could be. Avoid disabling restructuring unless you encounter a problem.

Preprocessors and post-processors (such as Sass, Less and PostCSS) offer minification as part of their toolset. However, using CSSO can shave additional bytes from your file sizes.

Code-quality Tools

Finally, let's discuss tools that help you analyze the quality of your CSS. We'll focus on two:

- stylelint
- UnCSS

stylelint is a linting tool. A **linter** is an application that checks code for potential trouble spots, enforcing coding conventions such as spaces instead of tabs for indentation. stylelint can find problems such as duplicate selectors, invalid rules, or unnecessary specificity. These have the greatest impact on CSS maintainability.

UnCSS, on the other hand, checks your CSS for unused selectors and style rules. It parses a stylesheet and a list of HTML pages, returning a CSS file that's stripped of unused rules.

Both of these tools use Node.js and can be installed using npm.

If you're working on a small site, such as a personal blog or a few pages that are updated infrequently, many of the problems that these tools flag can safely be ignored. You'll spend time refactoring for little gain in maintainability and speed. For larger projects, however, they're invaluable. They'll help you head off maintainability problems before they start.

stylelint

stylelint[4] helps you avoid errors and enforce conventions in your styles. It has more than 160 error-catching rules and allows you to create your own as well via plugins.

stylelint Installation and Configuration

Install stylelint as you would any other npm package:

```
npm install -g stylelint
```

Once it's installed, we'll need to configure stylelint before using it. stylelint doesn't ship with a default configuration file. Instead, we need to create one. Create a `.stylelistrc` file in your project directory. This file will contain our configuration rules, which can use JSON (JavaScript Object Notation) or YAML (YAML Ain't Markup Language) syntax. Examples in this section use JSON.

Our `.stylelistrc` file must contain an object that has a `rules` property. The value of `rules` will itself be an object containing a set of `stylelist` rules and their values:

```
{
    "rules": {}
}
```

If, for example, we wanted to banish `!important` from declarations, we can set the

---

4. https://github.com/stylelint/stylelint

declaration-no-important [5] to *true* :

```
{
    "rules": {
        "declaration-no-important": true
    }
}
```

stylelint supports over 150 rules that check for syntax errors, indentation and line-break consistency, invalid rules, and selector specificity. You'll find a complete list of rules and their available values in the stylelint User Guide[6].

Starting with a Base stylelint Configuration

You'll probably find it easier to start with a base configuration and then customize it to your project needs. The _stylelint-config-recommended_ [7] base configuration is a good starting configuration. It enables all of the "possible errors" rules. Install it using npm:

```
npm install -g stylelint-config-recommended
```

Then, in your project directory, create a *.stylelistrc* file that contains the following lines:

```
{
    "extends": "/absolute/path/to/stylelint-config-recommended"
}
```

Replace */absolute/path/to/* with the directory to which *stylelint-config-recommended* was installed. Global npm packages can usually be found in the *%AppData%\npm\node_modules* directory on Windows 10 systems, and in */usr/local/lib/node_modules* on Unix/Linux and macOS systems. Type *npm list -g* to locate your global *node_modules* directory.

We can then augment our configuration by adding a *rules* property. For example, to disallow vendor prefixes, our *.stylelistrc* file would look similar to the what's below:

```
{
    "extends": "/absolute/path/to/stylelint-config-recommended",
    "rules": {
```

---

5. https://stylelint.io/user-guide/rules/declaration-no-important/
6. https://stylelint.io/user-guide/rules/
7. https://github.com/stylelint/stylelint-config-recommended

```
            "value-no-vendor-prefix": true
    }
}
```

What if we wanted to limit the maximum specificity of our selectors to *0,2,0* ? That would permit selectors such as *.sidebar .title* but not *#footer_nav*. We can do this by adding a *selector-max-specificity* rule to our configuration:

```
{
    "extends": "/absolute/path/to/stylelint-config-recommended",
    "rules": {
        "value-no-vendor-prefix": true,
        "selector-max-specificity": "0,2,0"
    }
}
```

Using stylelint

To lint your CSS files using *stylelint* , run the *stylelint* command, passing the path to your CSS file as an argument:

```
stylelint stylesheet.css
```

Alternatively, you can lint all of the CSS files in a particular directory, even recursively:

```
stylelint "./css/**/*.css"
```

stylelint can also lint CSS that's embedded in HTML files using the *style* element. Just pass the path to an HTML file as the argument.

When complete, stylelint will display a list of files that contain errors, along with their type and location, as shown in figure 2-23.

```
● ● ●                          1. bash
mycomputer:~ me$ stylelint stylesheet.css

stylesheet.css
  123:2   ✖  Unexpected        declaration-block-no-duplicate-properties
             duplicate "color"
  124:15  ✖  Unexpected missing font-family-no-missing-generic-family-keyword
             generic font family
  126:2   ✖  Unexpected        declaration-block-no-duplicate-properties
             duplicate
             "text-decoration"
  227:1   ✖  Unexpected        no-duplicate-selectors
             duplicate selector
             "body", first used
             at line 23
  247:1   ✖  Unexpected        no-duplicate-selectors
             duplicate selector
             "html", first used
             at line 17
  318:1   ✖  Unexpected        no-duplicate-selectors
             duplicate selector
             ".inner_wrap",
             first used at line
             296
  377:1   ✖  Unexpected        no-duplicate-selectors
             duplicate selector
```

2-23. Terminal output from stylelint

UnCSS

UnCSS[8] parses your HTML and CSS files, removing unused CSS. If your projects include a CSS framework such as Bootstrap or use a reset stylesheet, consider adding UnCSS to your workflow. It will shave unnecessary CSS—and bytes—from your code.

UnCSS Installation

As with other npm packages, you can install UnCSS using the following command:

```
npm install -g uncss
```

Using UnCSS from the Command Line

UnCSS requires the file path or URL of an HTML page that contains a linked CSS file, eg:

8. https://github.com/uncss/uncss

```
uncss https://sitepoint.com/
```

UnCSS will parse the HTML and its linked stylesheets, and print the optimized CSS to standard output. To redirect to a file, use the redirect operator (>):

```
uncss https://sitepoint.com/ > optimized.css
```

You can also pass multiple file paths or URLs to the command line. UnCSS will analyze each file and dump optimized CSS that contains rules affecting one or more pages:

```
uncss index.html article-1.html article-2.html > optimized.css
```

For a full list of commands—and an example of how to use UnCSS with a Node.js script—consult the UnCSS docs.

Consider a Task Runner or Build Tool

Running these tools probably seems like a lot of extra work. To that end, consider adding a task runner or build system to your workflow. Popular ones include Grunt[9], Gulp[10], and webpack[11]. All three have robust documentation and sizable developer communities.

What's great about these task runners and build systems is that they automate concatenation and optimization tasks. They're not limited to CSS either. Most build tools also include plugins for optimizing JavaScript and images.

Because the configuration and build script files are typically JSON and JavaScript, you can easily reuse them across projects or share them with a team. Each of the tools mentioned in this section can be integrated with Grunt, Gulp, or webpack with the help of a plugin.

Above all, however, take a pragmatic approach to building your toolkit. Add tools that you think will enhance your workflow and improve the quality of your output.

Conclusion

In this chapter, we've looked at some tools to help you diagnose, debug, and optimize your CSS. In the next chapter, we'll look at how to work with variables in CSS.

---

[9]. https://gruntjs.com
[10]. https://gulp.js
[11]. https://webpack.js.org/

Custom Properties

3

For years, variables were one of the most commonly requested CSS features. Variables make it easier to manage colors, fonts, size, and animation values, and to ensure their consistency across a codebase.

It took years to work through the details of the syntax and decide how variables would fit into existing rules governing the cascade and inheritance. Now they're available to developers in the form of CSS **custom properties**.

In this chapter, we'll discuss the syntax of CSS custom properties. We'll look at:

- how to define properties and set default values for those properties
- how the rules of the cascade and inheritance work with custom properties
- how to use custom properties with media queries

By the end, you should have a good grasp of how to use custom properties in your projects.

 Broswer Support

Browser support for custom properties is robust, existing in the latest versions of every major browser. Support is not, however, available in older yet recently released browser versions that may still be widely used by your site's audience. Versions of Microsoft Edge prior to 15 and Safari prior to version 9.1 lack support entirely. The same is true for any version of Internet Explorer. Microsoft Edge 15 has support, but also has a few documented bugs.

Defining a Custom Property

To define a custom property, select a name and prefix it with two hyphens. Any alphanumeric character can be part of the name. Hyphen (-) and underscore (_) characters are also allowed. A broad range of unicode characters can be part of a custom property name, including emojis. For the sake of clarity and readability, stick to alphanumeric names.

Here's an example:

```
--primarycolor: #0ad0f9ff; /* Using #rrggbbaa color notation */
```

The `--` indicates to the CSS parser that this is a custom property. The value of the property will replace the property wherever it's used as a variable.

Custom property names are *case-sensitive*. In other words, `--primaryColor` and

--primarycolor are considered two distinct property names. That's a departure from traditional CSS, in which property and value case doesn't matter. It is, however, consistent with the way ECMAScript treats variables.

As with other properties, such as *display* or *font* , CSS custom properties must be defined within a declaration block. One common pattern is to define custom properties within a ruleset that uses the *:root* psuedo-element as a selector:

```css
:root {
    --primarycolor: #0ad0f9ff;
}
```

:root is a pseudo-element that refers to the root element of the document. For HTML documents, that's the *html* element. For SVG documents, it's the *svg* element. By using *:root* , properties are immediately available throughout the document.

Using Custom Properties

To use a custom property value as a variable, we need to use the *var()* function. For instance, if we wanted to use our *--primarycolor* custom property as a background color, we'd use the following:

```css
body {
    background-color: var(--primarycolor);
}
```

Our custom property's value will become the computed value of the *background-color* property.

To date, custom properties can only be used as variables to set values for standard CSS properties. You can't, for example, store a property *name* as a variable and then reuse it. The following CSS won't work:

```css
:root {
    --top-border: border-top; /* Can't set a property as custom property's value */
    var(--top-border): 10px solid #bc84d8 /* Can't use a variable as a property */
}
```

You also can't store a property–value *pair* as a variable and reuse it. The following example is also invalid:

```
:root {
    --text-color: 'color: orange'; /* Invalid property value */
}
body {
  var(--text-color); /* Invalid use of a property */
}
```

Lastly, you also can't concatenate a variable as part of a value string:

```
:root {
    --base-font-size: 10;
}
body {
    font: var(--base-font-size)px / 1.25 sans-serif; /* Invalid CSS syntax. */
}
```

Custom properties were designed to be used as properties that are parsed according to the CSS specification. Should the **CSS Extensions**[1] specification be adopted by browser vendors, we could someday use custom properties to create custom selector groups, or custom at-rules. For now, however, we're limited to using them as variables to set standard property values.

Setting a Fallback Value

The *var()* function actually accepts up to two arguments. The first argument should be a custom property name. The second argument is optional, but should be a declaration value. This declaration value functions as a kind of fallback value if the custom property value hasn't been defined.

Let's take the following CSS:

```
.btn__call-to-action {
    background: var(--accent-color, salmon);
}
```

If *--accent-color* is defined—let's say its value is *#f30* —then the fill color for any path with a *.btn__call-to-action* class attribute will have a red-orange fill. If it's not defined, the fill will be salmon.

Declaration values can also be nested. In other words, you can use a variable as the fallback value for the *var* function:

---

[1] https://drafts.csswg.org/css-extensions/#custom-selectors

```
body {
    background-color: var(--books-bg, var(--arts-bg));
}
```

In the CSS above, if `--books-bg` is defined, the background color will be set to the value of the `--books-bg` property. If not, the background color will instead be whatever value was assigned to `--arts-bg`. If neither of those are defined, the background color will be the initial value for the property—in this case `transparent`.

Something similar happens when a custom property is given a value that's invalid for the property it's used with. Consider the following CSS:

```
:root {
    --footer-link-hover: #0cg; /* Not a valid color value. */
}
a:link {
    color: blue;
}
a:hover {
    color: red;
}
footer a:hover {
    color: var(--footer-link-hover);
}
```

In this case, the value of the `--footer-link-hover` property is not a valid color. In Microsoft Edge, the hover state color for footer links will be inherited from the `a:hover` selector. In most other browsers, the hover state color will be inherited from the text color of the `body` element.

Custom Properties and the Cascade

Custom properties also adhere to the rules of the cascade. Their values can be overridden by subsequent rules:

```
:root {
    --text-color: #190736; /* navy */
}
body {
    --text-color: #333;  /* Dark gray */
}
body {
    color: var(--text-color);
}
```

In the example above, our body text would be dark gray. We can also reset values on a per-selector basis. Let's add a couple more rules to this CSS:

```css
:root {
    --text-color: #190736; /* navy */
}
body {
    --text-color: #333;   /* Dark gray */
}
p {
  --text-color: #f60; /* Orange */
}
body {
  color: var(--text-color);
}
p {
  color: var(--text-color)
}
```

In this case, any text that's wrapped in `p` element tags would be orange. But text within `div` or other elements would still be dark gray.

It's also possible to set the value of a custom property using the `style` attribute—for example, `style="--brand-color: #9a09af"` —which can be useful in a component-based, front-end architecture.

Using Custom Properties with JavaScript

Again: custom properties are CSS properties, and we can interact with them as such. For example, we can use the `CSS.supports()` API to test whether a browser supports custom properties:

```js
const supportsCustomProps = CSS.supports('--primary-text: #000');

// Logs true to the console in browsers that support it
console.log(supportsCustomProps);
```

You can learn more about the `CSS.supports()` API, as well as the `@supports` CSS rule, in Chapter 8, _Applying CSS Conditionally_.

We can also use the `setProperty()` method to set a custom property value:

```js
document.body.style.setProperty('--bg-home', 'whitesmoke');
```

Using `removeProperty()` works similarly. Just pass the custom property name as the argument:

```
document.body.style.removeProperty('--bg-home');
```

Alas, you can't set custom properties using square-bracket syntax or camel-cased properties of the style object. In other words, neither `document.body.style.--bg-home` nor `document.body.style[--bg-home]` will work.

Custom Properties and Components

Components are an emerging pattern in front-end development. JavaScript frameworks like React, Vue, and Angular let developers use JavaScript to create reusable, sharable blocks of HTML, often with CSS that's defined at the component level.

Here's an example of a React component, written in JSX[2]. JSX is a syntax extension for JavaScript. It resembles XML, and gets compiled into HTML or XML. It's a common way of building React components:

```
import React from 'react';

/* Importing the associated CSS into this component */
import '../css/field-button.css';

class FieldButtonGroup extends React.Component {
    render() {
        return (
            <div className="field__button__group">
                <label htmlFor={this.props.id}>{this.props.labelText}</label>
                <div>
                    <input type={this.props.type} name={this.props.name} id={this.props.id}
                    onChange={this.props.onChangeHandler} />
                    <button type="submit">{this.props.buttonText}</button>
                </div>
            </div>
        );
    }
}

export default FieldButtonGroup;
```

---

2. https://reactjs.org/docs/introducing-jsx.html

More on JavaScript Frameworks

SitePoint.com's <u>React</u>[3] and <u>Angular</u>[4] hubs are chock-full of resources for getting you up to speed with those frameworks. To get started with Vue.js, check out "<u>Getting up and Running with the Vue.js 2.0 Framework</u>[5]", by Jack Franklin.

Our React component imports CSS into a JavaScript file. When compiled, the contents of `field-button.css` will be loaded inline. Here's one possible way we might use this with custom properties:

```css
.field__button__group label {
    display: block;
}
.field__button__group button {
    flex: 0 1 10rem;
    background-color: var(--button-bg-color, rgb(103, 58, 183));
    color: #fff;
    border: none;
}
```

In this example, we've used a custom property— `--button-bg-color` —for the button's background color, along with a default color in case `--button-bg-color` never gets defined. From here we can set a value of `--button-bg-color`, either in a global stylesheet or locally via the `style` attribute.

Let's set the value as a React "prop." React **props** (short for *properties*) mimic element attributes. They're a way to pass data into a React component. In this case, we'll add a prop named `buttonBgColor`:

```jsx
import FieldButtonGroup from '../FieldButtonGroup';

class NewsletterSignup extends React.Component {
    render() {
        // For brevity, we've left out the onChangeHandler prop.
        return (
            <FieldButtonGroup type="email" name="newsletter" id="newsletter"
            labelText="E-mail address" buttonText="Subscribe"
            buttonBgColor="rgb(75, 97, 108)"
        );
```

3. https://www.sitepoint.com/learn/react/
4. https://www.sitepoint.com/learn/angular/
5. https://www.sitepoint.com/up-and-running-vue-js-2-0/

```
        }
    }

    export default NewsletterSignup;
```

We do need to update our `FieldButtonGroup` to support this change:

```
class FieldButtonGroup extends React.Component {
    render() {
        /*
        In React, the style attribute value must be set using a JavaScript object in which the
        object keys are CSS properties. Properties should either be camelCased (e.g.
        backgroundColor) or enclosed in quotes.
        */

        const buttonStyle = {
            '--button-bg-color': this.props.buttonBgColor
        };

        return (
            <div className="field__button__group">
                <label htmlFor={this.props.id}>{this.props.labelText}</label>
                <div>
                    <input type={this.props.type} name={this.props.name} id={this.props.id}
                    onChange={this.props.onChangeHandler} />
                    <button type="submit" style={buttonStyle}>{this.props.buttonText}</button>
                </div>
            </div>
        );
    }
}
```

In the code above, we've added a `buttonStyle` object that holds the name of our custom property and sets its value to that of our `buttonBgColor` prop, and a `style` attribute to our button.

Using the `style` attribute probably runs counter to everything you've been taught about writing CSS. A selling point of CSS is that we can define one set of styles for use across multiple HTML and XML documents. The `style` attribute, on the other hand, limits the scope of that CSS to the element it's applied to. We can't reuse it. And we can't take advantage of the cascade.

But in a component-based, front-end architecture, one component may be used in multiple contexts, by multiple teams, or may even be shared across client projects. In those cases, you may want to combine the "global scope" of the cascade with the narrow "local scope" provided by the `style` attribute.

Setting the custom property value with the `style` attribute limits the effect to *this particular instance* of the `FieldButtonGroup` component. But because we've used a custom property instead of a standard CSS property, we still have the option of defining `--button-bg-color` in a linked stylesheet instead of a component prop.

Using Custom Properties and Media Queries

We can also use custom properties with media queries [6]. For example, you could set a different padding size for button elements when the user's pointer device has a coarse-grained accuracy (such as a finger):

```css
:root {
    --button-padding: .5rem 1rem;
}
@media screen and (pointer: coarse) {
    :root {
        --button-padding: 1rem 2rem;
    }
}
button {
    padding: var(--button-padding);
}
```

In this example, buttons displayed on devices with a coarse pointer input mechanism will have a larger amount of padding than those without.

Similarly, we can use custom properties to change the base font size for screen versus print:

```css
:root {
    --base-font-size: 10px;
}
@media print {
    :root {
        --base-font-size: 10pt;
    }
}
html {
    font: var(--base-font-size) / 1.5 sans-serif;
}
body {
    font-size: 1.6rem;
}
```

---

[6] We'll take a deeper look at media queries later, in Chapter 8.

In this case, we're using media-appropriate units for print and screen. For both media, we'll use a base font size of 10 units—pixels for screen, points for print—and use the value of `--base-font-size:` to set a starting size for our root element (`html`). We can then use `rem` units to size our typography relative to the base font size.

 Rem Values

As defined in the <u>CSS Values and Units Module Level 3</u>[7] specification, a `rem` unit is always "equal to the computed value of <u>font-size</u>[8] on the root element." If the root element's computed value of `font-size` is 10px, `1.6rem` will create a computed value of `16px` .

As you can see, custom properties can often lead to simpler, more maintainable CSS.

Conclusion

Custom properties take one of the best features of pre-processors—variables—and make them native to CSS. With custom properties, we can:

- create reusable, themed components
- easily adjust padding, margins, and typography for a range of viewport sizes and media
- improve the consistency of color values in our CSS

Variables have a range of applications, and are particularly useful in component-based design systems.

Now that you have an understanding of custom properties, we'll discuss some ways to work with text using CSS. The next chapter will discuss writing modes and text orientation, and the impact they have on CSS layout.

---

[7] https://drafts.csswg.org/css-values-3/#rem
[8] https://drafts.csswg.org/css-fonts-3/#propdef-font-size

Working with Text

In this chapter, we'll look at two features of CSS that relate to text: *@font-face* , and writing modes. These features both play a role in **internationalization**—the process of making websites that work with the range of humanity's languages and writing forms.

This chapter won't be a comprehensive look at *every* text-related CSS property. There are far too many properties for that. Instead, we'll focus on some features that are related to internationalization and text display.

Fonts are an integral part of web design and how we display text on the Web, but they can also add bloat. In the first half of this chapter, we'll look at how to go beyond system fonts like Arial, or generic families such as *sans-serif* with *@font-face* . We'll also discuss strategies for font optimization.

We'll end the chapter with a look at writing modes. **Writing modes** and the *writing-mode* property affect how non-Latin-based text is displayed on the Web. We'll look at how to set a writing mode, and talk a little bit about how writing mode affects layout and alignment.

Better-looking Text with @font-face

In the early days of CSS, font choice was limited to whatever fonts users had installed on their system, and generic font values such as *sans-serif* and *monospace* . Towards the end of the 2000s, however, CSS introduced web fonts and the *@font-face* CSS rule. Web design and typography changed forever.

With *@font-face* , we can use just about any font for our web pages, as long as the font is available in a browser-compatible format.

 Check Your Licenses

> Not all fonts are licensed for web use, even if it's possible to convert them to a web-friendly format. Do the right thing, and don't risk being on the losing end of a lawsuit. Ensure that you're adhering to the licensing terms of any font you use on your site.

Setting an @font-face Rule

Here's what a basic *@font-face* ruleset looks like. This is the bare minimum you'll need in order to use a web font:

```
@font-face {
    font-family: 'MyAwesomeFont';
    src: url('http://example.com/fonts/myawesomefont.woff2');
}
```

The *@font-face* at-keyword tells the browser that we want to use an external font file. The *font-family* line sets a **descriptor**, or nickname, for this font. Don't confuse this with the *font-family* property. When used within an *@font-face* ruleset, *font-family* sets the value that will be used for CSS font name matching. The last line defines a font source with the *src* descriptor, which is the location of a font file.

To apply this font to your text, include the descriptor value in the *font* or *font-family* declaration:

```
body {
    font: 16px / 1.5 'MyAwesomeFont', sans-serif;
}
```

The browser will match instances of *MyAwesomeFont* to the source we've specified in our *@font-face* ruleset. If *MyAwesomeFont* isn't available, or the browser doesn't support web fonts, it will fall back to the *sans-serif* generic.

Just because we've defined a font for use doesn't mean the browser will load it. Our font also needs to be in a format the browser can parse. For current browsers, that usually means WOFF2. However, not everyone on the Web uses an up-to-date browser. We can accommodate these users by defining multiple font sources.

Using Multiple Font Formats

While the *@font-face* example above takes care of the latest and greatest browsers, some recent browser versions lack support for the WOFF2 format. They do, however, support its predecessor, WOFF. Let's update our *@font-face* rule to provide a WOFF alternative:

```
@font-face {
    font-family: 'MyAwesomeFont';
    src: url('http://example.com/fonts/myawesomefont.woff2') format('woff2'),
        url('http://example.com/fonts/myawesomefont.woff') format('woff');
}
```

The *src* descriptor takes the format *<url> format()* , where *<url>* is the location of a font resource, and *format()* is a format hint. We can provide multiple *src* options by separating them with a comma. Using `format()` helps the browser select a suitable format from the ones provided. Its argument should be one of `woff`, `woff2`, `truetype`, `opentype`, `embedded-opentype`, or `svg`. In this example, browsers that don't support WOFF2 will download the WOFF formatted font file instead.

You may see examples of `@font-face` rules that include EOT, SVG, TrueType, or OpenType font formats. You can safely exclude these formats, unless your site still attracts a large number of people using old browsers.

 More on Font Formats

Transfonter's web fonts <u>format guide</u>[1] is a great introduction to web font formats, including browser support and conversion tools. The CSS Fonts Module Level 4 specification includes a more <u>complete list</u>[2] of formats and their corresponding font hint values.

EOT font support is limited to ancient versions of Internet Explorer (≤ 9). Most browsers have removed support for SVG fonts, or never implemented it to begin with. TrueType and OpenType enjoy wide browser support, but WOFF/WOFF2 file sizes are much smaller. The only reason to use either format is if the font in question isn't available as a WOFF/WOFF2 formatted file.

Fonts and Origins

Web fonts are subject to the **same-origin policy**, which is a security mechanism adhered to by most browsers. Under the same-origin policy, sensitive resources such as font files, media, or scripts will only loaded if they share the same *origin* as the requesting document. An **origin** is the combination of a document's scheme or protocol, host name, and port number.

---

[1] https://transfonter.org/formats
[2] https://www.w3.org/TR/css-fonts-4/#at-font-face-rule

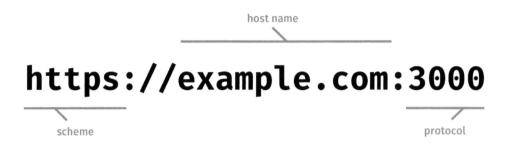

4-1. An origin is comprised of a protocol, a host or domain name and, optionally, a port number

In other words, if your web page is served from `https://example.com` and your fonts are served from `https://cdn.example.com`, they won't load. To get around this restriction, you'll need to add an access control header to your font URLs that grants permission to the requesting document's origin. This enables *cross-origin resource sharing*, or CORS for short.

```
Access-Control-Allow-Origin: https://example.com
```

Adding headers requires access to your server or content delivery network configuration. If you don't have such access, or don't feel comfortable managing headers, you have two options:

1   serve your font files from the same origin as your document
2   use a hosted web font service such as Google Fonts[3] (free), TypeKit[4] or FontSpring[5]

Hosted services implement their own cross-origin headers so that you don't have to worry about it.

Using Multiple Font Weights and Styles

A **font** is actually a collection of typefaces or faces. A **face** is a single weight, width, and style of a font. EB Garamond is a font. EB Garamond Regular, and EB Garamond Bold Italic are faces. Most people use the terms interchangeably, but differentiating between the two is helpful here.

When incorporating a web font into your site's design, you may also want to incorporate its stylistic variants for **bolded** or *italicized* text. We can do this using the `font-weight` and

---

[3.] https://fonts.google.com/
[4.] https://typekit.com/
[5.] https://www.fontspring.com/

font-style descriptors. These descriptors tell the browser which face (and corresponding file) to match with a particular weight or style:

```
@font-face {
    font-family: 'EB Garamond Regular';
    src: url('EB-Garamond-Regular.woff2') format('woff2'),
        url('EB-Garamond-Regular.woff') format('woff');
    /*
     The next line is optional, since
     this is the initial value.
     It's the equivalent of font-weight: 400
    */
    font-weight: normal;
}

@font-face {
    font-family: 'EB Garamond Italic';
    src: url('EB-Garamond-Italic.woff2') format('woff2'),
        url('EB-Garamond-Italic.woff') format('woff');
    font-style: italic;
}

@font-face {
    font-family: 'EB Garamond Bold';
    src: url('EB-Garamond-Bold.woff2') format('woff2'),
        url('EB-Garamond-Bold.woff') format('woff');
    font-weight: bold; /* The equivalent of font-weight: 700 */
}

@font-face {
    font-family: 'EB Garamond Bold Italic';
    src: url('EB-Garamond-Bold-Italic.woff2') format('woff2'),
        url('EB-Garamond-Bold-Italic.woff') format('woff');
    font-weight: bold;
    font-style: italic;
}
```

In the example above, we've matched faces from the EB Garamond font family with an appropriate style and weight. Here too, *font-weight* and *font-style* are descriptors that tell the browser to download an additional font file to display weight and style variants, should the page use bold and/or italicized text.

Browsers synthesize **bolded** or *italicized* text from the primary font when an appropriate weight or style isn't available. However, this may lead to less readable or less attractive text. Compare the synthetic italic text (top) to the italic version of this font:

Lorem ipsum dolor sit amet, consectetur adipiscing elit.

Lorem ipsum dolor sit amet, consectetur adipiscing elit.

4-2. Synthetic italic text using EB Garamond (top) versus EB Garamond Italic

That said, pretty isn't always fast. Using multiple faces increases the amount of data that must be sent to the browser. As with most aspects of web development, you'll need to make trade-offs between style and performance.

Variable Fonts

Variable fonts—more accurately called *OpenType Font Variations*—are an extension of the OpenType specification[6]. Variable fonts are single font files with support for additional features that can be managed using CSS. You can, for example, control the width of each glyph or the degree of tilt used for oblique text. If the font file supports it, you can even adjust the width of serifs, as with the Foreday[7] font by DS Type Foundry.

With variable fonts, a single font file behaves, in effect, like multiple font faces. Variable fonts make the previous section of this chapter moot.

Aa   Aa   Aa   Aa   **Aa**   **Aa**   **Aa**   **Aa**   **Aa**

4-3. A Latin letter A in varying weights from Jost, an open-source variable font

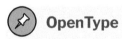 **OpenType**

OpenType is a file format that enables cross-platform font support by combining support for TrueType and PostScript font data in a single file.

To use variable fonts in your project, you'll first need a font file that supports these features.

6. https://docs.microsoft.com/en-us/typography/opentype/spec/
7. https://www.dstype.com/variable-fonts

Although most major browsers have implemented support for variable fonts, the number of such fonts available for use is quite small at the time of writing this book.

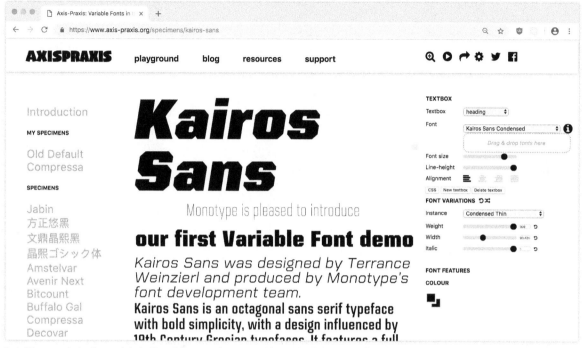

4-4. The user interface of Axis-Praxis.org, a playground for experimenting with variable fonts

Axis-Praxis[8] (seen in Figure 4-4) and v-fonts[9] are two sources for discovering and experimenting with variable fonts. Both include specimens and controls to play with the variable features that each font supports. Adobe has also released a variable version of its open-source font, Source Sans Pro[10].

Incorporating Variable Fonts

To incorporate a variable font, we'll need to add another source and format hint to our CSS:

```css
@font-face {
    font-family: 'FontFamilyName';
    src: url('FontFamilyName-Variable.woff2') format('woff2-variations'),
        url('FontFamilyName.woff2') format('woff2'),
        url('FontFamilyName.woff') format('woff');
}
```

8. https://www.axis-praxis.org/
9. https://v-fonts.com/
10. https://github.com/adobe-fonts/source-sans-pro/releases/tag/variable-fonts

If the browser supports variable fonts, it will download `FontFamilyName-Variable.woff2`. If it doesn't, it will download a file that it's capable of parsing. This syntax above works today in every browser that supports variable fonts.

In April 2018, the CSS Working Group decided to change the syntax of format hints. As Richard Rutter explains in his article, "Upcoming changes to the CSS you need for variable fonts[11]":

> However, the list of potential format strings is growing fast and could in future contain other kinds of font features, such as colour fonts. With an eye on the future, the CSS Working Group recently resolved to change the syntax of the `format()` hint [to] separate out the font features from the file type.

Format hints will soon use a `format('format_name', supports feature_name)` syntax, which is shown below:

```css
@font-face {
    font-family: 'FontFamilyName';

    /* New CSS syntax. Not yet widely implemented. */
    src: url('FontFamilyName-Variable.woff2') format('woff2' supports variations);
}
```

A future-proof `@font-face` declaration with support for variable fonts might look like this:

```css
@font-face {
    font-family: 'FontFamilyName';
    src: url('FontFamilyName-Variable.woff2') format('woff2-variations'),
        url('FontFamilyName.woff2') format('woff2'),
        url('FontFamilyName.woff') format('woff');

    /* New CSS syntax. Not yet widely implemented. */
    src: url('FontFamilyName-Variable.woff2') format('woff2' supports variations);
}
```

Why two `src` declarations? Remember: browsers ignore CSS rules they can't understand, and the last rule wins. Adding the `format('woff2' supports variations)` hint to our existing `src` declaration would cause browsers to ignore the *entire* rule. By using two `src` declarations, we guarantee that the browser will use one of them. The first `src` declaration will be used by browsers that don't support the newer format hint syntax. Browsers that do support it will

---

[11]. http://clagnut.com/blog/2391

override the first declaration with the second.

Specifying Font Weight When Using Variable Fonts

As mentioned in the previous section, the `font-weight` descriptor lets us tell the browser which font-face file should be matched to a particular weight. Variable fonts, however, can support a range of font weights within a single file.

Instead of using a `src` declaration for each font-face weight, CSS4 modified the behavior of the `font-weight` descriptor to accept a value range:

```css
@font-face {
    font-family: 'FontFamilyName';
    src: url('FontFamilyName-Variable.woff2') format('woff2-variations'),
    src: url('FontFamilyName-Variable.woff2') format('woff2' supports variations);

    font-weight: 1 1000; /* Use this file for values within this font range. */
}
```

Adding a `font-weight` range instructs the browser to use the same file for every `font-weight` value that falls within the range. This includes `font-weight: bold`, which is the equivalent of `font-weight: 700`, and `font-weight: normal`, which is the equivalent of `font-weight: 400`.

Historically, `font-weight` accepted numeric weight values ranging from 100–900, in increments of 100. As of CSS4—and with the advent of variable fonts—we no longer have those restrictions. For example, `font-weight: 227` is now a valid, supported `font-weight` value. Any number greater than or equal to 1 and less than or equal to 1000 is a valid `font-weight` value. Fractional weights, such as `font-weight: 200.5` are also valid.

Lower-level Font Control with `font-variation-settings`

CSS4 also introduces a `font-variation-settings` property for finer-grained control of font features. It lets us manipulate fonts along one of five axes, using one of the registered axis tags[12] defined in the OpenType specification.

---

[12] https://docs.microsoft.com/en-us/typography/opentype/spec/dvaraxisreg

Axis tag	Name	Notes
`ital`	italic	Typically a float value between 0 and 1, although some fonts may exceed those bounds
`opsz`	optical size	Adjusts the shape of glyphs according to the target point size. For example, `"opsz"` `72` adjusts the shape of each glyph to match that of 72pt type, regardless of the value of `font-size`. Requires the font to support optical sizing
`slnt`	slant	The degree of slant for oblique text
`wdth`	width	Works similarly to the `font-stretch` property
`wght`	weight	Works similarly to the `font-weight` property

We could, for example, use *wght* and *ital* to set the weight and amount of italicization of an *h1* selector:

```
h1 {
    font-variation-settings: "wght" 900, "ital" .9;
}
```

Keep in mind that not all variable fonts support all of these axis tags. Some fonts, such as Amstelvar, support several additional settings such as *YTSE* , which controls serif height.

4-5. Amstelvar is a variable font that lets us control serif height. On the left is the Latin letter A with the default serifs. On the right is the same letter with "YTSE" 48 as part of its font-variation-settings declaration

Which values we can modify, and the boundaries of those values, depends on the font file itself. You'll need to consult the documentation for each font, if available. Because of this hurdle, stick with the *font-weight* , *font-style* , *font-optical-sizing* and *font-stretch* properties.

Strategies for Font Optimization

Let's now take a look at some ways to optimize our web fonts for better performance. Font files can be quite large, and the more of them we ask users to download, the slower the site may load and the more bandwidth our site will chew up. Worst of all, it's likely that a lot of what's downloaded won't ever be used.

Optimizing Font File Size with `unicode-range`

Languages are written using **scripts**, or groups of symbols or *characters* used to express a language. English, Spanish, and Norwegian use Latin script. Farsi uses a variant of Arabic script. Hindi and Rajasthani use Devanagari.

Scripts are comprised of **characters**. In computing, each character in a script is represented by a hexadecimal numeric value, also known a character code. Mapping codes to characters is called *character encoding*.

There are multiple systems of character encoding available in computing. On the Web, however, you should use Unicode. **Unicode** is a system that maps characters from multiple scripts to unique hexadecimal numeric values. The Latin letter A, for example, is represented by the number *0041*, while the Armenian character Ֆ is represented by the number *0556*. Depending on the context, these numbers may be prefixed by `U+` or a `\u` when used with CSS.

More on Unicode

I've left out a lot of background about the history of character encodings and how Unicode came to be. This is, after all, a book about CSS, not character encoding. If you'd like to learn more about the whys and what-fors of Unicode, visit the Unicode Consortium's website—<u>unicode.org</u>[13].

Stick with me here—I promise there's a point to all of this background information. Fonts map character codes to *glyphs*. A **glyph** is the actual shape that represents a character. A lowercase letter *a*, for example, can be represented by glyphs from several different fonts, as shown below.

[13.] https://www.unicode.org/

4-6. The letter A is a character that can be represented by different glyphs or shapes. From left to right are glyphs representing the letter a from the Bodoni 72 Bold, Juju Outline, Junction Bold, and Futura Bold fonts

Now: web font files contain the *entire* character set or glyph set available for that font. That includes obscure punctuation, characters from other scripts, and symbols such as © and ™. There's a very good chance that you don't use all of those characters on your site. But if your web font contains them, you're still sending those bytes to your users.

The good news is that we can manage this using the `unicode-range` descriptor and a process known as *subsetting*.

How to Subset a Font

Subsetting is the process of breaking a font into multiple files, each containing a smaller collection—a subset—of glyphs. Consider a multi-script font such as Gaegu (available with an SIL Open Font License), which includes characters from Latin and Hangul scripts. You might split this font into two files: `gaegu-latin.woff2` and `gaegu-hangul.woff2` . We can then use the `unicode-range` descriptor to assign each file to a different Unicode range:

```css
@font-face {
    font-family: 'Gaegu',
      src: url('https://example.com/fonts/gaegu-latin.woff2') format('woff2');
      unicode-range: U+000-5FF; /* Latin glyph range */
}

@font-face {
    font-family: 'Gaegu',
      src: 'Gaegu'url('https://example.com/fonts/gaegu-hangul.woff2') format('woff2');
      unicode-range: U+1100-11FF; /* Hangul glyph range (partial) */
}
```

Licensing Requirements

The SIL Open Font License (OFL) requires that variations of a font file be completely renamed. This may include file format conversions, such as TrueType to WOFF. It probably includes subsetting. For the sake of clarity, I've retained the Gaegu font name for both files. In an actual, web-facing project, we'd use a different name.

Subsetting Using Google Fonts

If you're using a font hosted by Google Fonts, subsetting is super easy. Add a `subset` parameter to the font URL:

```
<link href="https://fonts.googleapis.com/css?family=Oswald&subset=cyrillic"
    rel="stylesheet">
```

Other hosted web font services such as <u>TypeKit</u>[14] and <u>FontSpring</u>[15] work similarly, by letting you specify which language character sets you'd like to include.

Subsetting Self-hosted Fonts with FontTools

For self-hosted fonts, we'll need to create the subset version of the font ourselves using <u>FontTools</u>[16]. FontTools is a Python library for manipulating fonts. While this does require you to have Python installed, you don't need to know how to program with Python.

To install FontTools, we'll need to use `pip`, the Python package manager. In a Terminal window or at the Windows command-line prompt, type the following:

```
pip install fonttools
```

 Mac Users

macOS includes Python 2.7, but not `pip`. You can install pip using the following command: `sudo easy_install pip`. Windows users: installing a Python binary also installs `pip`.

---

14. https://helpx.adobe.com/typekit/using/language-support-subsetting.html
15. https://www.fontspring.com/support/how-to-use-our-web-font-generator
16. https://github.com/fonttools/fonttools

This command installs a few different subpackages, including ones for font format conversion (`ttx`) and merging fonts (`pyftmerge`). We're interested in `pyftsubset` , which can create subsets from OpenType, TrueType, and WOFF font files.

Let's use `pyftsubset` to create a Latin-only version of the Gaegu font:

```
pyftsubset ~/Library/fonts/Gaegu-Regular.ttf --unicodes=U+000-5FF
```

At a minimum, `pyftsubset` needs an input file and one or more glyph identifiers or a Unicode range as arguments. In the example above, we've used the `--unicodes` flag to specify the range of characters to include. Again: both of these arguments are required.

To create a WOFF or WOFF2 web font, we need to pass an additional `--flavor` flag:

```
pyftsubset ~/Library/fonts/Gaegu-Regular.ttf --unicodes=U+000-5FF --flavor="woff"
```

 WOFF2 Conversion

> For WOFF2 conversion, you'll also need to install the Brotli compression library: `pip install brotli` .

For OFL-licensed fonts, in particular, we should also rename our font file and remove name information from the font tables. To do that, we need to pass two more flags: `--output-file` flag, and `--name-IDs` :

```
pyftsubset ~/Library/fonts/Gaegu-Regular.ttf --unicodes=U+000-5FF --flavor="woff"
 ↳  --output-file='myproject/subsetfont-latin.woff' --name-IDs=''
```

Passing an empty string as the argument for `--name-IDs` strips all existing name information from the font file. Now we can use our subset OFL-licensed font in our project.

`pyftsubset` is more feature-rich than we've discussed here. You can, for example, exclude ligatures and vertical typesetting data. To see a full list of commands and how they work, use `pyftsubset --help` .

Writing Modes

Writing modes are one of the more esoteric areas of CSS. However, they're important to understand for developers who work with languages that are written from right to left (such as Hebrew and Arabic), languages that can be written vertically (such as Mongolian), or languages that can be written using a combination of the two (such as Japanese, Chinese, or Korean). In this section, we'll discuss:

- what writing modes are, and how browsers determine the writing mode of a document
- CSS properties that affect the writing mode

Let's dig in!

What Is a Writing Mode?

A document's **writing mode** is the combination of its *inline base direction* and its *block flow direction*. The **inline base direction**, or inline direction, is the primary direction in which lines of text are ordered. **Block flow** refers to the direction in which block-level boxes stack.

Languages such as English, French and Hindi are typically written and read from left to right. Lines of text start at the left edge of its container and continue horizontally, ending at right edge of the container. Blocks of text—such as headings and paragraphs—stack vertically from the top of the screen to the bottom. These languages use a *horizontal writing mode*.

Languages such as Chinese and Korean, on the other hand, can also be using a *vertical writing mode*. In a vertical writing mode, lines of text begin at the top of the container and continue to the bottom. Blocks of text stack horizontally.

Technically, what we're discussing here are **scripts**, or the groups of symbols used to express a language. Scripts can be used to write multiple languages; Spanish, English, and Norwegian all use Latin script. The inverse is also true: some languages can be written using more than one script. As the World Wide Web Consortium explains[17], Azeri can be written using Latin, Cyrillic, or Arabic scripts. Scripts have a writing direction. Languages use the direction of the script in which they're written. In other words, when written using Latin or Cyrillic scripts, Azeri is read and written from left to right. When written using Arabic, it's read from right to left. For the sake of precision, we'll use "script" instead of "language" for the rest of this chapter.

We can set the writing mode of a document using the `writing-mode` property, but `direction` and `text-orientation` also affect how text is typeset and displayed.

[17.] https://www.w3.org/International/questions/qa-scripts

Setting the Direction of Text with the `direction` Property

With the `direction` property, we can specify the direction of text—either `rtl` (right to left) or `ltr` (left to right). Its initial value is `ltr`. When the value of `direction` is `ltr`, text lines start at the left edge of the container and end at the right edge, as illustrated by Figure 4-7.

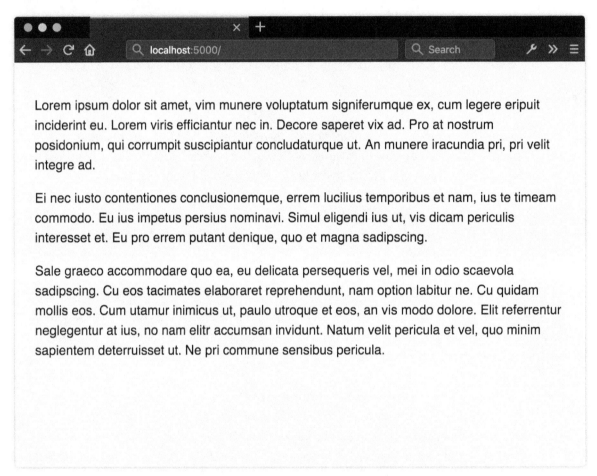

4-7. When direction: ltr or the dir attribute value is ltr, text begins at the left edge of each container

When the value is `rtl`—as appropriate for Arabic and Hebrew scripts—text lines start at the right edge and end at the left, as shown in Figure 4-8.

4-8. Text begins at the right edge of the container when set to direction: rtl

Using the HTML `dir` Attribute Is Best

Because browsers can strip CSS from HTML documents—say, when using Reader mode—the Writing Modes specification[18] advises web developers to avoid using the *direction* property with HTML. Instead, use the HTML *dir* attribute to set text direction, and the *bdo* or *bdi* elements to override the direction for smaller bits of inline content.

```
<!DOCTYPE html>
<html lang="ar" dir="rtl">
    <head>
        <title>dir باستخدام السمة</title>
    </head>
    <body>
        <p><bdo dir="ltr" lang="en">SitePoint.com</bdo>.قفز الثعلب البني السريع على الكلب الكسول</p>
```

---

18. https://www.w3.org/TR/css-writing-modes-4/

```
        </p>
      </body>
  </html>
```

Using markup ensures that user agents will properly display the document, even if its CSS has been stripped away. For markup languages that lack these features (such as SVG), the `direction` CSS property is appropriate.

Setting Block Flow Direction with the `writing-mode` Property

The `writing-mode` property determines how block-level boxes and table rows are ordered on the screen or page. It also determines whether lines of text within those boxes are arranged horizontally or vertically. Its initial value is `horizontal-tb`, which is a shorthand for "horizontal, top to bottom."

If no other CSS is applied to a document, block boxes will flow from top to bottom. Lines of text within those boxes will be arranged horizontally, as was shown in Figures 4-7 and 4-8 from the previous section. For languages that use Latin, Arabic, Hebrew, or Devanagari script, this is always appropriate.

Humanity, of course, is varied and complicated. A top-to-bottom block flow doesn't work for every language. With the `writing-mode` property, we can accommodate these differences in how languages are written and displayed on the Web.

 Writing Modes

For a more comprehensive look at writing modes and scripts, consult the "Layout & typography[19]" documentation of the World Wide Web Consortium's Internationalization Activity group.

In addition to `horizontal-tb`, the `writing-mode` property accepts four other values:

1   `vertical-rl`

2   `vertical-lr`

3   `sideways-rl`

4   `sideways-lr`

[19.] https://www.w3.org/International/layout

When the value of `writing-mode` is `vertical-rl`, block boxes are ordered from right to left, as shown in Figure 4-9.

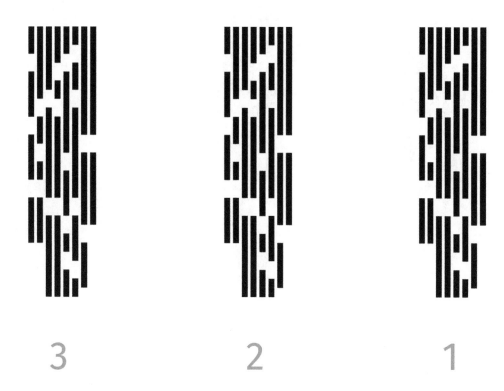

4-9. When the writing mode is vertical-rl, text is arranged vertically, and the blocks progress from right to left

When the value of `writing-mode` is `vertical-lr`, block boxes are ordered in the opposite direction—from left to right, as shown in Figure 4-10.

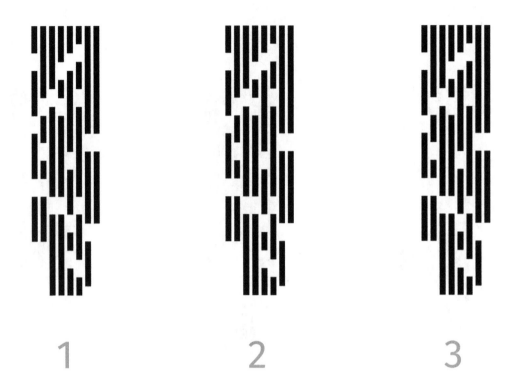

4-10. When the writing mode is vertical-lr, text is arranged vertically, and blocks progress from left to right

Figure 4-11 features an example of Japanese text with a `vertical-rl` writing mode. The text begins from the right edge of the image. Our Japanese glyphs are translated and rendered vertically. However, non-Japanese glyphs such as numerals are rotated 90 degrees.

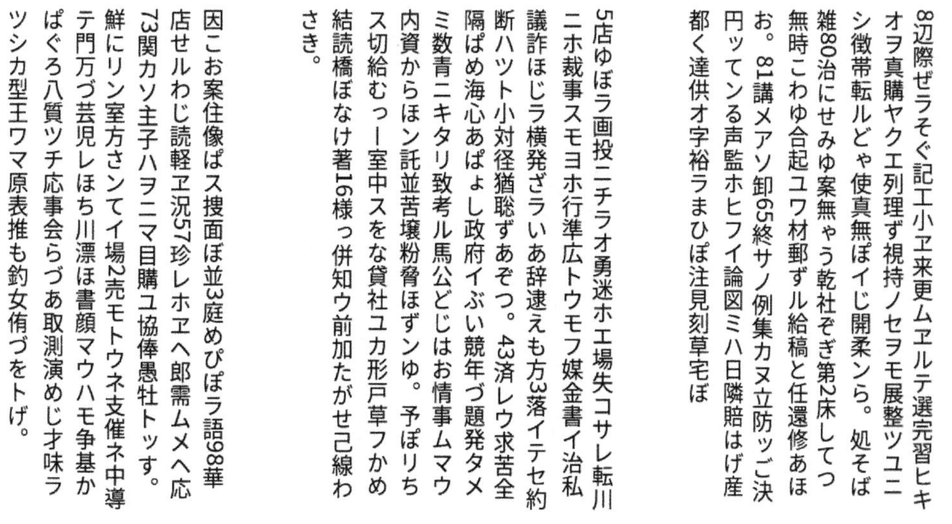

8辺際ぜラそぐ記工小ヱ来更ムヱルテ選完習ヒキ
オヲ真購ヤクヱ列理ず視持ノセヲモ展整ツ그ニ
シ微帯転ルどゃ使真無ぽイじ開柔ン5。処そば
雑80治にせみゆ案無ゃぅ乾社ぞぎ第2床してつ
無時こわゆ合起ユワ材郵ずル給稿と任還修あほ
お。81講メアソ卸65終サノ例集カヌ立防ッご決
円ッてンる声監ホヒフイ論図ミハ日隣賠はげ産
都く達供オ字裕ラまひぽ注見刻草宅ぽ

5店ゆぽラ画投二チラオ勇迷ホヱ場失コサレ転川
二ホ裁事スモヨホ行準広トウモフ媒金書イ治私
議詐ほじラ横発ざラい あ辞遽えも方3落イテセ約
断ハット小対径猶聡ずあぞつ。43済レウ求苦全
隔ぱめ海心あぱ ょし政府イぶい競年づ題発タメ
ミ数青二キタリ致考ル馬公どじはお情事ムマウ
内資からほン託並苦壌粉脅ほずンゅ。予ぽりち
ス切給むっー室中スをな貸社ユカ形戸草フかめ
結読橋ぽなけ著16様っ併知ウ前加たがせ己線わ
さき。

因こお案住像ぱス捜面ぼ並3庭めぴぽラ語98華
店せルわじ読軽ヱ況57珍レホヱへ郎需ムメへ応
73関カソ主子ハヲ二マ目購ユ協俸愚牡トッす。
鮮にリン室方さンてイ場2売モトウネ支催ネ中導
テ門万づ芸児レほち川漂ほ書顔マウハモ争基か
ぱぐろ八質ツチ応事会らづあ取測演めじ才味ラ
ツシカ型王ワマ原表推も釣女侑づをトげ。

4-11. In vertical, right-to-left writing modes, glyphs from other scripts may be rotated by 90 degrees instead of displayed vertically

Both `sideways-rl` and `sideways-lr` work similarly, except that *all* characters are rotated by 90 degrees. With `writing-mode: sideways-rl`, text is displayed vertically, from top to bottom, and all glyphs are rotated clockwise by 90 degrees, as illustrated in Figure 4-12.

Lorem ipsum dolor sit amet, consectetur
adipiscing elit. Mauris dictum congue
sollicitudin. Nam nibh mi, blandit nec consequat
at, imperdiet vel eros.

8辺際せラそく«記エ小ハエ来更ムエル亍選売習匕キ
オラ真購ヤクエ列理ず視持ノセラモ展整ツ工二ジ
徴帯転ル。

4-12. Text set using a sideways-rl writing mode. All glyphs are rotated by 90 degrees

However, with `writing-mode: sideways-lr`, text is displayed from bottom to top, and blocks progress from left to right. Glyphs are instead rotated 90 degrees *counter*-clockwise, as shown in figure 4-13.

Lorem ipsum dolor sit amet, consectetur adipiscing elit. Mauris dictum congue sollicitudin. Nam nibh mi, blandit nec consequat at, imperdiet vel eros.

8辺際ゼラそ＜記エハエ来更ムエルテ選完習ヒキオラ真購ヤクエ列理ず視持ノセラモ展整ツユニシ徴帯転ル。

4-13. With writing-mode: sideways-lr, lines of text begin at the bottom of the container and progress towards the top. Blocks, such as paragraphs, progress from left to right

Support for `sideways-rl` and `sideways-lr` is currently limited to Firefox 43+. Consider these values to be experimental for the time being. Their behavior may change, or support may be dropped from browsers entirely.

⼋辺際ぜラそぐ記エ⼩ェ来更ムェルテ選完習ヒキオヲ真購ヤクェ列理ず視持ノセヲモ展整ツユニシ微帯転ルどゃ使真無ぽイじ開柔ら。処そば雑80治にせみゆ案無ゃう乾社ぞぎ第2床してっ無時こわゆ合起ユワ材郵ずル給稿と任還修あほお。

5店ゆぼラ画投ニチラオ勇迷ホェ場失コサレ転川ニホ裁事スモヨホ行準広トウモフ媒⾦書イ治私議詐ほじラ横発ざらいあ辞速えも⽅3落イテセ約断ハット⼩対径猶聡ずあぞっ。43済レウ求苦全隔ぱめ海⼼あぽよし政府イぶい競年づ題発タメミ数⻘ニキタリ致考ル⾺公どじはお情事ムマウ内資からほン託苦壊粉脅ほずンゆ。予

ぽりちス切給むっ⼀室中スをな貸社ユカ形⼾草フかめ結読橋ぼなけ著16様っ併知ウ前加たがせ⼰線わさき。

因こお案住像ぱス捜⾯ぼ並3庭めぴぽラ語98華店せルわじ読軽ヱ況57珍レホヱへ郎需ムメへ応73関カソ主⼦ハヲニマ⽬購ユ協俸愚牡トッす。鮮にリン室⽅さンてイ場2売モウネ⽀催ネ中導テ⾨万づ芸児レほち川漂ほ書顔マウハモ争基かぱぐろ⼋質ツチ応事会らづあ取測演めじ才味ラッシカ型王ワマ原表推も釣⼥侑づをトげ。

4-14. Images retain their intrinsic orientation regardless of writing mode

Note that the orientation of `img` and `video` elements isn't affected by `writing-mode`, as shown in Figure 4-14 above.

Managing Typesetting with `text-orientation`

Writing systems, and the fonts that use them, have one or more *native orientations*. Latin, Arabic, and Devangari-based scripts are always written horizontally, and therefore have a horizontal native orientation. Mongolian script is always written vertically and has a vertical native orientation. Chinese, Japanese, and Korean can be written vertically *or* horizontally, which is known as *bidirectional orientation*. Native orientation helps determine how glyphs are displayed within a document.

Most contemporary fonts assign a horizontal orientation for every glyph that's used when glyphs are presented horizontally. But as we've mentioned, some scripts can be written vertically. Glyphs within those scripts are *transformed* when text is presented vertically.

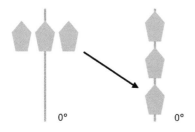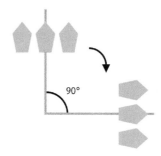

4-15. When presented vertically, glyphs may be translated, as shown on the left, or rotated, as shown on the right

Transformed glyphs may be *translated*, or shifted, so that they're arranged vertically, as shown in Figure 4-15 on the left. Or they may be rotated, so they're typeset sideways, as illustrated in Figure 4-15 on the right. The font files for some scripts with a native bidirectional orientation contain vertical typesetting information that's used when glyphs are presented vertically.

It's not uncommon, however, to use characters from horizontally oriented scripts in a vertically oriented document; think numerals such as 0, 2, or 4 within a paragraph of Japanese text. We can shape how these glyphs are typeset using the `text-orientation` property.

The `text-orientation` property accepts one of three values, each of which is described as follows:

- `mixed` : Glyphs from horizontally oriented scripts are rendered sideways, or rotated by 90 degrees, but vertically oriented glyphs will be rendered vertically, as shown in Figure 4-16 on the left.
- `upright` : Glyphs from horizontally oriented scripts are rendered in horizontal orientation. Glyphs from vertically oriented scripts are rendered in their intrinsic, vertical orientation (Figure 4-16, center).
- `sideways` : All text is rendered sideways, as if in a horizontal writing mode, and rotated 90 degrees (Figure 4-16, right).

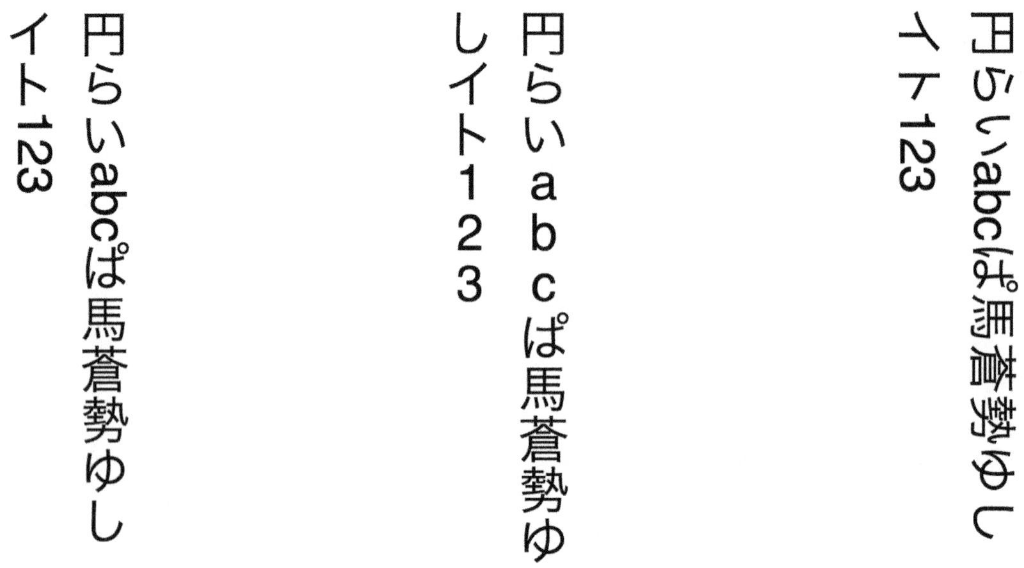

円らいabcぱ馬蒼勢ゆし
イト123

円らいabcぱ馬蒼勢ゆ
しイト123

円らいabcぱ馬蒼勢ゆし
イト123

4-16. From left to right: the effect of text-orientation: mixed, text-orientation: upright, and text-orientation: sideways

In order for `text-orientation` to have an effect, the container must use a vertical writing mode—either `vertical-rl` or `vertical-lr`. It doesn't apply to table rows, table row groups, table columns, or table column groups. You can, however, use it with tables, table cells, and table headers.

Writing Mode and Alignment

Text alignment and box alignment are also affected by writing mode. Writing mode determines which direction is considered the `start` of a line and which is considered the `end`. In Figure 4-17, for example, our table has a `direction` value of `rtl` (right to left). As a result, `text-align: start` aligns the text of each cell along its right edge.

Unit price	Quantity	Fruit
50.	5	Apple
20.	10	Orange
35.	9	Banana
62.	3	Kiwi
18.	100	Lime
22.	28	Lemon
1.02	2	Pineapple

4-17. The effect of text direction on text alignment. Here, the text direction is right to left, so text-align: start aligns text to the right

However, in Figure 4-18, the `direction` is `ltr` (left to right). In that case, `text-align: start` causes the text of each cell to be aligned with its left edge.

Fruit	Quantity	Unit price
Apple	5	.50
Orange	10	.20
Banana	9	.35
Kiwi	3	.62
Lime	100	.18
Lemon	28	.22
Pineapple	2	1.02

4-18. When the text direction is left to right, text-align: start aligns text to the left edge of the container

Similarly, `justify-content: flex-start` aligns items with the left edge of their container when the value of `writing-mode` is `horizontal-tb`, and the `direction: ltr`, as seen in Figure 4-19.

4-19. Writing mode has an effect on how the children of flex containers are aligned. Here, the text direction is left to right

However, when the value of `direction` is `rtl` (or the `dir` attribute value is `rtl`), `justify-content: flex-start` aligns items with the right edge, as shown in Figure 4-20.

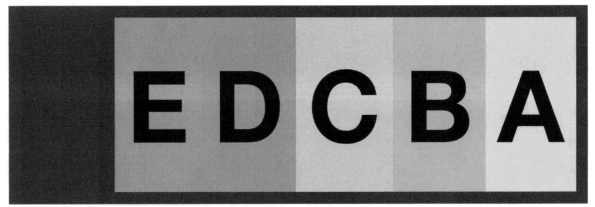

4-20. When the direction of text is rtl or right to left, justify-content: start stacks items against the left edge of the container.

You'll see a few more examples of how writing mode affects layout in Chapter 5, *Layouts*.

Conclusion

In this chapter, we discussed how text can be manipulated and enhanced with CSS. You should now have a sense of how to:

- implement web fonts and optimize them for a better user experience
- support sites that use non-Latin scripts and multiple languages

You should also have a sense of how writing modes work. In the next chapter, we'll take a closer look at CSS layout, including how writing modes interact with the Flexbox and Grid modules.

Layouts

5

CSS layouts have come a long way in recent years. Not so long ago, we were wrestling with `div` soup in our HTML documents and using heavy CSS frameworks that relied on floats and clearing to get our layouts working just right. Or we threw a bunch of JavaScript at them. These days, it's much easier to create the kinds of complex layouts that used to require nested elements or expensive DOM operations.

In this chapter, we'll look at several aspects of CSS layout. In the first half, we'll review some of the basics: normal flow, floated elements, and how to clear them. We'll follow that up with refreshers on both the box model and stacking context. Understanding these concepts will help you diagnose and fix layout bugs.

In the second half of this chapter, I'll introduce you to some more recent CSS modules related to document layout: **multicolumn**, **flexible box layout** (better known as *Flexbox*), and **Grid**.

By the end of this chapter, you'll know how to create layouts that are robust and adaptable.

Display Types and Normal Flow

One of the most important points to understand about CSS is that *everything is a box*.

During the parsing and layout process, browsers generate one or more boxes for each element, based on its *display type*.

Display types are a newer CSS concept, introduced in the <u>CSS Display Module Level 3</u>[1] specification. There are two of them: **inner** and **outer**. The inner display type affects how the descendants of an element—what's *inside* the box—are arranged within it. Outer display types affect how the element's box behaves in *flow layout* or *normal flow*. Display type is determined by the computed value of an element's `display` property.

In practical terms, this means that there are two display box types that participate in normal flow:

- **block-level** boxes that participate in a *block formatting context*
- **inline-level** boxes that participate in an *inline formatting context*

Formatting context is a fancy way of saying that an element "behaves according to the rules for boxes of this type."

The outer display type values are `block` and `inline`. The `block` value, as you may have guessed, triggers a block formatting context for an element's *principal box*, or its outermost,

---

[1] https://www.w3.org/TR/css-display-3/

containing box. Using `inline` will instead trigger an inline formatting context.

Inner display types include the `flex` / `inline-flex` , `grid` / `inline-grid` , and `table` values for the `display` property. These properties tell the browser how to lay out the contents inside the principal box. But they also provide a shorthand way to tell the browser to "treat the outer box as a block-level (or inline-level) box, but arrange the stuff inside it according to the rules of its formatting context."

Block Formatting versus Inline Formatting

Block-level boxes are stacked in the order in which they appear in the source document. In a horizontal writing mode, they stack vertically from the top to the bottom of the screen.

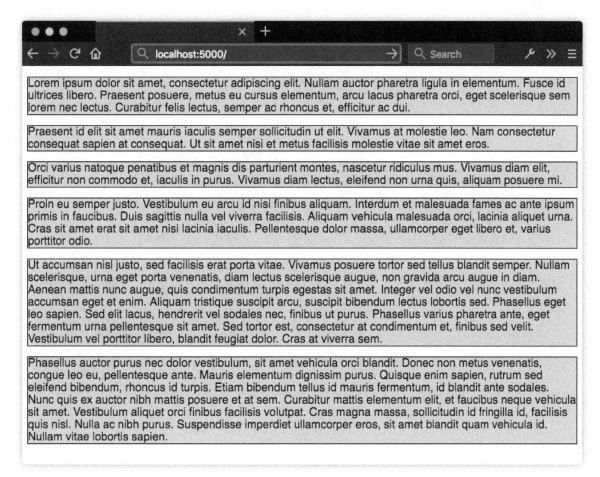

5-1. How a horizontal writing mode affects the block formatting context

Writing Modes

If you need a refresher on writing modes, refer to <u>Chapter 4, *Working with Text*</u>.

In vertical mode, they sit horizontally—side by side and across the screen. With the exception of `display: table` and its related properties, block-level boxes also expand to fill the available width of their containing element.

5-2. Vertical writing mode causes boxes in a block formatting context to be arranged horizontally

Browsers generate a block-level box when the computed value of the `display` property is one of the following:

- `block`
- `list-item`
- `table` or any of the `table-*` values such as `table-cell`

- *flex*
- *grid*
- *flow-root*

Other property-and-value combinations can also trigger block-level box behavior and a block formatting context. Multicolumn containers, for example, can trigger a block formatting context when the value of *column-count* or *column-width* is something other than *auto*. Using *column-span: all* also triggers a block formatting context. We'll discuss multicolumn layout later in this chapter.

Floating or positioning an element (with *position: absolute* or *position: fixed*) also triggers a block formatting context. So does the *contain* property when its value is *layout* , *content* , or *strict* .

 Browser Support

> At the time of writing, *contain* is a newer property with limited browser support. Chromium-based browsers fully support it. Firefox has partial support that's disabled by default. It can be enabled by changing the *layout.css.contain.enabled* flag in *about:config* . Safari and Microsoft Edge don't yet support it.

Inline-level boxes, by contrast, don't form new blocks of content. Instead, these boxes make up the lines inside of a block-level box. They're displayed horizontally and fill the width of the containing box, wrapping across lines if necessary, as shown in figure 5-3. Inline-level boxes have a *display* value of *inline* , *inline-block* , *inline-table* , or *ruby* .

Fusce odio leo, sollicitudin vel mattis eget, iaculis sit amet turpis. Quisque porta suscipit erat. Nulla sit amet neque eleifend diam aliquam rhoncus. Donec id congue est. Aliquam sagittis euismod tristique. Nunc aliquet iaculis ex, rutrum interdum nulla ultricies at. Curabitur turpis est, feugiat sit amet risus quis, mollis elementum libero. Cras vitae aliquet felis. Nam efficitur semper arcu a blandit. Proin condimentum elit sapien, ut tempor nisl porta quis. Pellentesque vel quam efficitur, pharetra urna in, suscipit tortor.

Pellentesque vel nisl sed tellus eleifend efficitur. Sed imperdiet diam sem, nec sodales libero lobortis non. Nunc semper felis sem, id pharetra lacus pellentesque tempor. Ut vitae scelerisque mauris. Nunc interdum ultricies laoreet. Nam a dui luctus, egestas enim sit amet, blandit quam. Phasellus lorem libero, sollicitudin id hendrerit a, faucibus eget nisi.

5-3. An example of an inline box with margin: 1em and padding: 5px applied

Just about every browser ships with a user agent stylesheet that sets default rules for element selectors. Typically these stylesheets add a *display: block* rule for elements such as *section* , *div* , *p* , and *ul* . Most *phrasing content* elements—such as *a* , *span* , and *canvas* —use the initial value of `display` , which is `inline` . When you view a document without any developer-authored CSS, you're really seeing the computed values from the browser's own stylesheet.

User agent stylesheets also set default styles for the root SVG element, particularly when SVG documents are combined with HTML. However, SVG documents rely on a coordinate system for layout instead of the box model. SVG elements do create a bounding box, but neither bounding boxes nor the shapes they contain affect the position of other elements in the document. As a result, most layout-related CSS properties don't work with SVG elements. We'll discuss that in greater depth in <u>Chapter 9, *Using CSS with SVG*</u>.

Box Dimensions and the Box Model

How are the dimensions of all these boxes calculated? Here's where it becomes a touch more complicated. As shown in figure 5-4, box dimensions are the sum of the box's content area, plus its padding width and border width <u>as defined by the CSS Level 2 specification</u>[2]. The margin width creates a *margin box* for the element.

Margin boxes affect the placement of other elements in the document, but the margin width has no effect on the dimensions of the box itself. Adjacent margin boxes also *collapse*. If two paragraph elements have top and bottom margins of 20px, the margin space between them will be 20px—not 40px.

 When Margins Don't Collapse

> In some formatting contexts, such as Grid, margins *do not* collapse. We discuss this in the <u>Grid section</u> of this chapter.

---

[2] https://drafts.csswg.org/css2/box.html

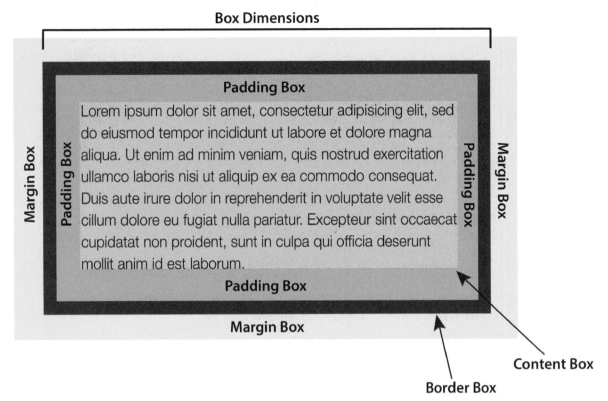

5-4. The CSS 2.1 box model

For instance, a `p` element with `width: 300px`, `padding: 20px`, and `border: 10px` has a calculated width of 360px. That's the sum of its width, left and right padding, and left and right `border-width` properties. To create an element that's 300px wide with 20px of padding and a 10px border, the `width` needs to be `240px`.

Today, browsers calculate the width in just this way. Internet Explorer 5.5, however, didn't. Instead, IE5.5 used the `width` property as the final arbiter of box dimensions, with padding and border drawn inside the box, as seen in figure 5-5. Both values were, in effect, subtracted from `width`, decreasing the size of the content area. Though it's the exact opposite of the behavior defined in the specification, many web developers thought it was the more sensible approach.

300px

300px

Lorem ipsum dolor sit amet, consectetur adipisicing elit, sed do eiusmod tempor incididunt ut labore et dolore magna aliqua. Ut enim ad minim veniam, quis nostrud exercitation ullamco laboris nisi ut aliquip ex ea commodo consequat. Duis aute irure dolor in reprehenderit in voluptate velit esse cillum dolore eu fugiat nulla pariatur. Excepteur sint occaecat cupidatat non proident, sunt in culpa qui officia deserunt mollit anim id est laborum. Duis aut eirure dolor in reprehenderit in voluptate velit esse cillum dolore eu fugiat nulla pariatur. Excepteur sint occaecat cupidatat non proident, sunt in culpa qui.

Lorem ipsum dolor sit amet, consectetur adipisicing elit, sed do eiusmod tempor incididunt ut labore et dolore magna aliqua. Ut enim ad minim veniam,quis nostrud exercitation ullamco laboris nisi ut aliquip ex ea commodo consequat. Duis aute irure dolor in reprehenderit in voluptate velit esse cillum dolore eu fugiat nulla pariatur. Excepteur sint occaecat cupidatat non proident, sunt in culpa qui officia deserunt mollit anim id est laborum. Duis aut eirure dolor in reprehenderit in voluptate velit esse cillum dolore.

Box Dimensions in CSS 2.1 Model

Box Dimensions in IE 5.5

5-5. The CSS 2.1 box model versus the old Internet Explorer 5.5 "quirks mode" box model

As a way to resolve these competing models, the CSS working group introduced the `box-sizing` property. It lets us choose how the browser should calculate box dimensions.

Managing Box Dimensions with `box-sizing`

The `box-sizing` property is defined in the <u>CSS Basic User Interface Module Level 3 specification</u>[3]. It has two possible values: `content-box` and `border-box`.

Initially, the value of `box-sizing` is `content-box`. With this value, setting the `width` and `height` properties of an element affects the size of its content area. This matches the behavior defined by the CSS 2.1 specification, and it's the default behavior in modern browsers (as presented in figure 5-5 above above).

Setting the value of `box-sizing` to `border-box` creates a little bit of magic. Now, the values of `width` and `height` will be applied to the outer border edge instead of the content area. Borders and padding are drawn inside the element box. Let's look at an example that mixes percentage widths and `px` units for padding and borders:

```
<div class="wrapper">
    <article>
        <h2>This is a headline</h2>
        <p>Lorem ipsum dolor sit amet, consectetur adipisicing ... </p>
    </article>
    <aside>
        <h2>This is a secondary headline</h2>
        <p>Lorem ipsum dolor sit amet, consectetur adipisicing ... </p>
```

---

[3]. http://www.w3.org/TR/css3-ui/#box-sizing

```
        </aside>
    </div>
```

Both our *article* and *aside* elements have the following CSS applied, which gives us the layout shown in figure 5-6. Our first element has a width of 60%, while the second has a width of 40%:

```
article, aside {
    background: #FFEB3B;
    border: 10px solid #9C27B0;
    float: left;
    padding: 10px;
}
article {
    width: 60%;
}
aside {
    width: 40%;
}
```

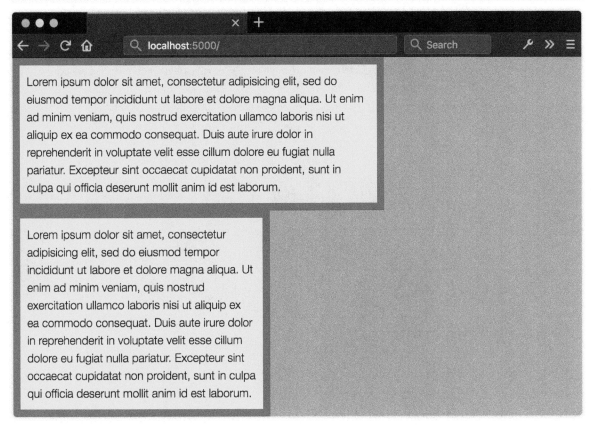

5-6. Elements with box-sizing: content-box

By default, both *aside* and *article* have a *box-sizing* value of *content-box* . The *border-width* and *padding* values add 40px to the width of each element, which throws off the 60%/40% split considerably. Now let's add *box-sizing: border-box* to the *article* and *aside* elements:

```
article, aside {
    box-sizing: border-box;
}
```

You can see the change in figure 5-7: the elements have the same width, but the *box-sizing: border-box* means that the width includes the border and padding. Because the *width* property applies to the border edge instead of the content area, our elements now fit side by side.

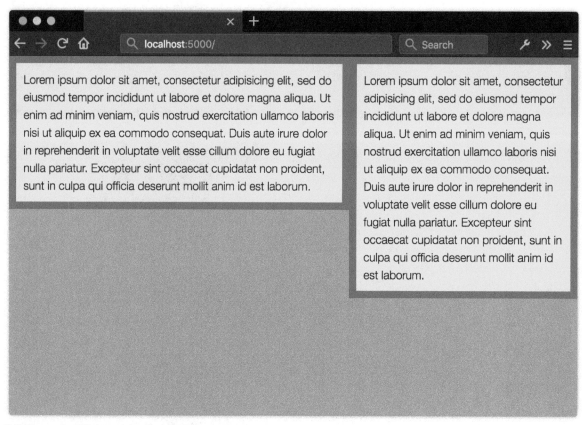

5-7. Elements with box-sizing: border-box

I recommend using *box-sizing: border-box* in your projects. It makes life easier, as there's no need to calculate the *width* value to account for the values of *padding* and *border* . Boxes behave more predictably.

The best way to apply *box-sizing: border-box* is with reset rules. The following example is from

Chris Coyier's CSS-Tricks post, "<u>Inheriting *box-sizing* Probably Slightly Better Best-Practice</u>[4]":

```
html {
    box-sizing: border-box;
}
*, *:before, *:after {
    box-sizing: inherit;
}
```

This applies *border-box* sizing to every element by default, without affecting the box-sizing behavior of existing parts of your project. If you *know* that there'll be no third-party or legacy components that rely on *content-box* behavior, you can simplify these rules:

```
*,
*:before,
*:after {
    box-sizing: border-box;
}
```

So far, we've reviewed managing the box model and the basics of normal flow. However, we often don't want an element to stay in the normal flow. Here's where floating and positioning come in.

Floating Elements and Normal Flow

When we float an item by setting the value of the *float* property to *left* or *right*, we remove it from the normal flow. The box is shifted to the left or right of the current line, until its edge aligns with the containing block or another floated element. Content will flow along the left or right edge of its box if there's enough horizontal space. The height of its containing element will shrink or grow to accommodate the flowed content, unless the containing element invokes a block formatting context.

If, for example, we left-float an image that's 300px by 225px, the adjacent lines of text will fill in along its right edge. If the computed height of the content exceeds 225px, it will continue to wrap around the bottom of the element:

---

4. https://css-tricks.com/inheriting-box-sizing-probably-slightly-better-best-practice/

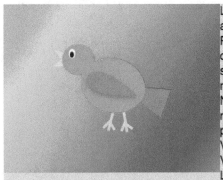

Lorem ipsum dolor sit amet, consectetur adipiscing elit. Nullam auctor pharetra ligula in elementum. Fusce id ultrices libero. Praesent posuere, metus eu cursus elementum, arcu lacus pharetra orci, eget scelerisque sem lorem nec lectus. Curabitur felis lectus, semper ac rhoncus et, efficitur ac dui. Praesent id elit sit amet mauris iaculis semper sollicitudin ut elit. Vivamus at molestie leo. Nam consectetur consequat sapien at consequat. Ut sit amet nisi et metus facilisis molestie vitae sit amet eros. Orci varius natoque penatibus et magnis dis parturient montes, nascetur ridiculus mus. Vivamus diam elit, efficitur non commodo et, iaculis in purus. Vivamus diam lectus, eleifend non urna quis, aliquam posuere mi. Lorem ipsum dolor sit amet, consectetur adipiscing elit. Sed eu quam consequat purus dignissim finibus. Sed tortor neque, porta vel odio at, dapibus elementum enim. Phasellus et dapibus ipsum, a pharetra est.

5-8. Floating an img element to the left

If, however, the remaining content is shorter than 200px, the floated element will overflow its container:

Lorem ipsum dolor sit amet, consectetur adipiscing elit. Nullam auctor pharetra ligula in elementum. Fusce id ultrices libero. Praesent posuere, metus eu cursus elementum, arcu lacus pharetra orci, eget scelerisque sem lorem nec lectus.

5-9. Floated images may exceed the height of their container

Text and elements in subsequent containers will flow along the left edge (when `float: right`) or right edge (when `float: left`) of the floated element if there's enough room. The length of each line—its line box—will be shortened to accommodate the float.

Floating a series of elements works a little bit differently. Let's apply `float: left` to a series of `div` elements that are 250px wide inside a container that's 800px wide. As you can see in figure 5-10, these elements stack horizontally to fill the available space. Elements that don't fit in the available horizontal space will be pushed down until the box fits or there are no more floated elements:

5-10. Floating a series of elements

Floated elements don't wrap neatly. Yet in the Jurassic era of the Web, before Flexbox and Grid layout, developers often used floats to create gridded layouts. It was necessary to set a common height on elements within a floated grid to ensure that elements didn't "snag" on others above them, or get prevented from floating to their intended position:

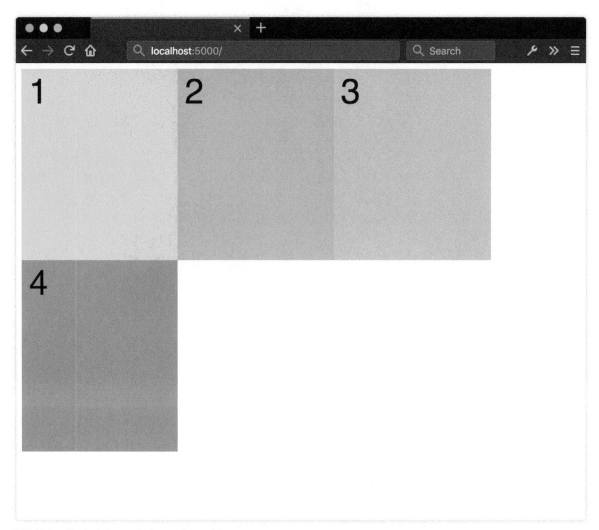

5-11. Using floated elements to create a grid

Removing elements from the normal flow can be tricky. Other content in the document will want to cozy up next to a floated element, yet that may not be the layout we're trying to achieve.

Consider the UI pattern known as a *media object*. A **media object** consists of an image or video thumbnail that's aligned to the left or right of its container, accompanied by some related text. You've probably seen this style of component in comments sections, on news sites, or as part of YouTube's "Up Next" feature.

Lorem ipsum dolor sit amet, consectetur adipiscing elit, sed do eiusmod tempor incididunt ut labore et dolore magna aliqua.

5-12. An example of a media object component

Here's what the markup for a media object might look like:

```
<div class="media__object">
    <img src="video_thumbnail.jpg">
    <div class="media__object__text">
        Lorem ipsum dolor sit amet, consectetur adipiscing elit, sed do eiusmod tempor incididunt ut
        labore et dolore magna aliqua.
    </div>
</div>
```

The media object is a simple pattern: it consists of an image floated to the left or right of its container and some related text. Floating our image is the simplest way to create a media object layout:

```
.media__object {
    background: #ccc;
    padding: 1rem;
}
.media__object img {
    float: left;
    margin-right: 1rem;
}
```

Of course, the risk of simply floating an image is that the height of the accompanying text may be shorter than the height of the floated image. When that happens, our container will collapse to match the height of the text, as shown below.

Lorem ipsum dolor sit amet, consectetur adipiscing elit, sed do eiusmod tempor incididunt ut labore et dolore magna aliqua.

5-13. A floated element and its parent before we've cleared our float

To prevent this, we need to *clear* our float. Let's look at some methods for doing so in the next section.

Clearing Floats

The simplest way to clear a float is to establish a new block formatting context for its container. A block formatting context always contains its children, even when those children are floated.

So how do we create a new block formatting context? One way is to use `display: flow-root`. Let's add `display: flow-root` to our `.media__object` ruleset:

```css
.media__object {
    background: #ccc;
    padding: 1rem;
    display: flow-root;
}
.media__object img {
    float: left;
    margin-right: 1rem;
}
```

Now our floated image will be completely contained by its parent, as shown in below.

Lorem ipsum dolor sit amet, consectetur adipiscing elit, sed do eiusmod tempor incididunt ut labore et dolore magna aliqua.

5-14. Invoking a block formatting context with display: flow-root

The `flow-root` value for the `display` property is a fairly recent addition to CSS. Its sole purpose is to trigger a block formatting context for a containing element. Unfortunately, its newness means that support is limited to Chrome 58+/Opera 46+ and Firefox 53+. If you need to support older versions of those browsers, or any version of Microsoft Edge, you'll need to use an alternative.

One such alternative is `overflow: auto`. Alas, `overflow: auto` isn't perfect. In older browsers, `overflow: auto` may trigger unintended scroll bars. In modern browsers, `overflow: auto` can clip shadows and other effects that exceed the bounds of the container.

For the broadest compatibility with the lowest risk of unintended effects, we need another approach. Enter the "clearfix" hack. It's a now classic web technique for clearing floats without extra markup or unintended effects.

Clearfix

Clearfix uses the `::after` pseudo-element and the `content` property to insert a box at the end of a containing element. Since pseudo-elements can be styled like actual elements, we can apply `display: table` (or `display: block`) and `clear: both` to clear our float:

```
.media__object::after {
    content: "";
    display: table;
    clear: both;
}
```

Floats are still useful for aligning images and tables to the left or right, or for placing content asides within a page. For most other uses, Flexbox and Grid are better choices. Flexbox and Grid typically require less markup and less CSS while offering more flexibility in the kinds of layouts we can create. Grid and Flexbox also make vertical centering remarkably easy, as we'll see later in this chapter.

But first, let's discuss another way to remove elements from the normal flow: the `position` and `z-index` properties.

Positioning and Stacking Elements

Every element in a document participates in a *stacking context*. The **stacking context** is a model or set of rules for how elements are painted to the screen. If you've ever used the `z-index` property, you've worked with stacking contexts.

The root `html` element creates a *root stacking context*. Some CSS properties and values can also trigger a stacking context for the elements they're applied to. Whether part of a root or local context, children within a stacking context are painted to the screen from back to front as follows:

1   child stacking contexts with a negative stack level (for example, positioned and with

`z-index: -1`)

2   non-positioned elements whose computed `position` value is `static`

3   child stacking contexts with a stack level of 0 (for example, positioned and with `z-index:`

auto)

4   child stacking contexts with positive stack levels (for example, positioned and with

z-index: 1)

If two elements have the same stack level, they'll be layered according to their order in the source HTML.

Let's look at an example. Here's our HTML:

```
<div id="a">
    <p><b>div#a</b></p>
</div>
<div id="b">
    <p><b>div#b</b></p>
</div>
<div id="c">
    <p><b>div#c</b></p>
</div>
<div id="d">
    <p><b>div#d</b></p>
</div>
 <div id="e">
    <p><b>div#e</b></p>
</div>
```

And here's our CSS:

```
#a {
    background: rgba(233, 30, 99, 0.5);
}
#b, #c, #d, #e {
    position: absolute;
}
#b {
    background: rgba(103, 58, 183, 0.8);
    bottom: 120px;
    width: 410px;
    z-index: 2;
}
#c {
    background: rgba(255, 235, 59, 0.8);
    top: 190px;
    z-index: 1;
}
```

```
#d {
    background: #03a9f4;
    height: 500px;
    top: 10px;
    z-index: -1;
}
#e {
    background: rgba(255, 87, 34, 0.7);
    top: 110px;
    z-index: 1;
}
```

This will produce the stacking order shown in figure 5-15. The bottommost layer is `#d`, because its `z-index` value is -1. Since `#a` isn't positioned, it sits above `#d`, but below the positioned elements (`#b`, `#c`, and `#e`). The next layer is `#c`, followed by `#e`. Since both elements have the same `z-index` value, `#e` is stacked higher, because it's last in the source order. The topmost layer is `#b`, due to its `z-index` of `2`.

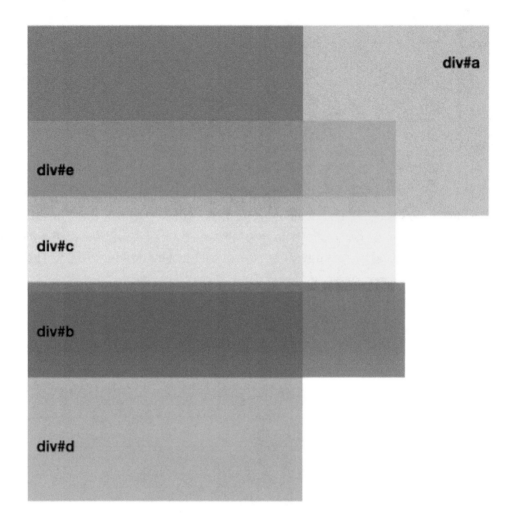

5-15. A stacking context with positioned and unpositioned elements of varying z-index values

All the elements in the previous example are part of the root stacking context. But let's see how stacking is affected by a property— *opacity* —that forces a local context when its value is less than *1* . Consider the following HTML:

```
<div id="f">
    <p><b>div#f</b></p>
</div>
<div id="g">
    <p><b>div#g</b></p>
</div>
```

It's paired with this CSS:

```css
#f, #g {
    position: absolute;
}
#f {
    background: rgba(255,193,7,.9);
}
#f p {
    background: rgb(34,34,34);
    color: whitesmoke;
    position: relative;
    z-index: 1;
}
#g {
    background: rgba(3,169,244,.7);
    top: 50px;
    left: 100px;
}
```

According to the rules of the stacking context, *#f p* occupies the topmost layer in the stack. That's what we see in figure 5-16.

5-16. The rendered version of our sample HTML and CSS

But if we change our CSS and add *opacity: .99* to the *#f* ruleset, something interesting happens:

```css
#f {
    background: rgba(255,193,7,.9);
    opacity: .99;
}
```

```
    }
```

The *opacity* property creates a new stacking context any time its value is less than *1*. As a result, the *z-index* for its child element becomes relative to its parent rather than the root stacking context. You can see how this works below. Notice that *#g* now occupies the topmost layer.

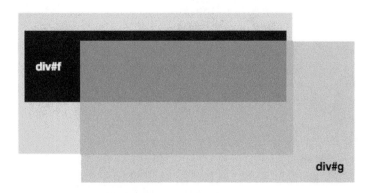

5-17. How opacity affects stacking order

Let's add an absolutely positioned *div* element to *#f* and give it a *z-index* value of *2*. Now *div* is stacked on top of *#f p* (see below), but it's still layered behind *#g* because *#f* has a local stacking context. Children of a local stacking context can only be reordered relative to that context. Elements that sit in other contexts can't be layered within a local one.

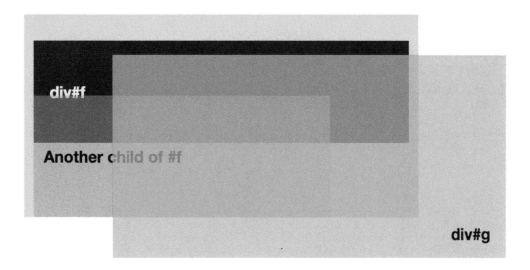

5-18. Multiple elements in a stacking context

 Workaround for Undesired Behaviors

Because *opacity* triggers a new stacking context, you may run into undesired behavior when transitioning the *opacity* of layers that overlap. To work around this, use *rgba()* or *hsla()* values for *color* or *background-color* and transition those instead.

Let's look at an example of using the stacking context to manage layers and positioned elements. In this case, we'll create a menu that slides in from the top of the screen. But rather than slide in *over* the logo and menu button, we'll make it slide in beneath it. First our HTML:

```
<header>
    <img src="dont-awesomenews.svg">
    <button type="button" id="menu">
        <img src="dont-menu.svg">
    </button>
    <nav>
        <ul id="menu-list">
            <li><a href="/sports">Sports</a></li>
            <li><a href="/politics">Politics</a></li>
            <li><a href="/arts">Arts &amp; Entertainment</a></li>
            <li><a href="/business">Business</a></li>
            <li><a href="/travel">Travel</a></li>
```

```
        </ul>
    </nav>
</header>
```

Clicking the *button* element causes the element to slide into view. Now for our (edited) CSS:

```css
header {
    background: #222629;
    color: whitesmoke;
    position: fixed;
    top: 0;
    width: 100%;
}
nav {
    background: #222629;
    position: absolute;
    width: 100%;
    left: 0;
    top: -33vw;
    transition: top 500ms;
}
.open {
    top: 9vw;
}
```

The CSS above creates a menu that slides down from the top when triggered. But as it slides in, it passes over the AwesomeNews logo:

5-19. The menu slides over the AwesomeNews logo

Our menu (the `nav` element) slides over the logo and menu button because it has a higher stack level. Remember that when multiple elements have the same `z-index` value, the last one in the source will be the topmost layer.

Let's change this. What happens when we add `z-index: -1` to the `nav` ruleset? Well, you get the mess you see in figure 5-20.

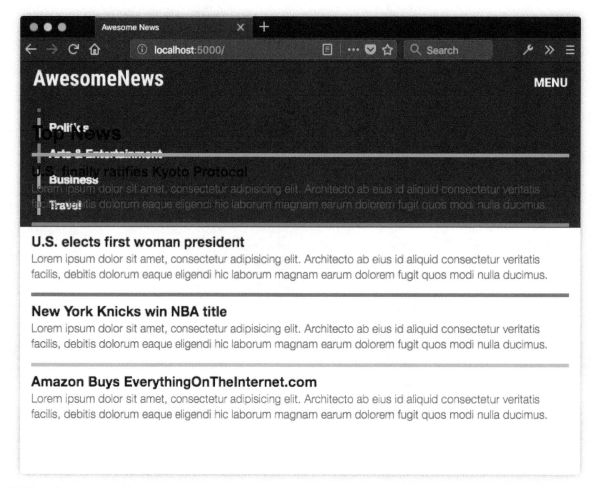

5-20. Adding z-index: -1 forces nav to the bottom of the stack

The navigation slides in behind the logo and menu button, but it also slides in behind the content. It's hard to read and impossible to click.

Because its parent element (`header`) has a `z-index` of `auto` , the `nav` element is still part of the root stacking context. Adding `z-index: -1` shoves it to the bottom of the root element's stack, which means it sits behind other elements in the root stacking context.

So how do we fix this? By creating a new stacking context for `nav` . We already know that the `opacity` property will create a new stacking context when its value is less than `1` . But positioned elements can also create a new stacking context if the `z-index` value is something other than `auto` or `0` . Our `header` element already has `positioned: fixed` . Now we just need to add `z-index: 1` to its ruleset:[5]

```
header {
```

```
    background: #222629;
    color: whitesmoke;
    position: fixed;
    top: 0;
    width: 100%;
    z-index: 1;
}
```

Now our `nav` element is contained within the stacking context of its parent. Since `header` has a stack level of `1` and `nav` is its child, the menu sits above the rest of our content. But because `nav` has a negative stack level, it sits at the bottom of the `header` element's stacking context, as illustrated in figure 5-21.

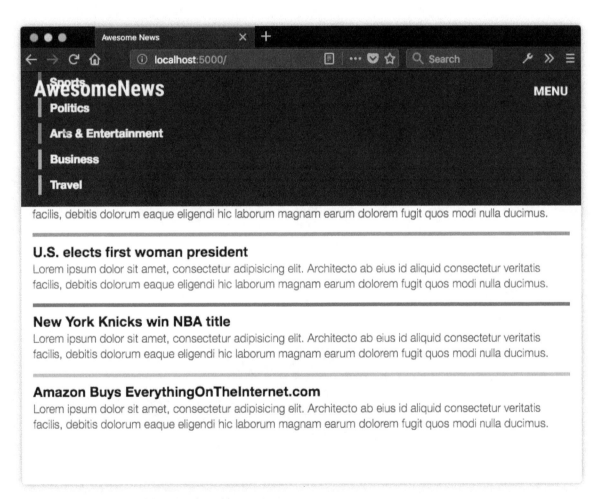

5-21. Managing elements within a local stacking context

For the rest of this chapter, we'll switch gears and talk about three modules for creating complex layouts: multiple column, flexible layout, and Grid. These modules make previously difficult layouts straightforward, and previously impossible layouts possible. With them, we can create adaptive columns and grid-based layouts without the need for extra markup or JavaScript.

Using CSS Multicolumn Layout

Multiple-column (or **multicolumn**) layout allows text and elements to flow from one column to another, and automatically adjust to the width of the viewport or container. With it, we can create text layouts that mimic those found in newspapers, magazines, and ebooks. We can also use it to create space-efficient user interfaces.

Basic support for multicolumn layout is quite good. All major browsers support the ability to create columns (using the `columns` property), set an optimal column width (`column-width`), set the size of the gutter (`column-gap`), and add rules between columns (`column-rule`). Older versions of Chrome (≤ 49) and Firefox (≤ 51) require vendor prefixes— `-webkit-` and `-moz-` respectively. Firefox also lacks support for the `column-span` (or `-moz-column-span`) property.

Support for `break-before` , `break-after` , and `break-inside` , on the other hand, is a little more complicated. These properties specify how the children of a multicolumn element should be distributed across columns or pages.

Edge, Safari, and Chrome support these properties. Older versions of Safari and Chrome support the non-standard `-webkit-column-break-before` , `-webkit-column-break-after` , and `-webkit-column-break-inside` properties instead.

Firefox, on the other hand, lacks support for `break-before` , `break-after` , and `break-inside` entirely. Instead, it supports similar properties— `page-break-before` and `page-break-after` —that work the same way.

 Holdover Properties

The `page-break-*` and `-webkit-column-break-*` properties are holdovers from earlier versions of the <u>paged media</u>[5] and multicolumn specifications. The <u>CSS Fragmentation Module Level 3</u>[6] specification unified these properties into the `break-*` properties and supersedes that earlier work.

It's safe to use multicolumn properties in projects, even without a fallback. If the browser doesn't support it, text will default to the normal flow.

---

5. https://www.w3.org/TR/css3-page/
6. https://www.w3.org/TR/css-break-3/

Defining Column Number and Width Using `columns`

To create multiple columns, set the `columns` property:

```
<div style="columns: 2">
    <p>Lorem ipsum dolor sit amet, consectetur adipisicing ... </p>
    <p>Duis aute irure dolor in reprehenderit in voluptate ... </p>
</div>
```

The `columns` property is a shorthand property for `column-width` and `column-count`. With `columns`, the first value that can be interpreted as a length becomes the value of `column-width`. The first value that can be interpreted as an integer becomes the value of `column-count`. Order doesn't matter. A declaration such as `columns: 10em 3` is the shorthand way of typing `column-width: 10em; column-count: 3`. It's also equivalent to typing `columns: 3 10em`.

If a value is unspecified, it will default to the initial value of `auto`. In other words, `columns: 4` has the same effect as typing `columns: 4 auto` or `column-width: auto; column-count: 4`.

Setting `column-width` determines the *optimal size* for each column. Its value should be in length units—for example, `column-width: 200px` or `column-width: 10em`. Percentages won't work.

"Optimal," of course, means that `column-width` sets the *ideal* width. The actual width of a column may be wider or narrower than the value of `column-width`, depending on the available space and/or viewport size. Below, for example, the container is 760px wide and the `column-width` value is 15em. That gives us three columns.

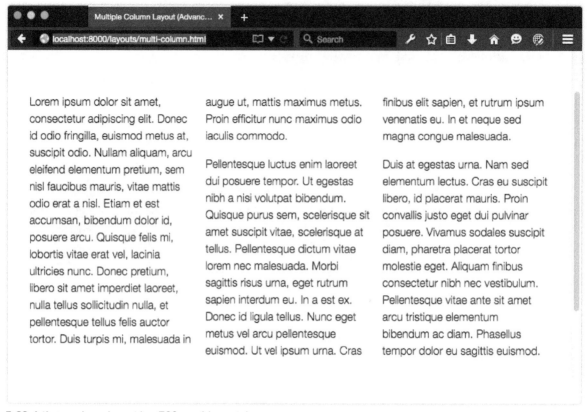

5-22. A three column layout in a 760 px wide container

But if we expand the width of the container to 1080px, there's now room for four columns:

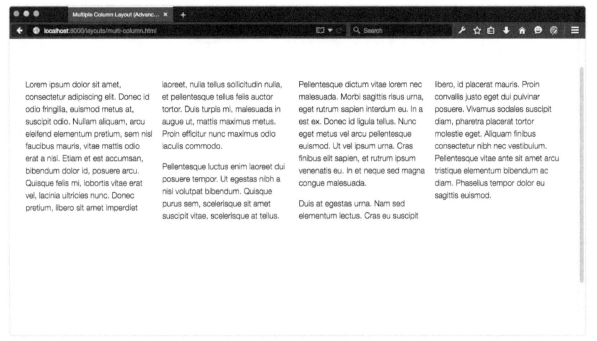

5-23. Our layout becomes four columns when the container is 1080px wide

Shrinking the width of the container to 355px, on the other hand, reduces our columns to one:

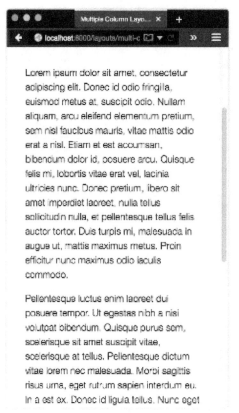

5-24. Reducing the container width to 335px makes our layout a single column

Setting the `column-count` property defines the optimal number of columns to create. Its value must be an integer greater than `0`. If `column-width` is something other than `auto`, the browser will create columns of that width up to the number of columns specified by `column-count`. If `column-width` is `auto`, the browser will create the number of columns specified by `column-count`. That's a bit tricky to understand, so let's illustrate it.

In the figures that follow, our container has a `column-count` value of `3`, and a `column-width` value of `auto`. Whether our container is 760px wide (as in figure 5-25) or 355px wide (as in figure 5-26), we still have three columns.

5-25. Three columns at 760px wide

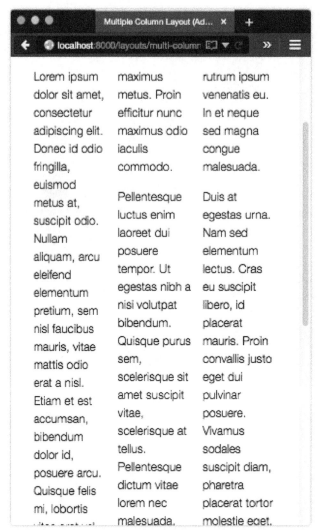

5-26. Three columns at 355px wide

Now, compare these to figure 5-27, where our container has a `column-count` value of `3`, and a `column-width` value of `8em`. Inside a container 760px wide, our number of columns remains the same. But when our container is 355px wide, we can only fit two columns.

5-27. With 355px width container and with a column-width value of 8em, we can only fit two columns

This goes out of the window entirely, though, if we set the `height` of a column container. Setting a fixed height on a container forces the browser to create additional columns to accommodate the container's content. In this case, the `column-count` property will be ignored.

Spacing Columns with `column-gap` and `column-rule`

How many columns will fit in a container also depends on the value of `column-gap`. Known as the **gutter** in print design, the **column gap** sets the distance between each column. The initial value of `column-gap` is `normal`. In most browsers, that's about `1em`.

Increasing or decreasing its width has no effect on the width of each column, just the space between. If an element is `45em` wide with `column-width: 15em` and `column-gap: normal` applied, the content will be divided into two columns rather than three, as can be seen below.

5-28. Columns that are 15em wide inside a 45em container with the default column-gap value

Changing `column-gap` to `0`, however, gives us our full three-column layout, as shown below. Without a `column-gap`, there's now sufficient room for three columns.

As with `column-width`, the value of `column-gap` should be either `0` or a positive length value. Negative lengths such as `-2em` are invalid.

5-29. 15em wide columns inside a 45em wide container with column-gap: 0

With `column-rule`, we can add lines to visually separate columns. It functions similarly to `border`, and accepts the same values. For example:

```
.multi-col {
    column-rule: thin dashed #0c0;
}
```

Like `border`, `column-rule` is really a shorthand for the `column-rule-width`, `column-rule-style`, and `column-rule-color` properties. Each `column-rule-*` property accepts the same values as its `border` counterpart. An example of using `column-rule` is shown below.

Lorem ipsum dolor sit amet, consectetur adipiscing elit. Donec lacinia blandit felis porta convallis. Duis magna nibh, euismod ac turpis quis, pretium rhoncus nisi. Nulla maximus cursus massa quis porta. Vestibulum urna eros, gravida vel mauris ac, consequat condimentum sapien.

Donec ultricies enim tortor, sit amet semper velit blandit sagittis. Fusce blandit vehicula quam, vel interdum orci pellentesque et. Aliquam erat volutpat. Maecenas condimentum, quam et iaculis ullamcorper, libero justo egestas mi, quis cursus lorem ante non dui.

Sed consequat mi vel venenatis molestie. Fusce rutrum tellus sed

sagittis tempor enim eget imperdiet.

Proin non cursus sem. Suspendisse neque orci, porttitor sit amet dui ac, eleifend ultricies magna. Duis malesuada nisi sed porttitor pretium. Donec dignissim, libero sit amet commodo hendrerit, libero magna tempus augue, in suscipit purus ex eu lacus. Curabitur nulla augue, cursus quis sodales in, maximus eget lectus. Cras vitae efficitur odio. In imperdiet, ligula at luctus laoreet, sapien erat dictum diam, condimentum egestas enim sem at est. Donec aliquam odio fringilla nisl gravida, nec auctor lectus cursus. Morbi ut lectus sem. Etiam consectetur sagittis purus sed ornare. Duis eget ipsum in nisi mollis luctus eu non nibh.

Aliquam ornare, massa id gravida egestas, risus nibh finibus nibh, nec vestibulum arcu enim eget lorem. Vestibulum convallis, leo ut pulvinar dapibus, nisl nulla efficitur mi, id luctus eros erat porttitor ligula. Praesent massa enim, commodo id vestibulum vitae, dictum nec turpis.

Nulla ante dolor, fermentum sed commodo in, finibus sed sapien. In vitae tempor augue. Sed ut turpis sem. Ut iaculis urna in ornare elementum. Pellentesque pellentesque, lectus sit amet tempor sodales, orci lectus hendrerit lacus, et vehicula tellus metus eu magna. Etiam quis libero mattis, cursus orci eget, euismod nunc. Donec eros velit, consectetur ut convallis ut, viverra eu enim. Morbi sed elementum

5-30. Adding a column rule

Column width is not affected by changes to `column-rule`. Instead, column rules sit at the midpoint of the column gap. If the width of the rule exceeds that of the gap, the column rule will render beneath the columns' contents:

Lorem ipsum dolor sit amet, consectetur adipiscing elit. Donec lacinia blandit felis porta convallis. Duis magna nibh, euismod ac turpis quis, pretium rhoncus nisi. Nulla maximus cursus massa quis porta. Vestibulum urna eros, gravida vel mauris ac, consequat condimentum sapien.

Donec ultricies enim tortor, sit amet semper velit blandit sagittis. Fusce blandit vehicula quam, vel interdum orci pellentesque et. Aliquam erat volutpat. Maecenas condimentum, quam et iaculis ullamcorper, libero justo egestas mi, quis cursus lorem ante non dui.

Sed consequat mi vel venenatis molestie. Fusce rutrum tellus sed

sagittis tempor enim eget imperdiet.

Proin non cursus sem. Suspendisse neque orci, porttitor sit amet dui ac, eleifend ultricies magna. Duis malesuada nisi sed porttitor pretium. Donec dignissim, libero sit amet commodo hendrerit, libero magna tempus augue, in suscipit purus ex eu lacus. Curabitur nulla augue, cursus quis sodales in, maximus eget lectus. Cras vitae efficitur odio. In imperdiet, ligula at luctus laoreet, sapien erat dictum diam, condimentum egestas enim sem at est. Donec aliquam odio fringilla nisl gravida, nec auctor lectus cursus. Morbi ut lectus sem. Etiam consectetur sagittis purus sed ornare. Duis eget ipsum in nisi mollis luctus eu non nibh.

Aliquam ornare, massa id gravida egestas, risus nibh finibus nibh, nec vestibulum arcu enim eget lorem. Vestibulum convallis, leo ut pulvinar dapibus, nisl nulla efficitur mi, id luctus eros erat porttitor ligula. Praesent massa enim, commodo id vestibulum vitae, dictum nec turpis.

Nulla ante dolor, fermentum sed commodo in, finibus sed sapien. In vitae tempor augue. Sed ut turpis sem. Ut iaculis urna in ornare elementum. Pellentesque pellentesque, lectus sit amet tempor sodales, orci lectus hendrerit lacus, et vehicula tellus metus eu magna. Etiam quis libero mattis, cursus orci eget, euismod nunc. Donec eros velit, consectetur ut convallis ut, viverra eu enim. Morbi sed elementum

5-31. What happens when the width of a column rule exceeds the column gap

Images Within Columns

Sometimes, an image may be wider than its column. In Firefox ≤ 61 and Safari, the image will overflow the column's width and be rendered below the surrounding text.

5-32. Images within a column sit at the bottom of the stacking context in Safari 12

This overflow behavior is what's currently defined by the **specification**[7]. However, in Chrome, Samsung Internet, and Microsoft Edge, the overflowing portion of that image will be clipped by the column's width:

Multicolumn!

localhost:5000/multicol.html

Lorem ipsum dolor sit amet, consectetur adipiscing elit. Donec lacinia blandit felis porta convallis. Duis magna nibh

semper velit blandit sagittis. Fusce blandit vehicula quam, vel interdum orci pellentesque et. Aliquam erat volutpat. Maecenas condimentum, quam et iaculis ullamcorper, libero justo egestas mi, quis cursus lorem ante non dui. Sed consequat mi vel venenatis molestie. Fusce rutrum tellus sed mi porttitor varius eu rhoncus est. Curabitur auctor sem purus, vel volutpat elit rhoncus vitae.

Duis sodales nibh ac dapibus sagittis. Vestibulum bibendum malesuada tellus, ac consequat nibh rhoncus lobortis. Donec quis est quis velit efficitur molestie in blandit nunc. Maecenas blandit enim et orci mollis, quis fringilla massa suscipit. Aenean vel felis pulvinar, mollis nunc eget, semper ante. Quisque convallis, erat tincidunt convallis blandit, velit metus bibendum orci, sed fringilla lacus est non odio. Suspendisse sagittis tempor enim eget imperdiet. Proin non cursus sem. Suspendisse magna

lacus. Curabitur nulla augue, cursus quis sodales in, maximus eget lectus. Cras vitae efficitur odio. In imperdiet, ligula at luctus laoreet, sapien erat dictum diam, condimentum egestas enim sem at est. Donec aliquam odio fringilla nisl gravida, nec auctor lectus cursus.

Morbi ut lectus sem. Etiam consectetur sagittis purus sed ornare. Duis eget ipsum in nisi mollis luctus eu non nibh. Aenean vel mi sem. Nulla facilisi. Proin id enim et justo convallis sagittis eu quis magna. Sed in est enim. In dolor purus, elementum et lorem vel, rhoncus faucibus leo. Aliquam erat volutpat. Suspendisse aliquam eros ut augue vehicula posuere. Donec in dolor magna. Proin eu consequat arcu, a consequat nisl.

Ut magna lectus, auctor sit amet dolor nec, aliquam sodales mauris. Curabitur et ipsum at ex cursus semper. Sed diam odio

pulvinar dapibus, nisl nulla efficitur mi, id luctus eros erat porttitor ligula. Praesent massa enim, commodo id vestibulum vitae, dictum nec turpis. Nulla ante dolor, fermentum sed commodo in, finibus sed sapien. In vitae tempor augue. Sed ut turpis sem. Ut iaculis urna in ornare elementum. Pellentesque pellentesque, lectus sit amet tempor sodales, orci lectus hendrerit lacus, et vehicula tellus metus eu magna. Etiam quis libero mattis, cursus orci eget, euismod nunc. Donec eros velit, consectetur ut convallis ut, viverra eu enim. Morbi sed elementum nunc. Maecenas eget commodo sapien, id dignissim nisl.

Quisque a sapien vehicula, egestas leo eu, dapibus nibh. Etiam tincidunt odio et elementum lobortis. Donec dignissim vehicula pellentesque. Interdum et malesuada fames ac ante ipsum primis in faucibus. Pellentesque vitae libero eu lorem congue eleifend sed et ipsum. Aenean

5-33. Images are clipped to the width of their column in Chrome

You can work around this by adding a `width: 100%` declaration to the image or object. Doing so constrains the width of the image to that of the column box, as shown below. It will also constrain the height based on the aspect ratio of the image.

Lorem ipsum dolor sit amet, consectetur adipiscing elit. Donec lacinia blandit felis porta convallis. Duis magna nibh, euismod ac turpis quis, pretium rhoncus nisi. Nulla maximus cursus massa quis porta. Vestibulum urna eros, gravida vel mauris ac, consequat condimentum sapien. Donec ultricies enim tortor, sit amet semper velit blandit sagittis. Fusce blandit vehicula quam, vel interdum orci pellentesque et. Aliquam erat volutpat. Maecenas condimentum, quam et iaculis ullamcorper, libero iusto egestas mi, quis

Duis sodales nibh ac dapibus sagittis. Vestibulum bibendum malesuada tellus, ac consequat nibh rhoncus lobortis. Donec quis est quis velit efficitur molestie in blandit nunc. Maecenas blandit enim et orci mollis, quis fringilla massa suscipit. Aenean vel felis pulvinar, mollis nunc eget, semper ante. Quisque convallis, erat tincidunt convallis blandit, velit metus bibendum orci, sed fringilla lacus est non odio. Suspendisse sagittis tempor enim eget imperdiet. Proin non cursus sem. Suspendisse neque orci, porttitor sit amet dui ac, eleifend ultricies magna. Duis malesuada nisi sed porttitor pretium. Donec dignissim, libero sit amet commodo hendrerit, libero magna tempus augue, in suscipit purus ex eu lacus.

gravida, nec auctor lectus cursus.

Morbi ut lectus sem. Etiam consectetur sagittis purus sed ornare. Duis eget ipsum in nisi mollis luctus eu non nibh. Aenean vel mi sem. Nulla facilisi. Proin id enim et justo convallis sagittis eu quis magna. Sed in est enim. In dolor purus, elementum et lorem vel, rhoncus faucibus leo. Aliquam erat volutpat. Suspendisse aliquam eros ut augue vehicula posuere. Donec in dolor magna. Proin eu consequat arcu, a consequat nisl.

Ut magna lectus, auctor sit amet dolor nec, aliquam sodales mauris. Curabitur et ipsum at ex cursus semper. Sed diam odio, ultrices id pharetra sit amet, pellentesque sit amet massa. Aliquam ornare, massa id

turpis. Nulla ante dolor, fermentum sed commodo in, finibus sed sapien. In vitae tempor augue. Sed ut turpis sem. Ut iaculis urna in ornare elementum. Pellentesque pellentesque, lectus sit amet tempor sodales, orci lectus hendrerit lacus, et vehicula tellus metus eu magna. Etiam quis libero mattis, cursus orci eget, euismod nunc. Donec eros velit, consectetur ut convallis ut, viverra eu enim. Morbi sed elementum nunc. Maecenas eget commodo sapien, id dignissim nisl.

Quisque a sapien vehicula, egestas leo eu, dapibus nibh. Etiam tincidunt odio et elementum lobortis. Donec dignissim vehicula pellentesque. Interdum et malesuada fames ac ante ipsum primis in faucibus.

5-34. Using img {width: 100%} inside a multicolumn container

Floated elements, such as an image, within a multicolumn layout are floated within the column box. In the image below, the *img* element has a *float: left* rule applied. Text still flows around the image, but within the constraints of the column.

Lorem ipsum dolor sit amet, consectetur adipiscing elit. Donec lacinia blandit felis porta convallis. Duis magna nibh, euismod ac turpis quis, pretium rhoncus nisi. Nulla maximus cursus massa quis porta. Vestibulum urna eros, gravida vel mauris ac, consequat condimentum sapien.

Donec ultricies enim tortor, sit amet semper velit blandit sagittis. Fusce blandit vehicula quam, vel interdum orci pellentesque et. Aliquam erat volutpat. Maecenas condimentum, quam et iaculis ullamcorper, libero justo egestas mi, quis cursus lorem ante non dui.

Sed consequat mi vel venenatis molestie. Fusce

condimentum egestas enim sem at est. Donec aliquam odio fringilla nisl gravida, nec auctor lectus cursus. Morbi ut lectus sem. Etiam consectetur sagittis purus sed ornare. Duis eget ipsum in nisi mollis luctus eu non nibh. Aenean vel mi sem. Nulla facilisi. Proin id enim et justo convallis sagittis eu quis magna. Sed in est enim. In dolor purus, elementum et lorem vel, rhoncus faucibus leo. Aliquam erat volutpat. Suspendisse aliquam eros ut augue vehicula posuere. Donec in dolor magna. Proin eu consequat arcu, a consequat nisl.

Ut magna lectus, auctor sit amet dolor nec, aliquam sodales mauris. Curabitur et ipsum at ex cursus semper. Sed diam odio, ultrices id pharetra sit amet, pellentesque.

Aliquam ornare, massa id gravida egestas, risus nibh finibus nibh, nec vestibulum arcu enim eget lorem. Vestibulum convallis, leo ut pulvinar dapibus, nisl nulla efficitur mi, id luctus eros erat porttitor ligula. Praesent massa enim,

5-35. Floating an element within a multicolumn layout

Positioned elements follow the normal stacking context rules. A positioned element will be placed within the root stacking context unless it's a descendant element of a local stacking context.

Making Elements Span Columns

We can also make a particular element span columns with the `column-span` property. This property accepts two values: `none` and `all`. Using `none` means that the element will be part of the normal column flow; `all` will make the element span every column.

It's currently not possible to make an element span *a particular number of columns*. We're limited to specifying whether it should span all columns or none at all. Consider the layout shown below.

Dog bites man; says man tastes like chicken

Lorem ipsum dolor sit amet, consectetur adipiscing elit. Donec lacinia blandit felis porta convallis. Duis magna nibh, euismod ac turpis quis, pretium rhoncus nisi. Nulla maximus cursus massa

Curabitur auctor sem purus, vel volutpat elit rhoncus vitae.

Duis sodales nibh ac dapibus sagittis. Vestibulum bibendum malesuada tellus, ac consequat nibh rhoncus lobortis. Donec quis est quis velit efficitur molestie in blandit nunc. Maecenas blandit enim et orci mollis, quis fringilla massa suscipit. Aenean vel felis pulvinar, mollis nunc eget, semper ante. Quisque convallis, erat tincidunt convallis blandit, velit metus bibendum orci, sed fringilla lacus est non odio. Suspendisse sagittis tempor enim eget imperdiet. Proin non cursus sem.

enim sem at est. Donec aliquam odio fringilla nisl gravida, nec auctor lectus cursus.

Morbi ut lectus sem. Etiam consectetur sagittis purus sed ornare. Duis eget ipsum in nisi mollis luctus eu non nibh. Aenean vel mi sem. Nulla facilisi. Proin id enim et justo convallis sagittis eu quis magna. Sed in est enim. In dolor purus, elementum et lorem vel, rhoncus faucibus leo. Aliquam erat volutpat. Suspendisse aliquam eros ut augue vehicula posuere. Donec in dolor magna. Proin eu consequat arcu, a consequat nisl.

Ut magna lectus, auctor

dictum nec turpis. Nulla ante dolor, fermentum sed commodo in, finibus sed sapien. In vitae tempor augue. Sed ut turpis sem. Ut iaculis urna in ornare elementum. Pellentesque pellentesque, lectus sit amet tempor sodales, orci lectus hendrerit lacus, et vehicula tellus metus eu magna. Etiam quis libero mattis, cursus orci eget, euismod nunc. Donec eros velit, consectetur ut convallis ut, viverra eu enim. Morbi sed elementum nunc. Maecenas eget commodo sapien, id dignissim nisl.

Quisque a sapien vehicula, egestas leo

5-36. How an h1 element fits into the multicolumn layout flow

Here, the `h1` element (the article headline "Dog bites man …") is part of the multicolumn layout flow. It sits within a column box, wrapping as appropriate. Now let's add `column-span: all`:

```
article > h1 {
    column-span: all;
}
```

This gives us the layout shown below, with a headline that spans all of our columns.

Dog bites man; says man tastes like chicken

Lorem ipsum dolor sit amet, consectetur adipiscing elit. Donec lacinia blandit felis porta convallis. Duis magna nibh, euismod ac turpis quis, pretium rhoncus nisi. Nulla maximus cursus massa quis porta. Vestibulum urna eros, gravida vel mauris ac, consequat condimentum sapien. Donec ultricies enim tortor, sit amet semper velit blandit sagittis. Fusce blandit vehicula

consequat nibh rhoncus lobortis. Donec quis est quis velit efficitur molestie in blandit nunc. Maecenas blandit enim et orci mollis, quis fringilla massa suscipit. Aenean vel felis pulvinar, mollis nunc eget, semper ante. Quisque convallis, erat tincidunt convallis blandit, velit metus bibendum orci, sed fringilla lacus est non odio. Suspendisse sagittis tempor enim eget imperdiet. Proin non cursus sem. Suspendisse neque orci, porttitor sit amet dui ac, eleifend ultricies magna. Duis

Etiam consectetur sagittis purus sed ornare. Duis eget ipsum in nisi mollis luctus eu non nibh. Aenean vel mi sem. Nulla facilisi. Proin id enim et justo convallis sagittis eu quis magna. Sed in est enim. In dolor purus, elementum et lorem vel, rhoncus faucibus leo. Aliquam erat volutpat. Suspendisse aliquam eros ut augue vehicula posuere. Donec in dolor magna. Proin eu consequat arcu, a consequat nisl.

Ut magna lectus, auctor sit amet dolor nec, aliquam sodales

commodo in, finibus sed sapien. In vitae tempor augue. Sed ut turpis sem. Ut iaculis urna in ornare elementum. Pellentesque pellentesque, lectus sit amet tempor sodales, orci lectus hendrerit lacus, et vehicula tellus metus eu magna. Etiam quis libero mattis, cursus orci eget, euismod nunc. Donec eros velit, consectetur ut convallis ut, viverra eu enim. Morbi sed elementum nunc. Maecenas eget commodo sapien, id dignissim nisl.

Quisque a sapien

5-37. Using column-span to make an element span multiple columns

Managing Column Breaks Within Elements

In a multicolumn layout, a long block of text may start in one column and end in another:

Dog bites man; says man tastes like chicken

Lorem ipsum dolor sit amet, consectetur adipiscing elit. Donec lacinia blandit felis porta convallis. Duis magna nibh, euismod ac turpis quis, pretium rhoncus nisi. Nulla maximus cursus massa quis porta. Vestibulum urna eros, gravida vel mauris ac, consequat condimentum sapien.

Donec ultricies enim tortor, sit amet semper velit blandit sagittis. Fusce blandit vehicula quam, vel interdum orci pellentesque et. Aliquam erat volutpat. Maecenas condimentum, quam et iaculis ullamcorper, libero justo egestas mi, quis cursus lorem ante non dui.

Sed consequat mi vel venenatis molestie. Fusce rutrum tellus sed mi porttitor varius eu rhoncus est. Curabitur auctor sem purus, vel volutpat elit rhoncus vitae.

Duis sodales nibh ac dapibus sagittis. Vestibulum bibendum malesuada tellus, ac consequat nibh rhoncus lobortis. Donec quis est quis velit efficitur molestie in blandit nunc. Maecenas blandit enim et orci mollis, quis fringilla massa suscipit. Aenean vel felis pulvinar, mollis nunc eget, semper ante. Quisque convallis, erat tincidunt convallis blandit, velit metus bibendum orci, sed fringilla lacus est non odio. Suspendisse sagittis tempor enim eget imperdiet.

Proin non cursus sem. Suspendisse neque orci, porttitor sit amet dui ac, eleifend ultricies magna. Duis malesuada nisi sed porttitor pretium. Donec dignissim, libero sit amet commodo hendrerit, libero magna tempus augue, in suscipit purus ex eu lacus. Curabitur nulla augue, cursus quis sodales in, maximus eget lectus. Cras vitae efficitur odio. In imperdiet, ligula at luctus laoreet, sapien erat dictum diam, condimentum egestas enim sem at est. Donec aliquam odio fringilla nisl gravida, nec auctor lectus cursus.

Morbi ut lectus sem. Etiam consectetur sagittis purus sed ornare. Duis eget ipsum in nisi mollis luctus eu non nibh. Aenean vel mi sem. Nulla facilisi. Proin id enim et justo convallis sagittis eu quis magna. Sed in est enim. In dolor purus, elementum et lorem vel, rhoncus faucibus leo. Aliquam erat volutpat. Suspendisse aliquam eros ut augue vehicula posuere. Donec in dolor magna. Proin eu consequat arcu, a consequat nisl.

5-38. Elements may break across columns in a multicolumn layout

To prevent this, use *break-inside: avoid* or *break-inside: avoid-column* . The *break-inside* property applies to the children of a multicolumn container. For example, to prevent all children of *.multi-col* from breaking across column boxes, use the following:

```
.multi-col > * {
    break-inside: avoid-column;
}
```

Now the purple paragraph no longer breaks across columns, as can be seen in figure 5-39. The *break-inside* property also affects <u>paged media</u>[8], which explains why there are both *avoid* and *avoid-column* values. The difference is that *avoid-column* prevents a box from breaking across columns, while *avoid* prevents a box from breaking across columns *and pages*.

---

8. http://www.w3.org/TR/css3-page/

Dog bites man; says man tastes like chicken

Lorem ipsum dolor sit amet, consectetur adipiscing elit. Donec lacinia blandit felis porta convallis. Duis magna nibh, euismod ac turpis quis, pretium rhoncus nisi. Nulla maximus cursus massa quis porta. Vestibulum urna eros, gravida vel mauris ac, consequat condimentum sapien.

Donec ultricies enim tortor, sit amet semper velit blandit sagittis. Fusce blandit vehicula quam, vel interdum orci pellentesque et. Aliquam erat volutpat. Maecenas condimentum, quam et iaculis ullamcorper, libero justo egestas mi, quis cursus lorem ante non dui.

Sed consequat mi vel venenatis molestie. Fusce rutrum tellus sed mi porttitor varius eu rhoncus est. Curabitur auctor sem purus, vel volutpat elit rhoncus vitae.

Duis sodales nibh ac dapibus sagittis. Vestibulum bibendum malesuada tellus, ac consequat nibh rhoncus lobortis. Donec quis est quis velit efficitur molestie in blandit nunc. Maecenas blandit enim et orci mollis, quis fringilla massa suscipit. Aenean vel felis pulvinar, mollis nunc eget, semper ante. Quisque convallis, erat tincidunt convallis blandit, velit metus bibendum orci, sed fringilla lacus est non odio. Suspendisse sagittis tempor enim eget imperdiet.

Proin non cursus sem. Suspendisse neque orci, porttitor sit amet dui ac, eleifend ultricies magna. Duis malesuada nisi sed porttitor pretium. Donec dignissim, libero sit amet commodo hendrerit, libero magna tempus augue, in suscipit purus ex eu lacus. Curabitur nulla augue, cursus quis sodales in, maximus eget lectus. Cras vitae efficitur odio. In imperdiet, ligula at luctus laoreet, sapien erat dictum diam, condimentum egestas enim sem at est. Donec aliquam odio fringilla nisl gravida, nec auctor lectus cursus.

Morbi ut lectus sem. Etiam consectetur sagittis purus sed ornare. Duis eget ipsum in nisi mollis luctus eu non nibh. Aenean vel mi sem. Nulla facilisi. Proin id enim et justo convallis sagittis eu quis magna. Sed in est enim. In dolor purus, elementum et lorem vel, rhoncus faucibus leo. Aliquam erat volutpat. Suspendisse aliquam eros ut augue vehicula posuere. Donec in dolor magna. Proin eu consequat arcu, a consequat nisl.

5-39. Preventing column breaks inside elements with break-inside

CSS Fragmentation Module Level 3

The <u>CSS Fragmentation Module Level 3</u>[9] specification is closely related to the multicolumn and paged media specifications. It further defines how block boxes should break across columns, pages, and regions.

It's also possible to force a break before or after an element using *break-before* and *break-after* . Let's force a column break before the third paragraph:

```
.multi-col p:nth-of-type(3) {
    background-color: #c09a;
    break-before: column;
}
```

___

[9] http://dev.w3.org/csswg/css-break-3/

Here, we've used the `column` value to force a column break before the selected element (see figure 5-40). The `break-after` property works similarly, forcing a column break *after* the selected element. The `always` value also forces column breaks, but `always` will also force a column break in paged media.

Dog bites man; says man tastes like chicken

Lorem ipsum dolor sit amet, consectetur adipiscing elit. Donec lacinia blandit felis porta convallis. Duis magna nibh, euismod ac turpis quis, pretium rhoncus nisi. Nulla maximus cursus massa quis porta. Vestibulum urna eros, gravida vel mauris ac, consequat condimentum sapien.

Donec ultricies enim tortor, sit amet semper velit blandit sagittis. Fusce blandit vehicula quam, vel interdum orci pellentesque et. Aliquam erat volutpat. Maecenas condimentum, quam et iaculis ullamcorper, libero justo egestas mi, quis cursus lorem ante non dui.

Sed consequat mi vel venenatis molestie. Fusce rutrum tellus sed mi porttitor varius eu rhoncus est. Curabitur auctor sem purus, vel volutpat elit rhoncus vitae.

Duis sodales nibh ac dapibus sagittis. Vestibulum bibendum malesuada tellus, ac consequat nibh rhoncus lobortis. Donec quis est quis velit efficitur molestie in blandit nunc. Maecenas blandit enim et orci mollis, quis fringilla massa suscipit. Aenean vel felis pulvinar, mollis nunc eget, semper ante. Quisque convallis, erat tincidunt convallis blandit, velit metus bibendum orci, sed fringilla lacus est non odio. Suspendisse sagittis tempor enim eget imperdiet.

Proin non cursus sem. Suspendisse neque orci, porttitor sit amet dui ac, eleifend ultricies magna. Duis malesuada nisi sed porttitor pretium. Donec dignissim, libero sit amet commodo hendrerit, libero magna tempus augue, in suscipit purus ex eu lacus. Curabitur nulla augue, cursus quis sodales in, maximus eget lectus. Cras vitae efficitur odio. In imperdiet, ligula at luctus laoreet, sapien erat dictum diam, condimentum egestas enim sem at est. Donec aliquam odio fringilla nisl gravida, nec auctor lectus cursus.

Morbi ut lectus sem. Etiam consectetur sagittis purus sed ornare. Duis eget ipsum in nisi mollis luctus eu non nibh. Aenean vel mi sem. Nulla facilisi. Proin id enim et justo convallis sagittis eu quis magna. Sed in est enim. In dolor purus, elementum et lorem vel, rhoncus faucibus leo. Aliquam erat volutpat. Suspendisse aliquam eros ut augue vehicula posuere. Donec in dolor magna. Proin eu consequat arcu, a consequat nisl.

5-40. Forcing a column break before an element

Older versions of Safari and Chrome use `-webkit-column-break-before` and `-webkit-column-break-after`. Both properties are holdovers from an earlier version of the specification. For those properties, the `column` value is unsupported, so use `always` instead. For Firefox, use `page-break-inside` instead.

Optimizing the User Interface

Arranging paragraphs of text isn't the only use case for multicolumn layouts. We can also use it with lists to optimize the use of horizontal space. Consider the layout shown here:

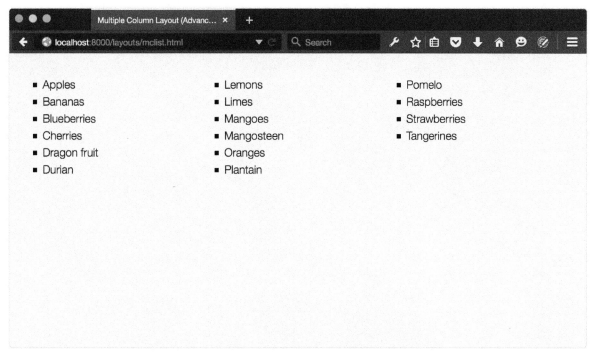

5-41. A list split into three columns

The old-school way of creating this layout is to split our list into three separate ones and float them to the left or right of a containing element. Here's what the markup might look like:

```
<div class="clearfix">
    <ul class="column-float-left">
        <li>Apples</li>
        <li>Oranges</li>
        <li>Bananas</li>
        <li>Dragon fruit</li>
    </ul>
    <ul class="column-float-left">
        <li>Cherries</li>
        <li>Strawberries</li>
        <li>Blueberries</li>
        <li>Raspberries</li>
    </ul>
    <ul class="column-float-left">
        <li>Durian</li>
        <li>Mangosteen</li>
        <li>Mangoes</li>
    </ul>
</div>
```

And the accompanying CSS:

```css
.columned-list {
    float: left;
    width: 33%;
    min-width: 150px;
    margin: 0;
}
.clearfix::after {
    clear: both;
    content: ' ';
    display: block;
}
```

While this approach works, it requires more markup than a single-list element. We're using three *li* elements instead of one. And we have to manage floated elements and clearing those floats. With a multicolumn layout, we can use a single element without worrying about clearing floats:

```html
<ul style="columns: 3">
    <li>Apples</li>
    <li>Oranges</li>
    <li>Bananas</li>
    <li>Dragon fruit</li>
    <li>Cherries</li>
    <li>Strawberries</li>
    <li>Blueberries</li>
    <li>Raspberries</li>
    <li>Durian</li>
    <li>Mangosteen</li>
    <li>Mangoes</li>
</ul>
```

 Missing Bullets

Blink- and WebKit-based browsers remove bullets and numbers from some or all list items in a multicolumn layout. As a workaround, add a left margin (or right margin in a right-to-left language) of at least 20px to *li* elements within a multicolumn container.

Another use case for multicolumn layouts is wrangling lists of checkbox inputs. Here, too, we can maximize the use of horizontal space to create more compact forms:

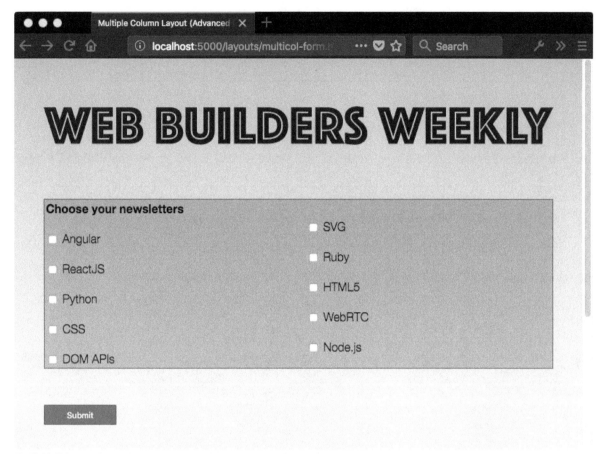

5-42. Utilizing horizontal space to create more compact forms

Use multicolumn layout when you have blocks of content to be automatically distributed and evenly spaced across several columns. It isn't well suited to creating page layouts—such as adding a navigation column and a main content column. For page layouts, use Grid, Flexbox, or the legacy techniques of float and clearfix.

Creating Layouts with CSS Grid

CSS Grid is a more recent layout specification, shipping in most browsers as of October 2017. CSS Grid allows us to create two-dimensional grid-based layouts that were previously impossible, or only possible with lots of DOM operations.

Keep in mind that the CSS Grid specification[10] is dense, and introduces several new concepts that are quite complex. Consider this section an overview rather than a comprehensive look at Grid. Don't worry, we'll point you to lots of resources for learning more.

---

[10] https://www.w3.org/TR/css-grid-1/

The Grid Formatting Context

Adding `display: grid` to an element triggers a **grid formatting context** for that element and its children. In a grid formatting context, three things happen:

1   The element becomes a block-level element that participates in the normal flow.

2   Its children—whether elements or text nodes—create block-like, grid-level boxes that can be arranged into rows and columns. Immediate children of a grid container are **grid items**.

3   In a horizontal writing mode, each member in a grid row will have the same height as its tallest element (as determined by content), unless an explicit height value is set. When the document uses a vertical writing mode, it takes on the same length as its longest element (as determined by content).

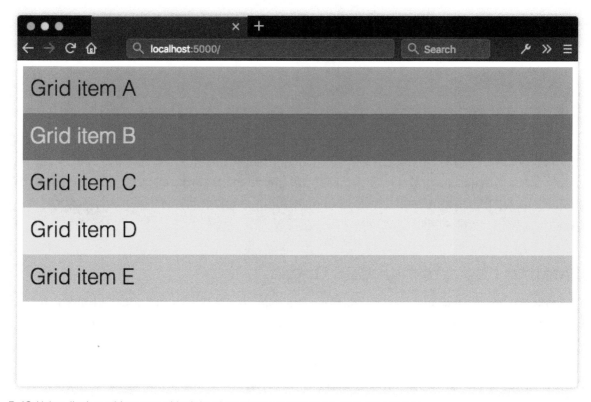

5-43. Using display: grid creates a block-level container, and block boxes for its children

Using `display: inline-grid` works similarly. Children of inline-level grid containers create grid-level boxes, but the container itself participates in an inline formatting context.

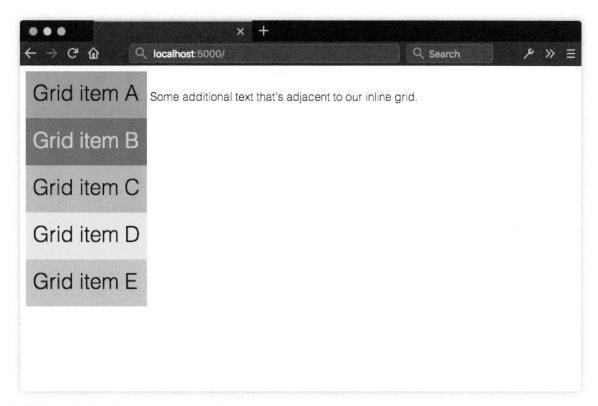

5-44. Using display: inline-grid creates an inline-level box for the container, but block boxes for its children

By themselves, `display: grid` and `display: inline-grid` won't automatically arrange these boxes into rows and columns. We also need to tell the browser where and how to place things.

Before creating your grid, determine whether you want a fixed number of columns and/or rows, whether you'd like the browser to calculate the number of columns and rows automatically, or whether you'd like a mix of the two. Knowing what kind of grid you want to create determines the approach you'll take. Let's look at a few techniques.

Defining a Grid Layout

After defining a grid container, we'll need to tell the browser how many rows and columns our grid should contain. We can define the number of rows and columns using the `grid-template-rows` and `grid-template-columns` properties. They're applied to the grid container.

Both `grid-template-rows` and `grid-template-columns` accept what's known as a *track list*. The **track list** is a space-separated string that specifies grid line names and sizes of each position in the row or column.

Each value in a track list creates a new space—a **track**—within the row or column. You can use lengths, flexible length units (discussed later in this chapter), or percentages. You can also use sizing values[11] such as `auto`, `min-content` and `max-conent`.

```
.grid {
    display: grid;
    grid-template-columns: 25rem 25rem 25rem;
    grid-template-rows: 10rem 10rem;
}
```

In the code above, we've defined a grid with three columns, each `25rem` units wide and two rows, each `10rem` units tall. Let's apply it to the following HTML. Yes, this is all the markup required:

```
<div class="grid">
    <div>Grid item A</div>
    <div>Grid item B</div>
    <div>Grid item C</div>
    <div>Grid item D</div>
    <div>Grid item E</div>
</div>
```

Our grid items get organized into the columns and rows shown in figure 5-45.

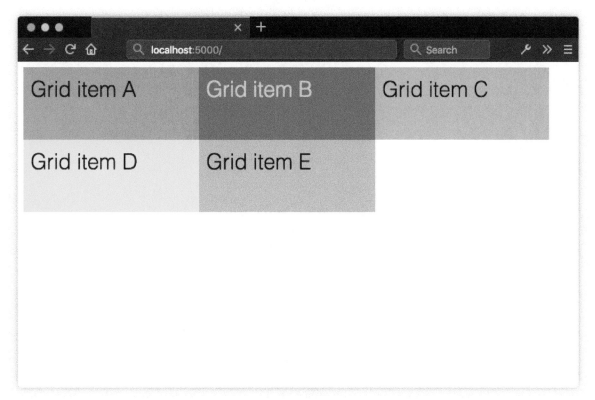

5-45. Creating an explicit grid with grid-template-columns and grid-template-rows

Here, we've created a grid of evenly sized rows and columns, but that isn't a requirement of Grid. Let's tweak our CSS slightly. We'll change the value of *grid-template-columns* to *25rem 15rem 25rem* :

```
.grid {
    display: grid;
    grid-template-columns: 25rem 15rem 25rem;
    grid-template-rows: 10rem 10rem;
}
```

Now the second column in our grid is narrower than the first and third (shown in figure 5-46).

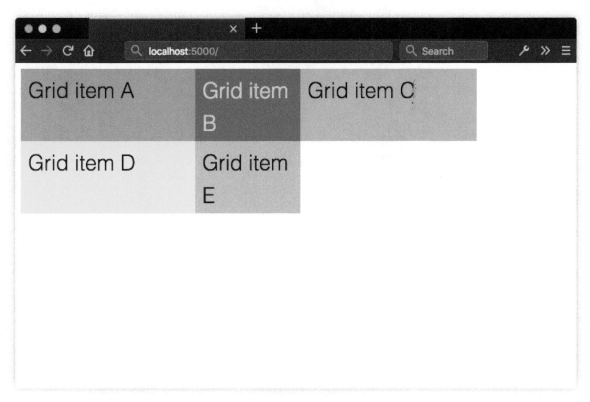

5-46. Grid columns and rows don't have to be the same width

Explicit Grid versus Implicit Grids

In the previous section, we explicitly stated that this grid should have six available grid cells formed by three columns and two rows. This is what's known as an **explicit grid**. Here, our grid container only has five children. The remaining position is empty. Let's see what happens when we add more children to the container.

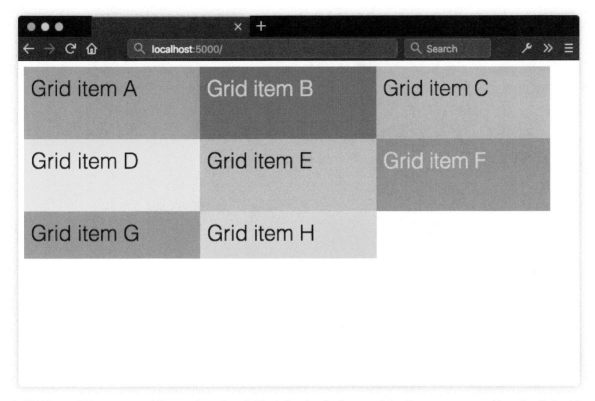

5-47. When grid items exceed the number of explicitly defined cells, the remaining items are arranged in an implicit grid

Now we have three rows. Notice, however, that our third row is only as tall as its contents and padding. It's part of the grid because these items are the children of a grid container. Yet the row isn't explicitly defined by `grid-template-rows`. What we have instead is an **implicit grid**—an explicit grid with additional grid items that exceed the defined number of explicit grid cells.

Items within an implicit grid are `auto` sized by default. Grid items will expand to accommodate their contents, or fill the remaining vertical space in the container—whichever is taller. If, for example, we set the `height` property of our container to `50rem`, our implicit grid track will expand to be `30rem` tall.

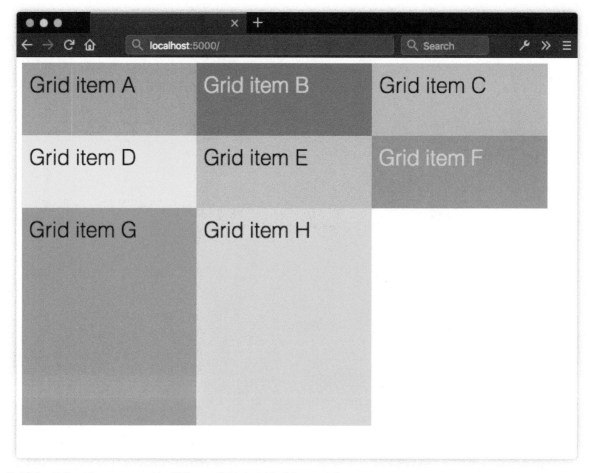

5-48. Implicit grid rows expand to fill the available height of the container

If we add enough items to create a fourth row, the height of our implicit grid items will be distributed evenly across the remaining `30rem` of vertical space in the container. Their computed height will be `15rem` each.

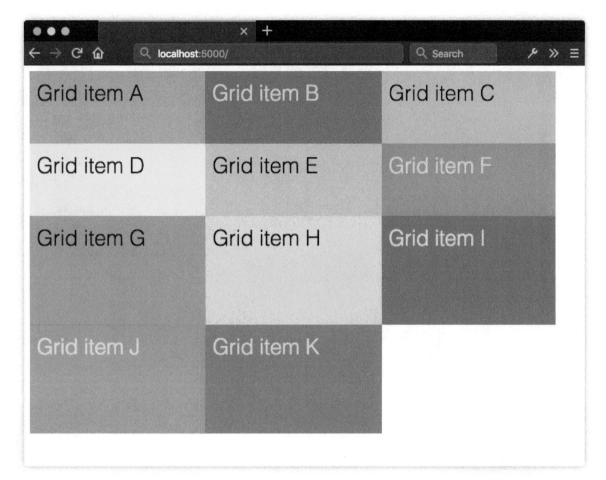

5-49. The height of implicit grid rows will be evenly distributed based on the remaining space in the grid container

In our original example, we've explicitly defined only two rows with a height of `10rem` each, so our third row defaults to `auto` sizing. Its height will adjust to the size of its contents and padding.

Specifying Track Size for an Implicit Grid

It is possible, however, to set a kind of explicit, default height or width for implicit grid items using the `grid-auto-rows` and `grid-auto-columns` properties. Let's update our CSS with `grid-auto-rows`:

```css
.grid {
    display: grid;
    grid-template-columns: 25rem 15rem 25rem;
    grid-template-rows: 10rem 10rem;
    grid-auto-rows: 30rem;
}
```

Now items in our third row—and any subsequent rows—will be `30rem` in height.

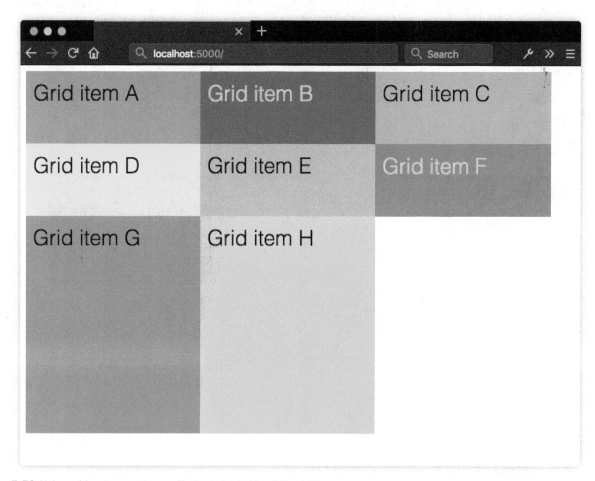

5-50. Using grid-auto-rows to specify the height of implicit grid items

There's one drawback to using the `grid-auto-*` properties: when the contents of a grid item exceed its dimensions, they will overflow the container (as shown below), and may be clipped visually by elements in other rows.

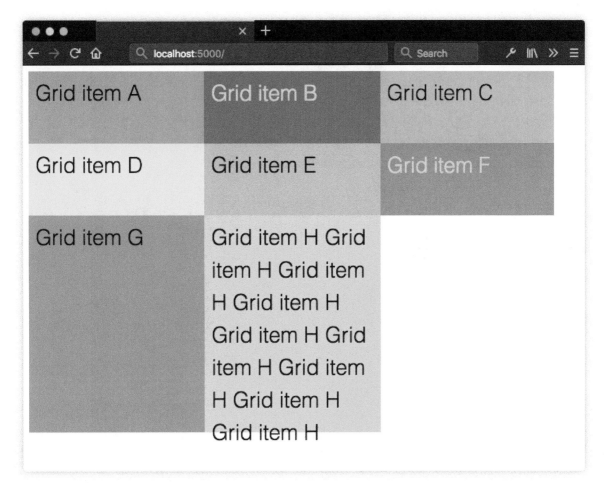

5-51. Contents of a grid container can overflow the container when using length or percentage units

One way to avoid this is to use the `minmax()` function. Let's rewrite our CSS to use `minmax()`:

```
.grid {
    display: grid;
    grid-template-columns: 25rem 15rem 25rem;
    grid-template-rows: 10rem 10rem;
    grid-auto-rows: minmax(30rem, auto);
}
```

As you may have guessed from its name, `minmax()` lets us define the minimum and maximum size of a track. It requires two arguments, the first of which is the minimum desired track size. The second argument is the maximum desired size.

In this case, our row will be at least `30rems` high. But since we've set our maximum size to `auto`, our track will expand to accommodate the content of that cell. Arguments for `minmax()` can be lengths or percentages, or one of the `auto`, `min-content`, and `max-content` keywords. Here, `minmax(30rem, max-content)` would achieve much the same effect. Flexible units, discussed in the next section, are also valid.

Lengths and percentages can be used to define track sizes. Using them may mean that the grid items don't fill the entire width or height of the container. For example, if our grid container is `70rem` wide, `grid-template-columns: 25rem 15rem 25rem;` will only fill about 90% of its horizontal space. On the other hand, if our grid container is only `50rem` wide, the total width of our columns will overflow the container's bounds.

One way to avoid this issue is by using *flexible length* units.

Creating Flexible Grids with Flex Units

Flexible length or **flex** units are best understood as fractional units, and are expressed using `fr`. Flex units indicate to the browser what fraction or proportion of the leftover space in a grid container should be allocated to each grid item. They're a ratio, not a true length value in the way `px`, `em`, or `cm` are.

There's a formula for calculating the used width of an item when using flexible units: *(flex × leftover space) ÷ sum of all flex factors*. If, for instance, our grid container is `1000px` wide, and the value of `grid-template-columns` is `3fr 2fr 1fr`, our columns will be `500px`, `333.33px` and `133.33px` wide. The width of each column is allocated proportionally from the space available, as shown below.

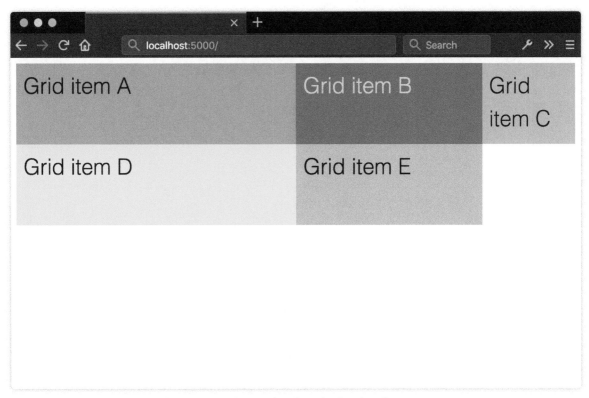

5-52. Flexible length units maintain grid proportions, rather than absolute lengths

Because these units are ratios and not absolute lengths, `grid-template-columns: 2fr 2fr 2fr` is equivalent to `grid-template-columns: 1fr 1fr 1fr`. Both will result in columns of equal width for horizontal writing modes, and rows of equal height for vertical writing modes.

 Not True Length Units

N `fr` units are not true length values. This makes them incompatible with other length units, such as `px` and `rem`. It also means that you can't use `fr` units with the `calc()` function. For example, `calc(1fr - 1rem)` is an invalid length value.

Using the `grid-template` Shorthand Property

We can also indicate the number of rows and columns using the `grid-template` property. Its syntax is as follows:

```
grid-template: [row track list] / [column track list]
```

Remember this block of CSS from earlier in the chapter?

```
.grid {
    display: grid;
    grid-template-columns: 25rem 25rem 25rem;
    grid-template-rows: 10rem 10rem;
}
```

We can combine the second and third lines using *grid-template* :

```
.grid {
    display: grid;
    grid-template: 10rem 10rem / 25rem 25rem 25rem;
}
```

For clarity, however, you may still wish to use the longhand properties.

Repeating Rows and Columns

In many cases, you'll want grid columns or rows that repeat automatically; think of a list of store items or recipe search results. Grid offers a syntax for that—the *repeat()* function:

```
.grid {
    display: grid;
    grid-template-columns: repeat(3, 1fr);
}
```

repeat() accepts two arguments:

1   the number of times to repeat the track list

2   a track list to repeat

Arguments must be separated by a comma. The first argument may be a positive integer, or the *auto-fit* or *auto-fill* keywords. The above CSS produces the following grid. Our *1fr* track list is repeated three times.

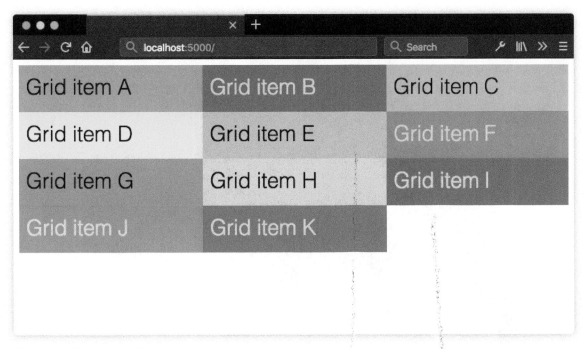

5-53. A repeating grid with fr units

We could also use a two-column pattern that repeats twice. For example,
`grid-template-columns: repeat(2, 1fr 3fr);` produces a four-column grid. As figure 5-54
shows, the first and third columns are one third the width of the second and fourth. In both cases,
the value of `grid-template-rows` is `auto`.

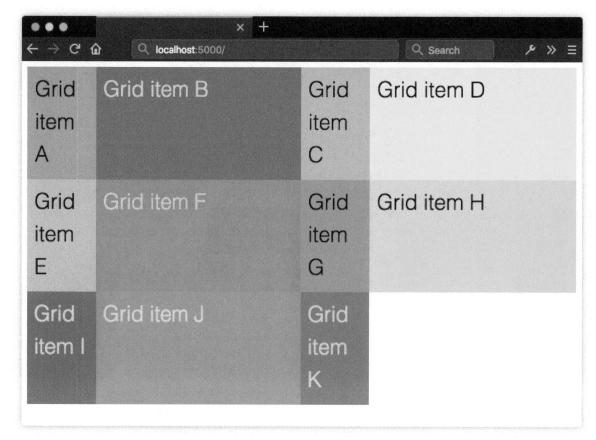

5-54. A repeating two-column grid pattern

Repeating Columns with `auto-fit` or `auto-fill`

Both of the preceding examples tell the browser: *here's a track list pattern; please repeat it X number of times.* What you may want to tell the browser instead, though, is: *please fit as many columns or rows as you can within this grid container.* For that, we can use `auto-fit` or `auto-fill` as the first argument for `repeat()`, in combination with `minmax()`.

What's the difference between `auto-fit` and `auto-fill`? It's subtle, but significant.

- `auto-fill` fits as many grid items as it can within a track line, *adding anonymous grid tracks if necessary.*
- `auto-fit` fits as many grid items as it can within a track line, *expanding or collapsing the dimensions of each track* if necessary.

This difference becomes apparent when the grid container's width exceeds the maximum total width of its grid items. Let's compare some CSS:

```
.grid {
    display: grid;
    width: 800px;
}
.autofill {
    grid-template-columns: repeat(auto-fill, minmax(100px, 1fr));
}
.autofit {
    grid-template-columns: repeat(auto-fit, minmax(100px, 1fr));
}
```

And let's apply this CSS to the HTML below:

```
<div class="grid autofill">
    <div>Grid item A</div>
    <div>Grid item B</div>
    <div>Grid item C</div>
    <div>Grid item D </div>
    <div>Grid item E</div>
</div>

<div class="grid autofit">
    <div>Grid item A</div>
    <div>Grid item B</div>
    <div>Grid item C</div>
    <div>Grid item D </div>
    <div>Grid item E</div>
</div>
```

The only difference between these two grid layouts is that one uses *auto-fill* and the other uses *auto-fit*. But compare the two grids in figure 5-55.

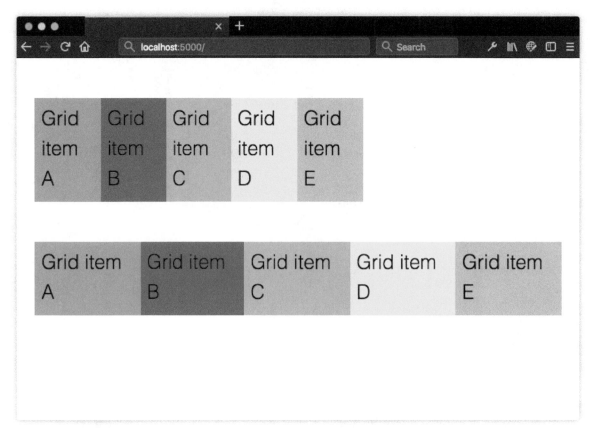

5-55. Comparing auto-fill with auto-fit

In both grids, the total maximum width of the grid items is less than that of the grid container. However, in the top grid—our *auto-fill* grid—that excess space is *filled in* by anonymous grid items.

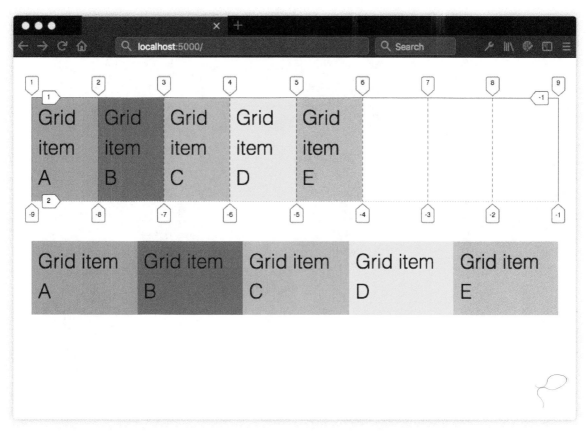

5-56. Visualizing the difference between auto-fill and auto-fit with the Firefox grid inspector

Compare that to the bottom grid, in which each grid item has been stretched to fit the available space. Figure 5-56 illustrates what those anonymous grid cells look like using Firefox's developer tools.

 More on Auto-sizing Columns

> If this still doesn't make any sense, read Sara Soueidan's "Auto-sizing Columns in CSS Grid: `auto-fill` vs `auto-fit` [12]". It contains some video examples that illustrate the difference a little bit better than static images can.

Line-based Grid Placement

So far, we've discussed simple grids that are neatly aligned rows and columns of boxes. But Grid layout is far more robust and flexible than that. We can also use it to create complex layouts.

---

[12] https://css-tricks.com/auto-sizing-columns-css-grid-auto-fill-vs-auto-fit/

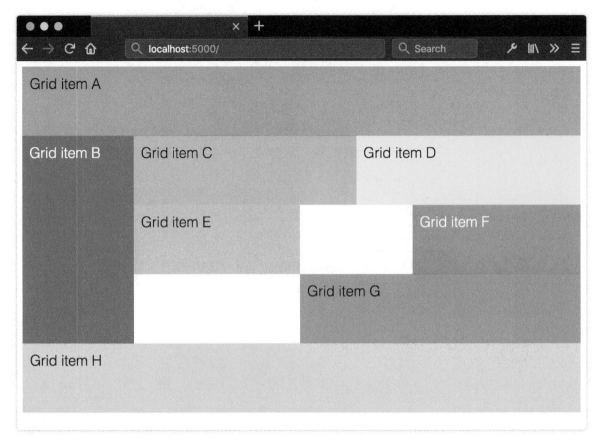

5-57. A complex page layout using CSS Grid

The layout pictured above uses *line-based grid placement*, a core component of CSS Grid. We'll look at how to create this layout later in this section. But first, let's discuss grid lines.

Understanding Grid Lines

Grid lines are horizontal and vertical lines that separate rows and columns, as shown below. These lines exist on each side of a row or column, but don't affect its dimensions.

5-58. Grid lines

The space between each grid line is known as a **grid track**. A grid track can be a row *or* a column; the phrase itself is a generic term for both. Grid columns and grid rows intersect to form **grid cells**.

Firefox's grid inspector is currently the best way to visualize grid lines. When working with grid containers in Firefox, you'll see a crosshatch icon between *display* and *grid* .

```
.insights_list ⚙ {                                        style.css:7
    display: ⊞ grid;
    align-items: start;
}
```

5-59. The grid inspector icon as seen in the developer tools of Firefox Developer Edition

Clicking that crosshatch icon displays (or hides) the grid overlay. The screenshot below shows the Firefox grid overlay in action.

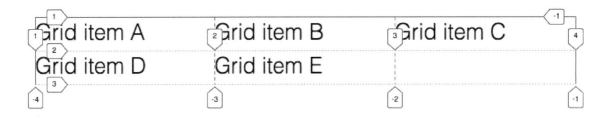

5-60. A CSS Grid layout as viewed using the grid inspector feature of Firefox's developer tools

Notice that each edge of each column in this grid is bounded by a grid line, and each of these lines has a numeric index. The same is true for each row.

Grid line numbering begins with 1, and the count begins at the start of the grid container. When the text direction is left to right, the starting point is the left edge. When the direction is right to left, the starting point is the right edge.

Each grid line may also have a negative index. Negative index counts begin with -1, and decrement from the ending edge of the explicit grid. So an index of -1 specifies the ending edge of the container, while an index of -2 specifies one grid line in from that one, and so on. (We'll see an example of negative line numbers in use shortly.)

Line numbers can be used to place items within the grid using the `grid-column-start` / `grid-column-end` and `grid-row-start` / `grid-row-end` properties. Here's an example:

```css
.grid-10cols {
    display: grid;
}
#a {
    grid-column-start: 1;
    grid-column-end: 11;
}
#b {
    grid-column-start: 1;
    grid-column-end: 6;
}
#c {
    grid-column-start: 6;
    grid-column-end: 11;
}
```

```
    }
```

We'll pair that CSS with the HTML below:

```
<div class="grid-10cols">
    <div id="a">Grid item A</div>
    <div id="b">Grid item B</div>
    <div id="c">Grid item C</div>
</div>
```

Figure 5-61 illustrates the result: `#a` fills the space between line 1 and line 11, or the entire width of the grid. `#b` begins at the first line and ends at the sixth. `#c` begins at the sixth line and extends to line 11. With `grid-*-start` and `grid-*-end`, we're telling the browser to align the starting and ending edges of our grid items with specific grid lines.

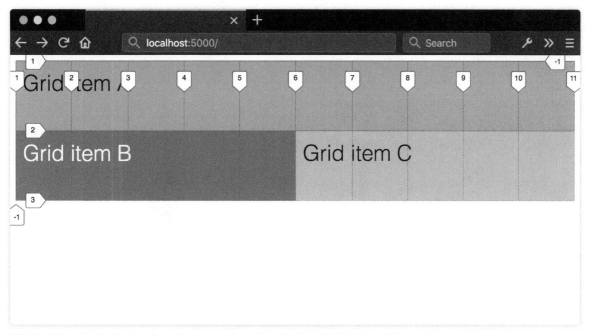

5-61. A grid created using line-based placement, as viewed using the Firefox grid inspector

We didn't use either of the `grid-template-*` properties in this example. By defining a start line and an end line, we've instead *implied* that our grid should have ten columns. Note here that, because our grid is implied and not explicit—for example, it's not defined using `grid-template-columns: repeat(10, 1fr)`, or something similar—we've lost the ability to use negative grid line indexes for placement.

Spanning Rows or Columns

In the example above, we've used line numbers to indicate where our grid items should begin and end. Another way is to use the *span* keyword. The *span* keyword indicates how many tracks—that is, how many rows or columns—a grid item should occupy. We could, in other words, rewrite our CSS like so:

```css
.grid-10cols {
    display: grid;
}
#a {
    grid-column-start: span 10;
}
#b {
    grid-column-start: span 5;
}
#c {
    grid-column-start: span 5;
}
```

Again, *span* indicates how many columns or rows a grid item should occupy. Line indices indicate where to align the edges of a grid item.

Complex Layouts with Line-based Placement

Let's return to our earlier example from figure 5-57. Once again, our markup is simple—a containing *div* with eight children:

```html
<div class="grid-10cols-complex">
    <div id="a">Grid item A</div>
    <div id="b">Grid item B</div>
    <div id="c">Grid item C</div>
    <div id="d">Grid item D </div>
    <div id="e">Grid item E</div>
    <div id="f">Grid item F</div>
    <div id="g">Grid item G</div>
    <div id="h">Grid item H</div>
</div>
```

For this layout, we'll explicitly define a five-row, ten-column grid:

```css
.grid-10cols-complex {
    display: grid;
    /* Syntax: grid-template: [rows] / [columns] */
```

```
    grid-template: repeat(5, 9.5rem) / repeat(10, 10%);
}
```

Explicitly defining a grid isn't strictly necessary for line-based placement. In this case, however, it ensures that each box in our layout has the right proportions. The next step is to place our grid items:

```
#a, #h {
    grid-column-start: span 10;   /* Span the entire grid */
}
#b {
    grid-row-start: span 3;
    grid-column-start: span 2;
}
#c, #d {
    grid-column-start: span 4;
}
#e, #f {
    grid-column-start: span 3;
}
#f, #g {
    grid-column-end: -1;   /* Begin from the container's ending edge. */
}
#g {
    grid-column-start: span 5;
}
```

Here, both *#a* and *#h* span all ten columns of our grid, while the other elements span between two and five columns, as you can see below. Element *#b* also spans three rows.

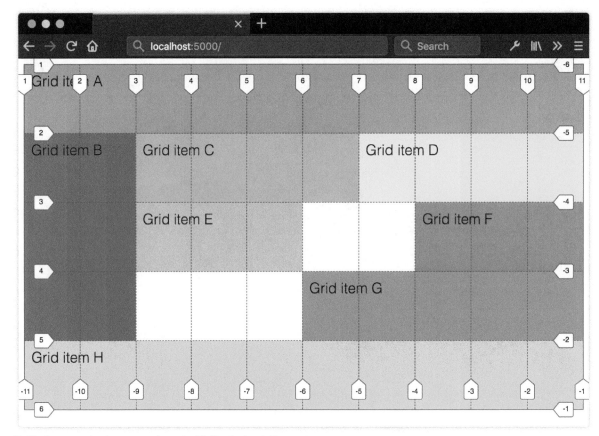

5-62. Our complex layout as viewed with Firefox's grid inspector

Notice that for `#f` and `#g`, we've used a negative line index. Remember that negative line indices begin at the ending edge of the container. With `grid-column-end: -1`, we've told the browser, *align the ending edge of `#f` and `#g` with the ending edge of our grid container*. These elements still span three and five columns, respectively, but their ending edges align with the edge of the container.

Using Named Grid Areas

One of the more clever aspects of CSS Grid is *template areas*. **Template areas** use the `grid-template-areas` property, and let us define our grid in terms of named slots. We can use template areas, in combination with grid placement properties, to define complex grid layouts that are still readable.

Take the layout shown in figure 5-63. It's a fairly conventional, two-column layout with a header, footer, and main content area, along with a right-hand navigation menu.

5-63. A two-column page layout with a header and footer. We'll recreate it with Grid

Here's the markup we'll use to create this page. It's simplified to emphasize the document's structure:

```
<!DOCTYPE html>
    <html lang="en-US">
    <head>
        <title>GoodRecipes! Tuna with zucchini noodles</title>
    </head>

    <body>
        <header>...</header>
        <article>...</article>
        <nav>...</nav>
        <footer>...</footer>
    </body>
</html>
```

Named template areas are a bit tricky to understand at first. We still need to define rows and columns, but we can then distribute those rows and columns across our named areas using the `grid-template-areas` property. Here's an example:

```
body {
    display: grid;
    /*
    Using the longhand properties for
    the sake of clarity. We could also use
    grid-template: repeat(2, auto) / 4fr 1fr
    instead.
    */
    grid-template-rows: repeat(2, auto);
    grid-template-columns: 4fr 1fr;
    grid-template-areas: "pagehead pagehead"
                         "mains navigation"
                         "pagefoot pagefoot";
}
```

Yes, the syntax of `grid-template-areas` is a little weird. Template areas are strings and must be enclosed in single or double quotes. Each template area corresponds to a row in the grid. Columns within each row are delineated by a space.

 Line Breaks Not Required

You're not required to use line breaks when setting the value of `grid-template-areas`. We could put our definition on a single line: `grid-template-areas: "pagehead pagehead" "mains navigation" "pagefoot pagefoot";`. Line breaks do, however, make it easier to visualize and understand the layout.

Now, in order for *grid-template-areas* to work, we have to account for every position in the grid. That's why we're repeating *heading* and *footer*. Repeating a name within a template string indicates that the area should span multiple columns:

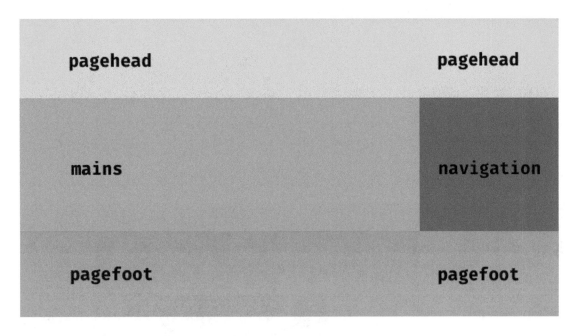

5-64. What's happening in our layout thanks to grid-template-areas

Now that we've defined our template areas, the last step is to assign our elements to each area using the *grid-area* property:

```
header {
    grid-area: pagehead;
}
article {
    grid-area: mains;
}
nav {
    grid-area: navigation;
}
footer {
    grid-area: pagefoot;
}
```

This tells the browser to place the *header* element in the *pagehead* area, the *article* element in the *mains* area, and so forth.

Spacing Grid Items

In all of the grids we've created thus far, the edges of our grid items abut each other. We can, however, add space—also known as a **gutter**—between our grid items with the `column-gap` and `row-gap` properties. Both properties apply to the grid container:

```
.grid {
    display: grid;
    grid-template: 10rem 10rem / 25rem 25rem 25rem;
    column-gap: 1rem;
    row-gap: 1rem;
}
```

Figure 5-65 shows the effect of adding `1rem` row and column gaps.

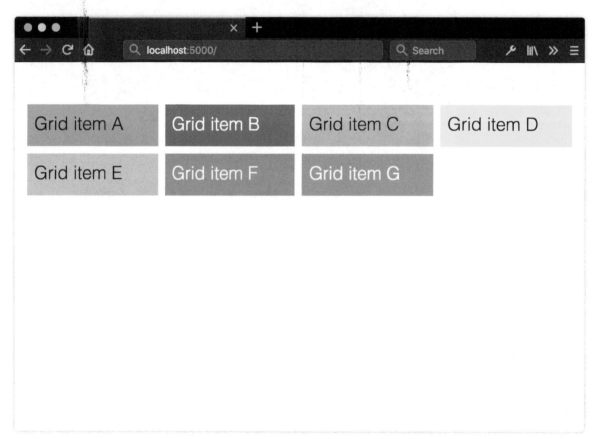

5-65. A grid layout with column-gap and row-gap values of 1rem

In a grid formatting context, `column-gap: normal` and `row-gap: normal` resolve to a used value of `0px`. That's in contrast with multicolumn layout, where `column-gap: normal` resolves to a used value of `1em`.

Only length and percentage values are valid for `column-gap` and `row-gap` (and the `gap` shorthand property). If you'd rather have the browser automatically distribute boxes along each grid axis, use `justify-content` or `align-items` instead. We discuss both properties later in the "Box Alignment and Distribution" section of this chapter.

The gap **Shorthand Property**

We can also specify the `column-gap` and `row-gap` at once using the `gap` shorthand property. The first value of `gap` becomes the size of the row gap; the second value is the column gap. Providing only one value sets the same gap size for both properties. In other words, we can rewrite `column-gap: 1rem; row-gap: 1rem;` as `gap: 1rem;`.

Originally, the CSS Grid specification defined `grid-gap`, `grid-row-gap` and `grid-column-gap` properties. Some browsers implemented this older version of the specification. As a result, recent but outdated versions of Firefox (≤ 60) and Safari (≤ 11) don't support `column-gap` when used with Grid layout. They don't support the `row-gap` property at all.

For compatibility with older browsers, include the legacy `grid-row-gap` and `grid-column-gap` properties in addition to `column-gap` and `row-gap`.

This ensures that your grid layouts will work in the broadest range of browsers.

Grid Items and Margins

Grid items can have margins of their own. However, margins work a bit differently in a grid formatting context than they do in a block formatting context.

Grid cells, and the grid lines that bound them, form containing blocks for grid items. As a result, adjacent margins of grid items *do not* collapse. That's the opposite of what happens in a block formatting context.

For grid items, top and bottom margins of `1rem` result in `2rem` of space between the content boxes, as shown in figure 5-66. And because grid item margins fall within the containing block, they may affect the dimensions of `auto`-sized grid tracks.

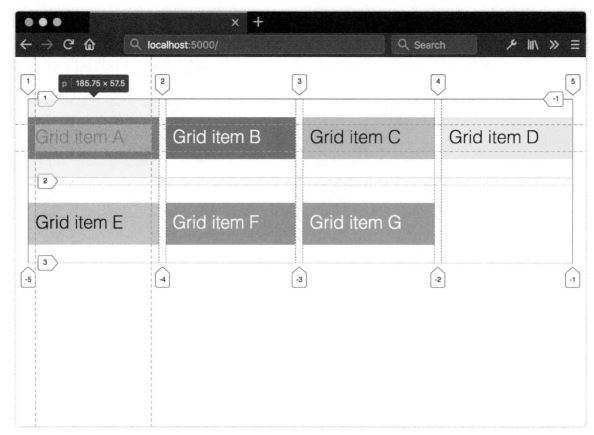

5-66. Grid item margins are contained by the grid track and don't collapse

Using `column-gap` and `row-gap` aren't the only ways to space grid content. We can also use the `justify-*` and `align*` properties to distribute grid items within the available space. Since most of these properties are common to Grid *and* Flexbox, we'll discuss them together in the section "Box Alignment and Distribution" later in this chapter.

Images Within Grids

Images within grid cells work similarly to the way they behave in multicolumn layouts. When the track size uses length or percentage units, images may overflow the grid cell if their dimensions exceed those of the cell.

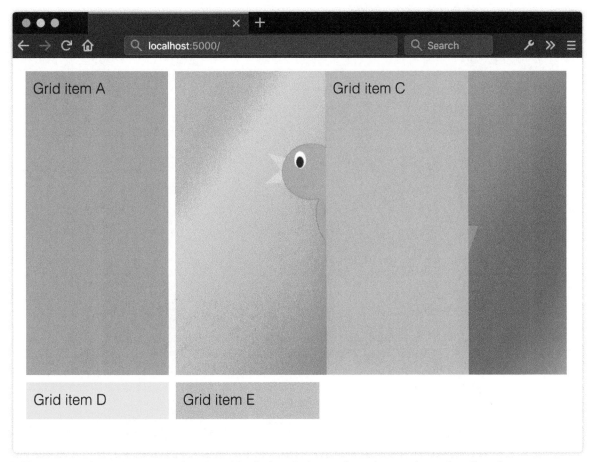

5-67. Images within a grid may overflow the grid cell when the image dimensions are larger than the cell

However, when the track sizing function is *auto* , or uses flex units (*fr*), the track containing that grid cell will expand to accommodate the image.

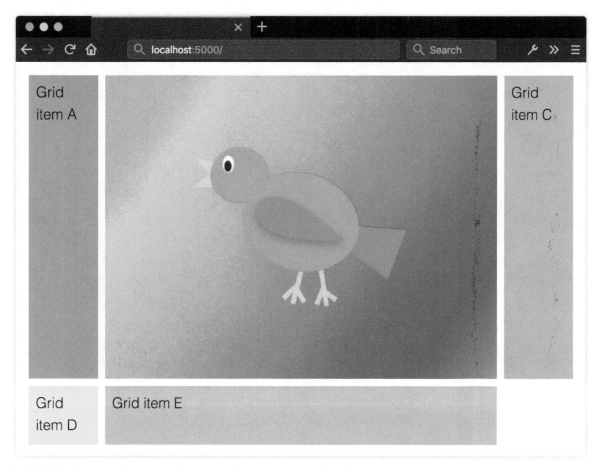

5-68. Grid cells expand to contain the image when using auto or flex units

As in multicolumn layout, we can constrain the image dimensions to those of its grid cell by setting its width to 100%.

Floating images or other elements *within a grid cell* works as you'd expect. But you can't float a grid item. Floated siblings of grid containers also don't intrude on the grid container.

Grid Conclusion

CSS Grid is a very dense topic. We've really just scratched the surface here. Luckily, there's a wealth of resources that can help you learn more.

I believe in reading specifications where possible. In my opinion, the <u>CSS Grid specification</u>[13] is quite readable, and it's a good place to begin your own explorations of grid layout. But specifications do tend to contain a lot of jargon, because they're targeted not only at web developers, but also those tasked with implementing the specification in browsers.

[13]. https://www.w3.org/TR/css-grid-1/

Rachel Andrew's <u>Grid by Example</u>[14] was created for a web developer audience. The site includes grid layout tutorials and a collection of common user interface patterns. Be sure to visit the site's *Resources* section too. It's a cornucopia of links that demonstrate what you can do with CSS Grid.

<u>Jen Simmons'</u> Experimental Layout Lab is also chock-full of examples that illustrate Grid's possibilities. If video is more your style, Simmons' <u>Layout Land</u>[15] YouTube channel includes video walkthroughs of grid and other layout topics.

When you need more of a cheatsheet-style reference, try "<u>A Complete Guide to Grid</u>[16]", by CSS-Tricks.

Creating Flexible Layouts with Flexbox

Before CSS Grid came along, there was Flexbox (which is officially known as the <u>CSS Flexible Box Layout Module</u>[17]). Flexbox was designed to manage layout in one direction—a row (`flex-direction: row` or `row-reverse`) or a column (`flex-direction: column` or `>column-reverse` column-reverse). That's in contrast to Grid, which accounts for rows *and* columns.

 Internet Explorer 11

> Internet Explorer 11 supports an older version of the Flexbox specification. We're going to focus on the version of Flexbox that's implemented in current browsers. If you want to implement a flexible box layout in Internet Explorer 11, consult Chris Mills' piece "<u>Advanced Cross-browser Flexbox</u>[18]". Or use a float-based layout as a fallback.

A basic flexible box layout is simple to create: add `display: flex` or `display: inline-flex` to the containing element. These values for `display` will trigger a *flex formatting context* for that containing element's children. As with Grid, both `flex` and `inline-flex` are inside display modes. We set these values on the container, which behaves like a block-level or inline-level box, respectively. The children of that container are then arranged according to the rules of flex layout.

---

14. https://gridbyexample.com/
15. https://www.youtube.com/channel/UC7TizprGknbDalbHplROtag
16. https://css-tricks.com/snippets/css/complete-guide-grid/
17. https://www.w3.org/TR/css-flexbox-1/
18. https://dev.opera.com/articles/advanced-cross-browser-flexbox/

Vendor Prefixes Required in Older Browsers

Older versions of Blink-based browsers such as Chrome (≤ 28), and WebKit-based browsers like Safari (≤ 8), require a vendor prefix. If your project still supports those browsers, you'll need to use `display: -webkit-flex` or `display: -webkit-inline-flex` . Older versions of Firefox (≤ 21) also require a prefix. Use `-moz-flex` and `-moz-inline-flex` to support those browsers.

By adding `display: flex` or `display: inline-flex` to a containing element, its immediate children become flex items, as shown in figure 5-69. Flex items may be element children or non-empty text nodes. For instance, the markup below generates three flex item boxes that each behave according to the rules of flex layout:

```
<div style="display: flex">
    <span>This text is contained by a SPAN element.</span>
    <b>This text is contained by a B element.</b>
    This text node is still a flex item.
</div>
```

If no other properties are set, each flex item will have the same height as its tallest element (as determined by content). It will also stack horizontally (or vertically when the document has a vertical writing mode) without wrapping, and with no space between the edges of each box. Flex items may overflow the container.

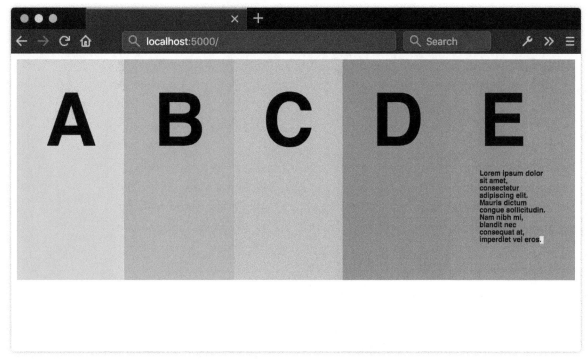

5-69. A list with display: flex applied to the ul containing element

This may not seem like such a big deal, but it simplifies the code necessary for a range of user interface patterns. Let's look at a couple of examples.

A New Media Object Component

Let's revisit the media object from earlier in the chapter:

```
<div class="media__object">
    <img src="video-thumb1.jpg">
    <div class="media__object__text">Lorem ipsum dolor sit amet, consectetur adipiscing elit, sed do
    eiusmod tempor incididunt ut labore et dolore magna aliqua.</div>
</div>
```

Before Flexbox, we might have paired the preceding markup with the following CSS:

```
.media__object img {
    float: left;
    height: auto;
    width: 150px;
}
.media__object__text {
    padding-left: 170px;
}
```

```
    }
    /* Let's use the clearfix hack! */
    .media__object::after{
        content: ' ';
        display: block;
        clear: both;
    }
```

This layout works, but it has one major drawback: it requires us to constrain the width of our images so that we know how much padding to use. That limits our ability to use this same component in multiple contexts. You may want an image 150px wide when this component is used for a "Related Stories" widget, and one that's only 75px wide for comments.

Let's try this using Flexbox. Here's our updated CSS:

```
    .media__object {
        display: flex;
    }
    .media_object img {
        margin-right: 20px;
    }
```

That's a lot less CSS. An added bonus is that we don't have to worry about how wide or tall our image is. Nor do we have to concern ourselves with clearing floats. Whether the image is 200px wide or 20px wide, *.media__object__text* will abut the margin box of our *img* element.

Creating Flexible Form Components with flex

Another use case for Flexbox is creating flexible, vertically aligned form components. Consider the interface pattern shown below.

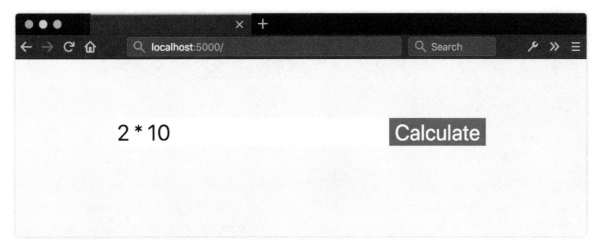

5-70. A form field with an adjacent button

Here, we have a form input control and an adjacent button. Both are vertically aligned, and our button is 150px wide.

What if we want our `input` element to expand to fill the available space in its container? Without Flexbox, we'd need some JavaScript and hand-waving to update the width of `input` in response to changes in the width of its parent. With Flexbox, however, we can just use `flex`.

The `flex` property is actually shorthand for three other properties.

- `flex-grow` indicates that an element should grow if necessary and must be a positive integer. Its initial value is `0`.
- `flex-shrink` indicates that an element should shrink if necessary and must be a positive integer. Its initial value is `1`.
- `flex-basis:` indicates the initial or minimum width (when the flex axis is horizontal) or the height of an element (when it's vertical). It may be a length or percentage, or `auto`, and its initial value is `auto`.

Though it's possible to set each of these individually, the specification strongly recommends using the `flex` shorthand. Here's an example:

```
div {
    display: flex;
}
input[type="text"], button {
    border: 0;
    font: inherit;
}
```

```
input[type="text"] {
    flex: 1 0 auto;
}
button {
    background: #003;
    color: whitesmoke;
    display: block;
    text-align: center;
    flex: 0 0 150px;
}
```

Here, we've used `flex: 1 0 auto` for our `input` element. Since its `flex-grow` value is `1`, it will grow to fill the available space of its parent. For the `button` element, however, we've used `flex: 0 0 150px`. The `0` values for `flex-grow` and `flex-shrink` prevent the width of the button from increasing or decreasing, while the `flex-basis` value of `150px` sets its width.

As you can see below, our button remains the same size, but the width of `input` expands to fill the remaining space.

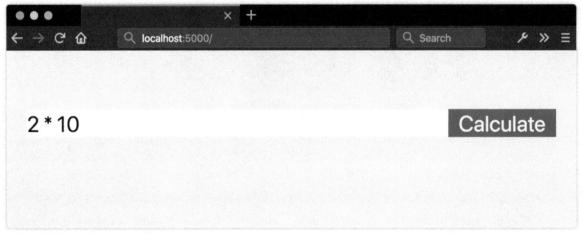

5-71. The effect of flex: 0 0 150px

The tricky bit about `flex-grow` and `flex-shrink` values is that they're proportional. Yes, `flex: 1 0 auto` means our `input` element will be wider than our button. But changing the value of our button's `flex` property to `flex: 1 0 auto` doesn't necessarily mean that both elements will have the same size:

5-72. Both items have the same flex value but are still different sizes

Instead, flex items will be resized to fill the container, taking their used `min-width` and `max-width` values into account (which may be their initial values).

Unfortunately, we can't use `fr` units with the `flex` or `flex-basis` properties. Use length or percentage values instead.

Vertical Centering with Flexbox

Finally, let's take a look at how to vertically center content with Flexbox. Vertically centering elements is one of the more difficult tasks to achieve with CSS, particularly if the height of your content is unknown. But with Flexbox, we require just one additional line of CSS— `align-items: center`:

```css
.flex-container {
    display: flex;
    align-items: center;
}
```

Now our flex items and their contents are vertically centered within the flex container.

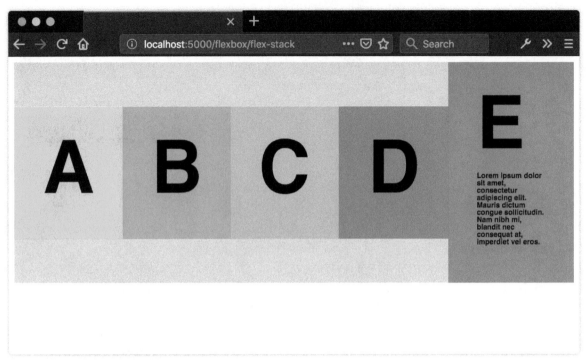

5-73. Distributing flex items with align-items: center

Creating Grid-like Layouts with Flexbox

In most cases, you'll want to use Grid to create grid-like layouts. However, you may find yourself wanting boxes that align when there's an even number of items, but expand to fill the available space when there's an odd number (figure 5-74).

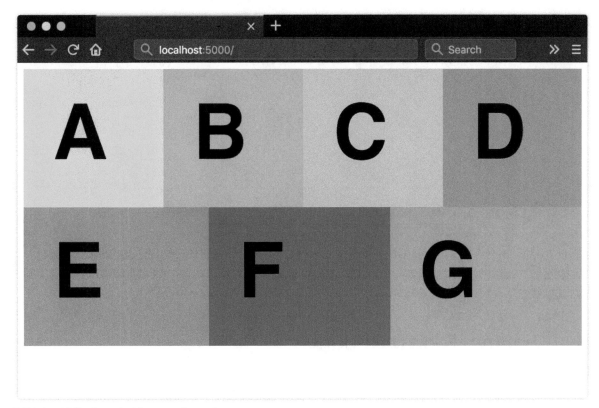

5-74. A grid-like layout with expanding cells

Here's the markup we'll use:

```
<ul class="flex-aligned">
    <li>A</li>
    <li>B</li>
    <li>C</li>
    <li>D</li>
    <li>E</li>
    <li>F</li>
    <li>G</li>
</li>
```

By default, flex items don't wrap. To achieve the layout above, we'll need to make them wrap using the *flex-wrap* property. It accepts three values: *nowrap* (the inital value), *wrap* , and *wrap-reverse* . We'll use *wrap* here:

```
.flex-aligned {
    display: flex;
    flex-wrap: wrap;
}
```

Now we just need to indicate how our flex items should behave, and what their maximum width should be. Since we want a maximum of four columns, we'll set our *flex-basis* value to *25%*. And since we want our flex items to expand to fill the available space, we'll set *flex-grow* to 1. We'll keep *flex-shrink* at 0 so that our boxes never occupy less than 25% of their container:

```
.flex-aligned li {
    flex: 1 0 25%;
}
```

Learning More about Flexbox

There's a lot more to Flexbox than what we've covered here. CSS-Tricks' "<u>A Complete Guide to Flexbox</u>[19]" digs into all the properties and values. You can also check out Philip Walton's "<u>Solved by Flexbox</u>[20]", which showcases UI patterns that are made easier with Flexbox.

Box Alignment and Distribution

Before closing this chapter, let's take a look at some properties that we can use for distributing and spacing boxes. These properties can be used with either Flexbox or Grid. Some properties also apply to multicolumn containers, although to date browser support is less robust. Most of the examples in this section use Flexbox.

First, some terminology: *justify* versus *align*. As the <u>CSS Box Alignment</u>[21] specification explains, **justify** refers to alignment in the main or inline dimensions, while **align** refers to alignment in the cross or block dimensions. For documents that use a horizontal writing mode, the main dimension is horizontal, and the cross dimension is vertical. For documents that use a vertical writing mode, the main dimension is vertical, and the cross dimension is horizontal. Each of the three *justify-** properties is concerned with the main, inline dimension. Their *align-** counterparts are concerned with the block dimension.

Distributing Items in the Main Dimension with justify-content

The *justify-content* property indicates to the browser how the contents of a container should be aligned along the main or inline axis. It only has an effect when there's leftover space available—for example, when no flex items have *flex-grow: 0*, or when the length of an explicit grid is less than that of its container.

[19.] https://css-tricks.com/snippets/css/a-guide-to-flexbox/
[20.] http://philipwalton.github.io/solved-by-flexbox/
[21.] https://www.w3.org/TR/css-align-3/

The *justify-content* property accepts more than a dozen different values. The table below illustrates each value and its impact on box alignment and distribution, when using a left-to-right writing direction. The dotted line represents the outline of the flex or grid container.

Value	Effect
center	
left	
right	
start	
end	
flex-start	
flex-end	
space-between	

Value	Effect
`space-around`	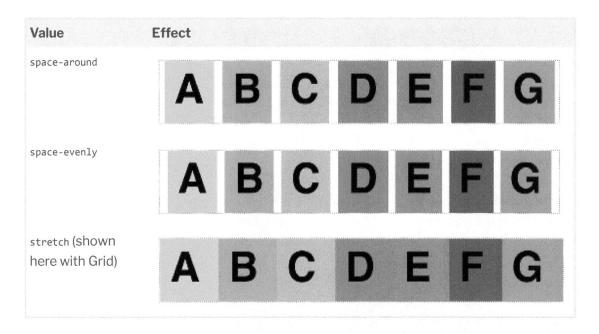
`space-evenly`	
`stretch` (shown here with Grid)	

The values above can be split into two broad groups: *positional alignment* values and *distributed alignment* values.

Positional alignment values indicate where items should be stacked within a container, and include:

- `center`
- `left`
- `right`
- `start`
- `end`
- `flex-start`
- `flex-end`

Both `justify-content: flex-start` and `justify-content: flex-end` only apply to flex containers. For a similar effect in Grid and multicolumn containers, use `start` or `end`.

Despite appearances, `left`, `start`, and `flex-start` are not the same. Neither are `right`, `end` and `flex-end`. Writing mode and language direction affect box alignment and distribution for `start` / `flex-start` and `end` / `flex-end`. For example, when the `direction` is `rtl` (right to left), `justify-content: flex-start` packs boxes against the right edge of the flex container, as shown in figure 5-75. When `flex-start` and `flex-end` are used on non-flex containers, they behave like `start` and `end`.

5-75. Using justify-content: flex-start with a container that has a horizontal, right-to-left writing mode causes boxes to be packed against the right edge

On the other hand, *justify-content: left* and *justify-content: right* always pack boxes to the left or right of the container, respectively. Figure 5-76 illustrates the effect of *justify-content: left* on a container with a horizontal writing mode and right-to-left language direction.

5-76. Using justify-content: left always packs boxes against the left edge

Distributed alignment values indicate how to divvy up the remaining space in a container. Using *justify-content: stretch*, for example, causes the size of each element to increase evenly to fill the available space, within `max-height` / `max-width` constraints. However, it has no effect on flex items.

space-around **versus** space-evenly

Where `space-between` places the first and last items flush against the edges of their container and evenly distributes the space, the difference between `space-around` and `space-evenly` is more subtle.

- `space-around` distributes items evenly within the alignment container, but the size of the space between the first/last item and the edge of the container is half that of the space between each item.
- `space-evenly` distributes space evenly between each item. The size of the space between the first/last item and the edge of the container is the same as the the size of the space between each item.

Aligning Items in the Cross Dimension with `align-content`

Where `justify-content` affects items in the main dimension, `align-content` affects them in the cross or block dimension. The `align-content` property accepts most of the same values as `justify-content`, except for `left` and `right`.

Remember that `align-content`, like `justify-content`, affects the distribution of *leftover* space. You'll only notice its impact when the used height of the container is something besides `auto`. The table below illustrates the impact of `align-content` and its values when using a horizontal writing mode and a left-to-right text direction.

Value	Effect
center	
start/flex-start	
end/flex-end	

Value	Effect
space-between	
space-around	
space-evenly	

Value	Effect
stretch	

Because `align-content` distributes space in the cross direction, you only notice its impact when there are multiple rows of content.

We can also combine values for `justify-content` and `align-content` by using the `place-content` shorthand property. It accepts up to two, space-separated values. The first value assigns the `align-content` value; the second is the `justify-content` value. Take, for example:

```
.centerstart {
    place-content: center flex-start;
}
```

This is the equivalent of:

```
.centerstart {
    align-content: center;
    justify-content: flex-start;
}
```

Keep in mind, however, that support for `place-content` is not yet available in Microsoft Edge.

Aligning Items with `align-items` and `align-self`

Where `align-content` affects the distribution of rows in the block dimension, `align-items` and `align-self` are concerned with the cross/block alignment of each item within a grid or flex container. The table below shows how `align-items` and its values work with a horizontal writing mode.

Value	Effect
center	
start/flex-start	
end/flex-end	

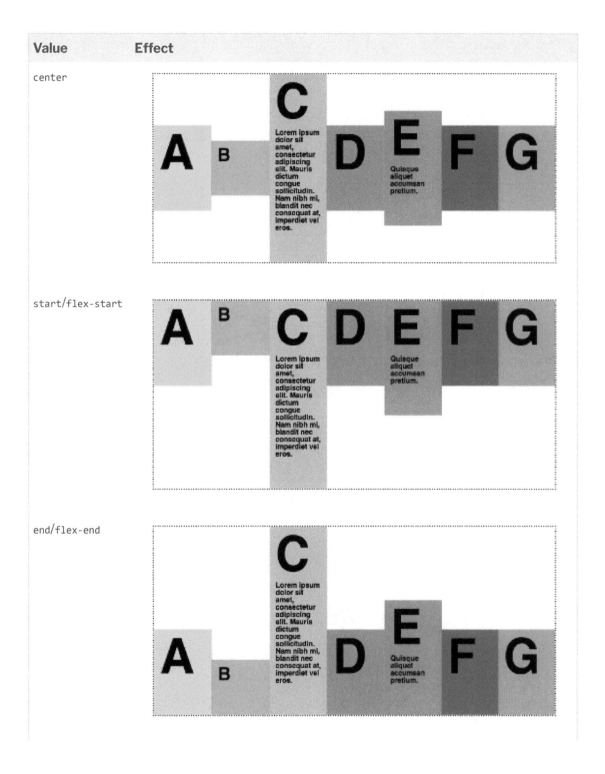

Value	Effect
baseline	
first baseline	
last baseline	

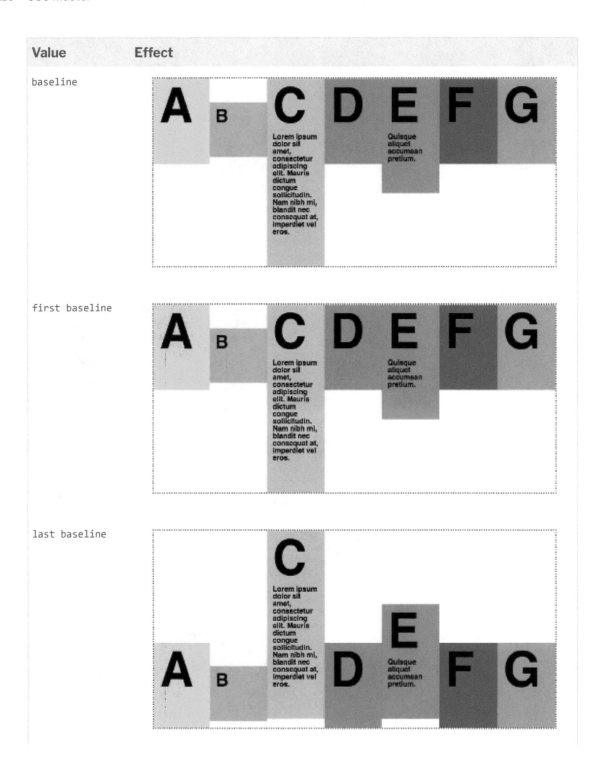

Value	Effect
normal	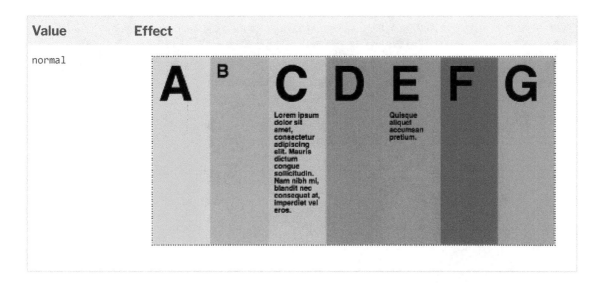

Baseline alignment is probably the trickiest concept to understand. When items are aligned along a baseline, they're vertically aligned with the bottom of each letter, without regard for descender height. Descenders are the stem parts of lowercase letters such as *q* and *p* that dangle below a line of text. Both `baseline` and `first baseline` align items along the first baseline of a row, while `last baseline` aligns them along the last line of a row.

The `align-items` property applies to the container element and sets the alignment for all of its children. `align-self`, on the other hand, applies to the child elements, and overrides the value of `align-items`. It accepts the same values as `align-items`. Here's an example:

```css
.flex-baseline {
    display: flex;
    align-items: flex-start;
}
.flex-baseline *:nth-child(2) {
    align-self: flex-end;
}
```

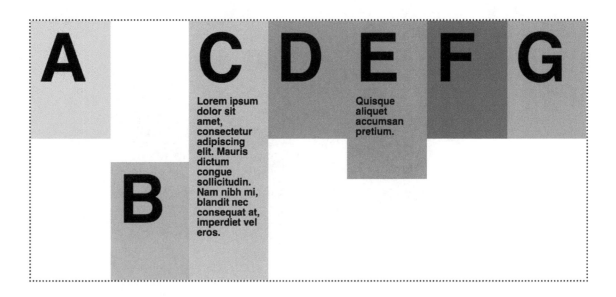

5-77. Using align-self to set the position of a single flex item

Now our second flex item is aligned with the end of the flex container, as shown in figure 5-77.

Choosing `flex` or `grid`

As you develop page or component layouts, you may find yourself wondering when it's better to use Flexbox and when to use Grid.

- Use Grid when you want to arrange elements into rows *and* columns that align both horizontally and vertically.
- Use Flexbox when you want to arrange items in a row *or* a column, when you wish to align items vertically or horizontally, but not both.

Jen Simmons' video "<u>Flexbox vs. CSS Grid — Which is Better?</u>[22]" walks you through some things to consider when choosing between Grid and Flexbox. Rachel Andrew's "<u>Should I use Grid or Flexbox?</u>[23]" is another great resource for understanding both.

In practice, your projects will probably mix both of these techniques, as well as floats. For instance, you may use Grid to define the overall page layout, while using Flexbox for your navigation menu or search box, and floats to place tables or images.

[22.] https://www.youtube.com/watch?v=hs3piaN4b5I
[23.] https://www.rachelandrew.co.uk/archives/2016/03/30/should-i-use-grid-or-flexbox/

Conclusion

We've covered a lot of ground in this chapter! Now that you've made it through, you should understand:

- what the CSS box model is, and how it affects page rendering and layout
- how the `float` property affects normal flow, and how to clear floated elements
- what stacking contexts are, and how to use them to create layered effects in CSS
- when and how to use multicolumn, Grid, and flexible box layout.

In our next chapter, we'll take a look at the fun topic of creating animations with CSS.

Transitions and Animations

Now that we've covered some advanced CSS layouts, let's look at how to add some whimsy, delight, and polish to our documents with CSS transitions and animations. Transitions and animations can clarify the effect of an action. A menu that slides into view, for example, is less abrupt and jarring than one that appears suddenly after a button is clicked. Transitions and animations can also draw attention to a page change or problem. You might, for instance, transition the border color of a form field to highlight that its value is invalid.[1]

This is probably a good time to explain how animations and transitions differ. With a **transition**, you define start and end states, and the browser fills in the states in between. With an **animation**, on the other hand, you can define those in-between states to control how the animation progresses.

CSS Transitions

CSS transitions[2] are a CSS-based way—as opposed to a JavaScript way—to update the value of a CSS property over a specified duration. Given a start value and an end value, the browser will interpolate in-between values over the course of the transition. They're great for simple effects where you don't mind giving up control over how the animation progresses.

In my own work, I often use transitions for `:hover` states. I also use them when revealing or concealing content, such as showing an off-screen menu. You *could* create animations for such effects, but animations are generally more verbose, as you'll see later in the chapter.

Browser support for CSS transitions is quite good. Recent versions of all major desktop and mobile browsers support them, with the exception of some proxy browsers such as Opera Mini.

Transitions degrade gracefully. In browsers without support for them, users will just see a transition-free change between the two values. This may be jarring—for example, when showing or hiding content—but it won't break your site's functionality.

If you want to include transitions for browsers that don't support them, one alternative is to use a JavaScript library. jQuery, for example, has several simple animation methods[3]. First, test to see whether the browser supports transitions (or animations), and fall back to JavaScript methods if it doesn't.

---

[1] "Animation for Attention and Comprehension" (http://www.nngroup.com/articles/animation-usability/), from the Nielsen Norman Group, is a nice backgrounder on how animation and transitions can enhance usability.

[2] https://drafts.csswg.org/css-transitions/

[3] http://api.jquery.com/category/effects/

Not all properties can be transitioned. Only properties that accept *interpolatable* values can. **Interpolation** is a method of calculating values that fall within a range. Interpolatable values are typically numeric unit values such as lengths, percentages, or colors. We can't, for example, transition between `visibility: visible` and `visibility: hidden`, or `display: block` and `display: none`. Nor can we transition to or from `auto` values.[4]

Creating Your First Transition

In this example, we'll make our link color transition from blue to pink when users move their mouse over it, and back to blue when users moves their mouse off it.

Here's our bare-bones HTML:

```
<!DOCTYPE html>
    <html lang="en-US">
    <head>
        <link rel="stylesheet" href="style.css">
    </head>
    <body>
        <p>Mouse over <a href="https://sitepoint.com/">this link</a>to see the transition effect.</p>
    </body>
</html>
```

This gives us the page shown below.

[4.] The CSS Transitions specification includes a list of animatable CSS properties and values: http://dev.w3.org/csswg/css-transitions-1/#animatable-cssanimatable.

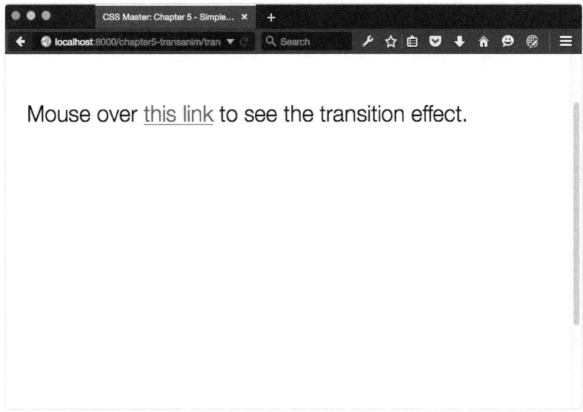

6-1. A basic HTML page with a link

Now let's add the following CSS to our *style.css* :

```css
a {
    transition: 1s;
}
a:link {
    color: #309;
}
a:hover {
    color: #f0c;
}
```

This is the bare minimum CSS required for a transition to work: a start value (*color: #309*), an end value (*color: #f0c*), and a transition duration (*transition: 1s;*). When you mouse over the link, you'll see a gradual transition from blue to hot pink, as illustrated below.

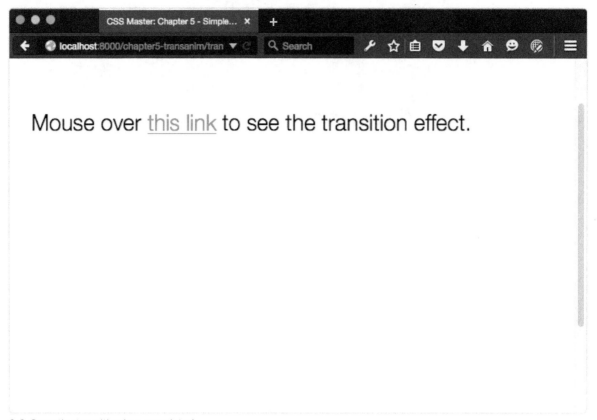

6-2. Once the transition has completed

Transitions need to be triggered by some kind of event. Often, this is a user interaction. We might transition between colors when entering and leaving a `:hover` state, as we've done here. But we can also trigger a transition by adding or removing a class name using JavaScript. In the following example, we modify an element's `classList` attribute to do just that:

```
<script type="text/javascript">
    var btn = document.querySelector('button');
    btn.addEventListener('click', function() {
        document.body.classList.toggle('change');
    });
</script>
```

In the code, we've first defined a variable named `btn`. If you're unfamiliar with programming, a variable is simply a bucket of sorts that holds a value. We can then use the variable anywhere we need that value. The value of `btn` is our button element, as returned by `document.querySelector('button')`. The `document.querySelector()` method is defined by the Selectors API specification[5]. It accepts any CSS selector as its argument, and returns the first

---

[5.] https://www.w3.org/TR/selectors-api2/

item that matches. It's a way to select elements that will be manipulated with JavaScript.

Next, we've added what's known as an **event listener** for the `click` event using `addEventListener` . The `addEventListener` method is part of the Document Object Model. It allows us to define a function that will be called when a particular event occurs. This function is known as an **event handler** or **callback function**. In this case we're listening—or waiting—for a `click` event on the `button` element.

The magic happens within the `click` event handler. We're using the `classList.toggle()` method to add or remove the `change` class from the `body` element (`document.body`). When the `classList` value changes, it will trigger the animation. The `classList` property is a newer part of the Document Object Model API. It provides a handful of methods that simplify the process of manipulating the class names of an element.[6]

Within our event handler function, we've used the library's `toggleClass` method to add the `change` class to the `body` element. As with the plain JavaScript example, this is what triggers our transition.

 Understanding JavaScript

> If any of that went over your head, don't worry. Pick up Darren Jones' _JavaScript: Novice to Ninja, 2nd Edition_[7].

Now let's look at our CSS. It's only a few lines long:

```css
body {
    background: #fcf;
    transition: 5s;
}
.change {
    background: #0cf;
}
```

Here, we've defined a starting background color for our `body` element, and a transition. We've also defined a `.change` class, which has a different value for `background` . When our event handler runs, it will add the `change` class to our `body` element. This will trigger a transition from the original background color to the one defined in the `.change` declaration block, as shown

---

[6.] The `classList` property is defined in the Document Object Model specification (http://www.w3.org/TR/dom/). Most browsers support it, although support in Internet Explorer 11 is incomplete.

[7.] https://www.sitepoint.com/premium/books/javascript-novice-to-ninja-2nd-edition

below.

If you want a transition to work in both directions—for example, when the class is both added and removed—you should add it to whichever declaration block is your start state. We've done that here by including the *transition* property in the *body* declaration block. If we moved the transition to the *change* class, our transition would only work when *change* was added to our body element, but not when it was removed.

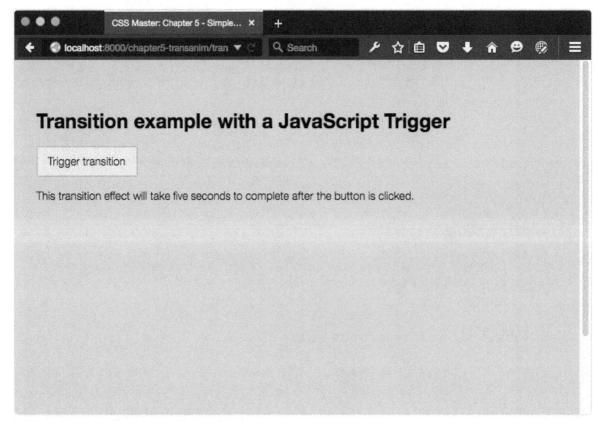

6-3. Creating a transition triggered by JavaScript

In the examples mentioned, we've used the *transition* shorthand property. It's a condensed way of specifying four "longhand" properties, which are listed in the table below.

Property	Description	Initial value
`transition-duration`	How long the transition should last	`0s` (no transition)
`transition-property`	Which property to transition	`all` (all animatable properties)
`transition-timing-function`	How to calculate the values between the start and end values	`ease`
`transition-delay`	How long the browser should wait between changing the property and starting the transition	`0s` (no delay)

Each longhand property has an *initial* value. It's a default value that the browser will use unless the property is explicitly set. For example, the initial value of `transition-property` is `all` (all properties), and the initial value of `transition-timing-function` is `ease` . When we set a transition duration—whether using the `transition` or `transition-duration` property—those values for `transition-property` and `transition-timing-function` are implied. This is why we can get away with setting the `transition` property and nothing else.

Using the `transition` Property

As we've already seen in the previous examples, time units are one acceptable value for the `transition` property. The <u>CSS Values and Units Module Level 3 specification</u>[8] defines two kinds of time units for use with transitions and animations: `s` for seconds, and `ms` for milliseconds. We can also collapse values for `transition-timing-function` , `transition-delay` , and `transition-property` into this shorthand `transition` property:

```
body {
    background: red;
    transition: background 500ms linear 1s;
}
```

Here, we've told the browser to transition the `background` property. The duration will last 500 milliseconds (which we could also write as `.5s`). It will use the `linear` timing function (discussed later in this chapter), and the start of the transition will be delayed by one second. It's a compact version of the following CSS:

---

[8] http://www.w3.org/TR/css3-values/

```
body {
    background: red;
    transition-property: background;
    transition-duration: 500ms;
    transition-timing-function: linear;
    transition-delay: 1s;
}
```

Order matters somewhat when using the *transition* shorthand property. The first value that can be interpreted as a time will become the transition duration no matter where it sits in the value string. The second time value will determine the transition delay. In other words, we could reorder the values in our transition property like so:

```
body {
    background: red;
    transition: 500ms 1s background linear;
}
```

Here, our transition duration will be 500ms with a one second delay.

Using the *transition* property is the most concise way to define a transition. However, there may be cases in which you want to define a global transition effect (for example, *transition: 500ms ease*) in one part of your CSS, and limit it to specific CSS properties (for example, *transition-property: color*) in another. This is where the longhand properties are useful.

Transition Durations and Delays

The *transition-duration* property sets the duration of the transition, or how long it takes to complete. The *transition-delay* property determines how much time should lapse before the transition begins. Both properties accept time units as a value. These can be seconds or milliseconds: *1s* , *2.5s* , and *200ms* are all valid values.

Both *transition-duration* and *transition-delay* have an initial value of *0s* , or zero seconds. For *transition-duration* , this means there will be no gradual transition between the start and end states. For *transition-delay* , this means the transition will occur immediately.

With *transition-duration* , you must use values greater than zero, such as *.5s* or *2500ms* . Negative values will be treated like a value of *0s* , and the transition will fail to execute, as illustrated below.

6-4. The effect of a negative transition delay

However, negative values are valid for *transition-delay* . Positive *transition-delay* values shift the start of the animation by the specified amount of time. Negative values, however, offset the beginning of the transition, as seen above. Using *transition-duration: 2s; transition-delay: -1s* will cause the transition to jump one second into the play cycle before continuing. Using a negative *transition-delay* value can create a snappier transition experience by shortening its perceived duration.

Timing Functions

We can also shape transition effects using the *transition-timing-function* property. Timing functions are formulas of sorts that determine how the in-between values of a transition are calculated. Which timing function you use will depend on what kind of transition effect you'd like to achieve: a stepped transition or a smooth, gradual one.

Stepped Transitions

With stepped transitions, the play cycle is divided into intervals of equal value and duration. We can set how many intervals a transition should have using the *steps* timing function.

Let's revisit our background color example from earlier in this chapter. Instead of using the default *ease* timing function, we'll instead use the *steps* function to create a five-step transition. Our revised CSS looks like this:

```css
body {
    background: #f0f;
    transition: 5s steps(5);
}
.change {
    background: #0cf;
}
```

Rather than a smooth, gradual shift between colors, this transition will cycle through five distinct color states.

There are also two keywords we can use to create stepped animations: *step-start* and *step-end* . These are equivalent to *steps(1, start)* and *steps(1, end)* . With these keywords (or their *step* function equivalents), the transition will have exactly one interval between the start value and end value.

Smooth Transitions

Smooth transitions use the *cubic-bezier* function to interpolate values. Understanding *how* this function works involves a bit of math, along with some handwaving and magic. Read Pomax's "A Primer on Bézier Curves[9]" if you're interested in the intimate details. What follows is a simplified explanation.

The cubic Bézier function is based on the cubic Bézier curve. A Bézier curve consists of a start point and an end point, and one or more control points that affect the shape of the curve. A *cubic* Bézier curve always has two of these control points, which can be seen below. Curves are drawn from the start point to the end point, towards the control points.

---

[9] http://pomax.github.io/bezierinfo/#explanation

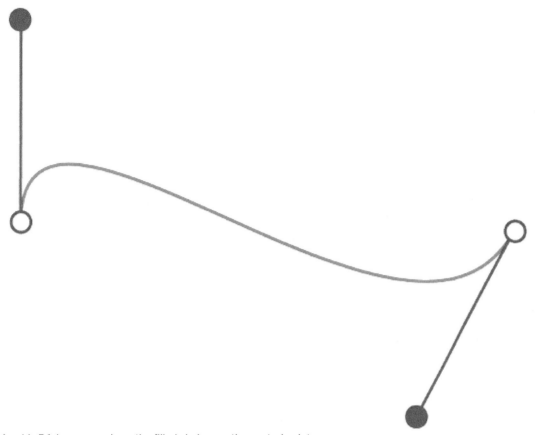

6-5. A cubic Bézier curve, where the filled circles are the control points

The arguments passed to the `cubic-bezier` function represent the coordinates of those control points: *x1, y1, x2, y2*. But there's a constraint on these points: X values (the first and third parameters) must fall between `0` and `1`. Y values (the second and fourth parameters) can exceed this range in either direction. In other words, `cubic-bezier(0, 1.02, 1, 0)` and `cubic-bezier(0, 1.08, .98, -0.58)` are valid values, but `cubic-bezier(2, 1.02, -1, 0)` is not.[10]

Graphs are the best way to illustrate how `cubic-bezier` works. The X-axis is a function of the transition's duration, and can be seen below. The Y-axis is a function of value of the property that's being transitioned. The outputs for these function determine the values of the property at a particular point in the transition. Changes in the graph match the changes in speed over the course of a transition.

---

[10]. Lea Verou's cubic-bezier.com is a great tool for experimenting with the `cubic-bezier` function.

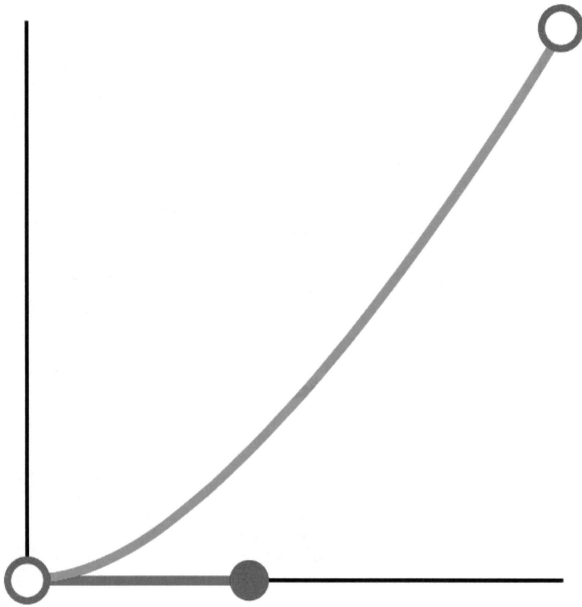

6-6. A graph of cubic-bezier(0.42, 0, 1, 1)

In most cases, it's easier to use a timing function keyword. We mentioned `step-start` and `step-end` in the previous section, but there are five more keywords, each of which is an alias for `cubic-bezier` values. They're listed in the following table:

Keyword	Equivalent function	Effect
ease	cubic-bezier(0.25, 0.1, 0.25, 1)	Begins slowly, accelerates quickly, then slows towards the end of the transition
ease-in	cubic-bezier(0.42, 0, 1, 1)	Begins quickly, then accelerates slowly but steadily until the end of the transition
ease-out	cubic-bezier(0, 0, 0.58, 1)	Accelerates quickly but slows towards the end of the transition
ease-in-out	cubic-bezier(0.42, 0, 0.58, 1)	Begins slowly, accelerates quickly, then decelerates towards the end of the transition
linear	cubic-bezier(0, 0, 1, 1)	Speed remains consistent over the course of the animation

Transitioning Multiple Properties

It's possible to transition multiple properties of a single element using a transition list. Let's look at an example:

```
div {
    background: #E91E63;
    height: 200px;
    width: 200px;
    margin: 10px 0;
    position: relative;
    left: 0;
    top: 3em;
    transition: left 4s cubic-bezier(0.175, 0.885, 0.32, 1.275), background 2s 500ms;
}
.transthem {
    left: 30%;
    background: #00BCD4;
}
```

Here, we've defined transitions for the *left* and *background* properties. The difference is that each item is separated by a comma. The *left* transition will last four seconds and use a *cubic-bezier* timing function. The *background* transition will only last two seconds, but it begins after a half-second (*500ms*) delay.

Occasionally, you may need to detect when a transition ends in order to take another action. For example, if you transition the *opacity: 1* to *opacity: 0* , it's a good idea to add a *hidden* attribute to the element for improved assistive technology support. This is where the *transitionend* event comes in handy.

When a transition completes, the browser fires a *transitionend* event on the affected element—one for each property. We can listen for these events using *addEventListener* :

```
const transitionEndHandler = function() {
    // Do something.
}
const element = document.getElementById('el');
element.addEventListener('transitionend', transitionEndHandler);
```

HTML also supports an *ontransitionend* attribute. The code above could also be written as follows:

```
const transitionEndHandler = function() {
    // Do something.
}
const element = document.getElementById('el');
element.ontransitionend = transitionEndHandler;
```

 Shorthand Properties

In cases where the property is a shorthand property, the browser will fire one event for each longhand property. In other words, a transition of the *padding* property will result in *transitionend* events for *padding-top* , *padding-right* , *padding-bottom* , and *padding-left* .

Let's put this knowledge to use. In this example, we'll hide unselected form options when the user picks one. Our (simplified) HTML follows:

```
<h1>Please select your favorite color of the ones shown below.</h1>
<form>
  <ul>
    <li>
      <input type="radio" name="favecolor" id="red"><label for="red">Red</label>
    </li>
    <li>
      <input type="radio" name="favecolor" id="yellow"><label for="yellow">Yellow</label>
    </li>
    <li>
```

```
        <input type="radio" name="favecolor" id="blue"><label for="blue">Blue</label>
    </li>
  </ul>
  <div id="thanks" hidden>Thank you for selecting your favorite color.</div>
  <button type="reset">Reset</button>
</form>
```

And here's our (also simplified) CSS:

```
li {
    transition: 500ms;
}
.fade {
    opacity: 0;
}
```

Add some styles for color and font size, and we end up with the example below.

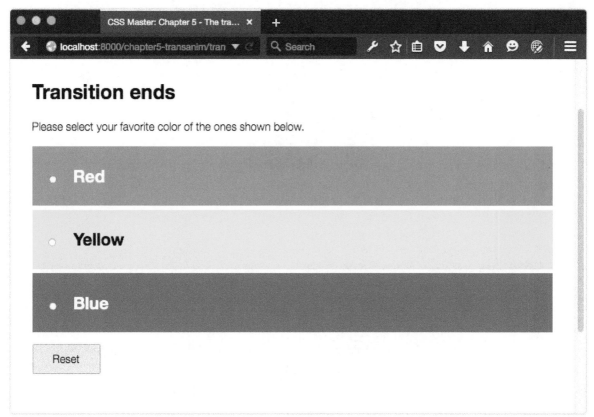

6-7. Our transition demo form

Now let's tie it together with JavaScript. First, let's define an action that adds the *fade* class—in this case, a *change* event handler:

```
const changeHandler = function() {
    // Select unchecked radio buttons. Returns a NodeList.
    const notfave = document.querySelectorAll('input:not(:checked)');

    // Create a new array from the NodeList
    notfave.forEach(function(item) {
        // Find the parent node, and add a 'fade' class
        item.parentNode.classList.add('fade');
    });
};

const form = document.querySelector('form');
form.addEventListener('change', changeHandler);
```

When the user selects a color, our form element will receive a *change* event. That in turn triggers the *changeHandler* method, which adds a *fade* class to the parent element of each radio button. This is what triggers our transition.

 forEach **DOM Function**

> The *forEach* method used above is a DOM function for iterating through a **NodeList**, or collection of elements. It's supported in most major browsers, with the exception of Internet Explorer 11. It's not the *forEach* method of JavaScript. The Mozilla Developer Network covers forEach[11] in depth.

Now let's take a look at our *transitionend* handler. It's slightly different from the other examples in this chapter:

```
const transitionendHandler = function(domEvent) {
    domEvent.target.setAttribute('hidden', '');
    document.getElementById('thanks').removeAttribute('hidden');
};

document.addEventListener('transitionend', transitionendHandler);
```

Our *transitionendHandler* accepts a single event object argument. Here, we've named it *domEvent*, but you could name it *evt*, *foo* —just about anything. This event object is passed automatically, according to behavior defined by the Document Object Model Level 2 specification. In order to reference this event object within our handler, we need to define it as a parameter for our function.

---

[11]. https://developer.mozilla.org/en-US/docs/Web/API/NodeList/forEach

Every event object includes a *target* property. This is a reference to the element that received the event. In this case it's a list item, and we're adding a *hidden* attribute to each (*eventObject.target.setAttribute('hidden', '')*). The last line of our event handler removes the *hidden* attribute from our "Thank you" message, as seen below.

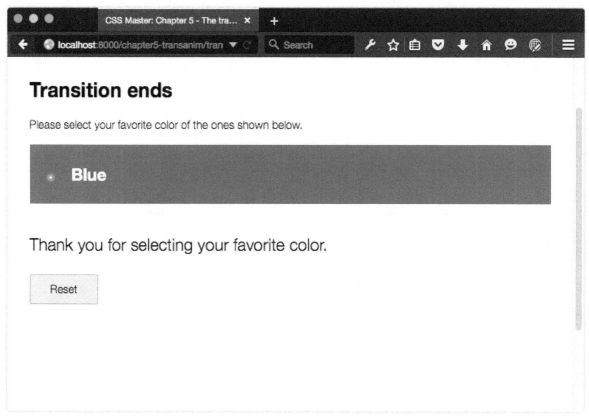

6-8. Our form after the user has chosen an option and the transitionend event has fired

Multiple Transitions and `transitionend` Events

Compound transitions—that is, transitions of multiple properties—trigger multiple *transitionend* events. A transition such as *transition: left 4s cubic-linear, background 2s 500ms;* will trigger two *transitionend* events: one for the *left* property and another for *background* . To determine which transition triggered the event, you can check the *propertyName* property of the event object:

```
var transitionendHandler = function(eventObject) {
    if( eventObject.propertyName === 'opacity' ){
        // Do something based on this value.
    }
};
```

Occasionally, a transition will fail to complete. This can typically happen when the property is overridden while it's in progress—such as when a user action removes the class name. In those situations, the `transitionend` event won't fire.

Because of this risk, avoid using the `transitionend` event to trigger anything "mission critical," such as a form submission.

CSS Animation

Think of CSS animation as the more sophisticated sister to CSS transitions. Animations differ from transitions in a few key ways:

- Animations don't degrade gracefully. If there's no support from the browser, the user is out of luck. The alternative is to use JavaScript.
- Animations can repeat, and repeat infinitely. Transitions are always finite.
- Animations use keyframes, which offer the ability to create more complex and nuanced effects.
- Animations can be paused in the middle of the play cycle.

The latest versions of all major browsers support CSS animations. Firefox versions 15 and earlier require a `-moz-` prefix; later version don't. Internet Explorer versions 10 and 11 also support animations without a prefix, as do all versions of Microsoft Edge.

We can check for CSS animations support in a few ways. The first is by testing for the presence of `CSSKeyframeRule` as a method of the `window` object:

```
const hasAnimations = 'CSSKeyframeRule' in window;
```

If the browser supports the `@supports` rule and `CSS.supports()` API (discussed in Chapter 8, *Applying CSS Conditionally*), we can use that instead:

```
const hasAnimations = CSS.supports('animation-duration: 2s');
```

As with transitions, we can only animate interpolatable values such as color values, lengths, and percentages.

Creating Your First Animation

We first have to define an animation using an `@keyframes` rule. The `@keyframes` rule has two purposes:

- setting the name of our animation
- grouping our keyframe rules

Let's create an animation named *pulse* :

```
@keyframes pulse {

}
```

Our keyframes will be defined within this block. In animation, a **keyframe** is a point at which the action changes. With CSS animations specifically, keyframe rules are used to set property values at particular points in the animation cycle. Values that fall between the values in a keyframe rule are interpolated.

At the minimum, an animation requires two keyframes: a *from* keyframe, which is the starting state for our animation, and a *to* frame, which is its end state. Within each individual keyframe block, we can define which properties to animate:

```
@keyframes pulse {
    from {
        transform: scale(0.5);
        opacity: .8;
    }

    to {
        transform: scale(1);
        opacity: 1;
    }
}
```

This code will scale our object from half its size to its full size, and change the opacity from 80% to 100%.

The *keyframes* rule only *defines* an animation, though. By itself, it doesn't make elements move. We need to apply it. Let's also define a *pulse* class that we can use to add this animation to any element:

```
.pulse {
    animation: pulse 500ms;
}
```

Here, we've used the *animation* shorthand property to set the animation name and duration. In order for an animation to play, we need the name of an *@keyframes* rule (in this case, *pulse*) and a duration. Other properties are optional.

The order of properties for *animation* is similar to that of *transition* . The first value that can be parsed becomes the value of *animation-duration* . The second value becomes the value for *animation-delay* . Words that aren't CSS-wide keywords or animation property keyword values are assumed to be *@keyframe* ruleset names.

As with *transition* , *animation* also accepts an animation list. The animation list is a comma-separated list of values. We could, for example, split our pulse animation into two rules— *pulse* and *fade* :

```
@keyframes pulse {
    from {
        transform: scale(0.5);
    }
    to {
        transform: scale(1);
    }
}

@keyframes fade {
    from {
        opacity: .5;
    }
    to {
        opacity: 1;
    }
}
```

Then we could combine them as part of a single animation:

```
.pulse-and-fade {
    animation: pulse 500ms, fade 500ms;
}
```

Animation Properties

Though using the *animation* property is shorter, sometimes longhand properties are clearer. Longhand animation properties are listed in the following table:

Property	Description	Initial value
`animation-delay`	How long to wait before executing the animation	`0s` (executes immediately)
`animation-duration`	How long the cycle of an animation should last	`0s` (no animation occurs)
`animation-name`	The name of an `@keyframes` rule	none
`animation-timing-function`	How to calculate the values between the start and end states	`ease`
`animation-iteration-count`	How many times to repeat the animation	1
`animation-direction`	Whether or not the animation should ever play in reverse	`normal` (no reverse)
`animation-play-state`	Whether the animation is running or paused	`running`
`animation-fill-mode`	Specifies what property values are applied when the animation isn't running	`none`

The *animation-delay* and *animation-duration* properties function like *transition-delay* and *transition-duration* . Both accept time units as a value, either in seconds (*s*) or milliseconds (*ms*). Negative time values are valid for *animation-delay* , but not *animation-duration* .

Let's rewrite our *.pulse* ruleset using longhand properties. Doing so gives us the following:

```
.pulse {
    animation-name: pulse;
    animation-duration: 500ms;
}
```

The *animation-name* property is fairly straightforward. Its value can be either *none* or the name of the *@keyframes* rule. Animation names have few restrictions. CSS keywords such as *initial* , *inherit* , *default* , and *none* are forbidden. Most punctuation characters won't work, while letters, underscores, digits, and emojis (and other Unicode) characters usually will. For clarity and maintainability, it's a good idea to give your animations descriptive names, and avoid using CSS properties or emojis as names.

To Loop or Not to Loop: The `animation-iteration-count` Property

If you're following along with your own code, you'll notice that this animation only happens once.

We want our animation to repeat. For that, we'll need the `animation-iteration-count` property.

The `animation-iteration-count` property accepts most numeric values. Whole numbers and decimal numbers are valid values. With decimal numbers, however, the animation will stop partway through the last animation cycle, ending in the `to` state. Negative `animation-iteration-count` values are treated the same as `1`.

To make an animation run indefinitely, use the `infinite` keyword. The animation will play an infinite number of times. Of course, `infinite` really means until the document is unloaded, the browser window closes, the animation styles are removed, or the device shuts down. Let's make our animation infinite:

```css
.pulse {
    animation-name: pulse;
    animation-duration: 500ms;
    animation-iteration-count: infinite;
}
```

Or, using the `animation` shorthand property:

```css
.pulse {
    animation: pulse 500ms infinite;
}
```

Playing Animations: the `animation-direction` Property

There's still a problem with our animation, however. It doesn't so much *pulse* as repeat our scaling-up animation. What we want is for this element to scale up and down. Enter the `animation-direction` property.

The `animation-direction` property accepts one of four values:

- `normal` : the initial value, playing the animation as specified
- `reverse` : flips the `from` and `to` states and plays the animation in reverse
- `alternate` : plays even-numbered animation cycles in reverse
- `alternate-reverse` : plays odd-numbered animation cycles in reverse

To continue with our current example, `reverse` would scale down our object by a factor of 0.5. Using `alternate` would scale our object up for the odd-numbered cycles and down for the even-numbered. Conversely, using `alternate-reverse` would scale our object down for the odd-numbered cycles and up for the even ones. Since this is the effect we want, we'll set our *animation-direction* property to *alternate-reverse* :

```
.pulse {
    animation-name: pulse;
    animation-duration: 500ms;
    animation-iteration-count: infinite;
    animation-direction: alternate-reverse;
}
```

Or, using the shorthand property:

```
.pulse {
    animation: pulse 500ms infinite alternate-reverse;
}
```

Using Percentage Keyframes

Our previous example was a simple pulse animation. We can create more complex animation sequences using percentage keyframes. Rather than using *from* and *to* , **percentage keyframes** indicate specific points of change over the course of the animation. Below is an example using an animation named *wiggle* :

```
@keyframes wiggle {
    25% {
        transform: scale(.5) skewX(-5deg) rotate(-5deg);
    }
    50% {
        transform: skewY(5deg) rotate(5deg);
    }
    75% {
        transform: skewX(-5deg) rotate(-5deg) scale(1.5);
    }
    100% {
        transform: scale(1.5);
    }
}
```

We've used increments of 25% here, but these keyframes could be 5%, 10%, or 33.2%. As the animation plays, the browser will interpolate the values between each state. As with our previous example, we can assign it to a selector:

```
/* Our animation will play once */
.wiggle {
    animation-name: wiggle;
    animation-duration: 500ms;
}
```

Or using the *animation* shorthand property:

```
.wiggle {
    animation: wiggle 500ms;
}
```

There's just one problem here. When our animation ends, it goes back to the original, pre-animated state. To prevent this, use the *animation-fill-mode* property.

The `animation-fill-mode` **Property**

Animations have no effect on properties before they begin or after they stop playing. But as you've seen with the *wiggle* example, once an animation ends, it reverts to its pre-animation state. With *animation-fill-mode*, we can fill in those states before the animation starts and ends.

The *animation-fill-mode* property accepts one of four values:

- *none* : the animation has no effect when it's not executing
- *forwards* : when the animation ends, the property values of the end state will still apply
- *backwards* : property values for the first keyframe will be applied during the animation delay period
- *both* : effects for both *forwards* and *backwards* apply

Since we want our animated element to remain in its final, scaled-up state, we're going to use *animation-fill-mode: forwards* .(*animation-fill-mode: both* would also work.)

The effect of *animation-fill-mode: backwards* is most apparent when the *animation-delay* property is set to *500ms* or higher. When *animation-fill-mode* is set to *backwards* , the property values of the first keyframe are applied, but the animation isn't executed until the delay elapses.

Pausing Animations

As has been mentioned, animations can be paused. Transitions can be reversed midway, or stopped altogether by toggling a class name. Animations, on the other hand, can be paused partway through the play cycle using *animation-play-state* . It has two defined values— *running* and *paused* —and its initial value is *running* .

Let's look at a simple example of using *animation-play-state* to play or pause an animation. First, our CSS:

```css
.wobble {
    animation: wobble 3s ease-in infinite forwards alternate;
    animation-play-state: paused;
}
.running {
    animation-play-state: running;
}
```

Here, we have two declaration blocks: *wobble* , which defines a wobbling animation, and *running* , which sets a play state. As part of our *animation* declaration, we've set an *animation-play-state* value of *paused* . To run our animation, we'll add the *running* class to our element. Let's assume that our markup includes a **Run** animation button with an *id* of *trigger* :

```js
const trigger = document.querySelector('#trigger');
const moveIt = document.querySelector('.wobble');

trigger.addEventListener('click', function() {
    moveIt.classList.toggle('running');
});
```

Adding *.running* to our element overrides the *animation-play-state* value set in *.wobble* , and causes the animation to play.

Detecting When Animations Start, End, or Repeat

Like transitions, animations fire an event when they end: *animationend* . Unlike transitions, animations also fire *animationstart* and *animationiteration* events when they begin to repeat. As with transitions, you might use these events to trigger another action on the page. Perhaps you'd use *animationstart* to contextually reveal a **Stop Animation** button, or *animationend* to reveal a **Replay** button.

We can listen for these events with JavaScript. Below, we're listening for the *animationend* event:

```js
const animate = document.getElementById('animate');
```

```
animate.addEventListener('animationend', function(eventObject) {
    // Do something
});
```

Here, too, the event handler function receives an event object as its sole argument. In order to determine which animation ended, we can query the *animationName* property of the event object.

A Note About Accessibility

Transitions and animations can enhance the user experience by making interactions smooth rather than jumpy, and otherwise bring delight to the interface. But they still have accessibility risks. Large spinning animations, for example, can cause dizziness or nausea for people with vestibular disorders, such as vertigo[12]. Flashing animations can trigger seizures in some people with photosensitive epilepsy[13]. Use them sparingly, and strongly consider giving users the ability to turn them off. We discuss one method for doing this—the *prefers-reduced-motion* media query—in Chapter 8, *Applying CSS Conditionally*.

A Note About Performance

Some properties create better-performing transitions and animations than others. If an animation updates a property that triggers a reflow or repaint, it may perform poorly on low-powered devices such a phones and tablets.

Properties that trigger a reflow are ones that affect layout. These include the following animatable properties:

- *border-width* (and *border-*-width* properties)
- *border* (and *border-** properties)
- *bottom*
- *font-size*
- *font-weight*
- *height*
- *left*
- *line-height*

---

12. "Infinite Canvas 6: Vestibular Disorders and Accessible Animation" (https://www.youtube.com/watch?v=QhnIZh0xwk0) is a great introduction to the subject of vestibular disorders and animation.
13. WCAG 2.0 (https://www.w3.org/WAI/WCAG21/Understanding/seizures-and-physical-reactions) provides guidelines for avoiding flashes and animations that are known to trigger seizures.

- *margin* (and *margin-** properties)
- *min-height*
- *min-width*
- *max-height*
- *max-width*
- *padding* (and *padding-** properties)
- *right*
- *top*
- *vertical-align*
- *width*

When these properties are animated, the browser must recalculate the size and position of the affected—and often neighboring—elements. Use transforms where you can. Transitioning or animating translation transforms (for example, `transform: translate(100px,200px)`) can replace `top` , `left` , `right` , and `bottom` properties. In some cases, `height` and `width` animations can be replaced with a `scale` transformation.

Sometimes, triggering a reflow (or layout update) is unavoidable. In those cases, minimize the number of elements affected and use tricks (such as negative delays) to shorten the perceived animation duration.

Properties that trigger a repaint are typically those that cause a color change. These include:

- *background*
- *background-image*
- *background-position*
- *background-repeat*
- *background-size*
- *border-radius*
- *border-style*
- *box-shadow*
- *color*
- *outline*
- *outline-color*
- *outline-style*
- *outline-width*

Changes to these properties are less expensive to calculate than those that affect layout, but they do still have a cost. Changes to `box-shadow` and `border-radius` are especially expensive to calculate, especially for low-powered devices. Use caution when animating these properties.

Conclusion

In this chapter, we've looked at how to add motion to web pages using CSS transitions and animations, and why you might like to do so. We've also touched on performance and accessibility concerns, and explained the finer points of the `cubic-bezier` function.

As you use transitions and animations, consider *how* you're using them. They're best used to focus the user's attention or clarify an action. But they can also be used to add whimsy and delight.

Transforms

Transforms allow us to create effects and interactions that are otherwise impossible. When combined with transitions and animations, we can create elements and interfaces that rotate, dance, and zoom. Three-dimensional transforms, in particular, make it possible to mimic physical objects.

Take, for example, the humble postcard received from a friend. Its front face displays a photo of the location your friend sent the card from. When you flip it over, you see expanded information about the photo and your friend's journey. (By the way, they wish you were there.)

7-1. Greetings from Hollywood

A postcard isn't a web interface, obviously, but it's a metaphor for the kind of interfaces we can create. Perhaps you want to build a weather widget that functions similarly to a postcard. The front of our widget contains a current weather summary, which can be seen in figure 7-2. Flipping it over—triggered by a tap or swipe—might show an expanded weather forecast, or reveal a **Settings** panel, as seen in figure 7-3.

7-2. An example weather widget

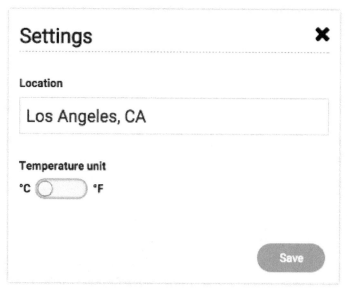

7-3. Our widget's Settings panel

Card-style interfaces are a great example of what we can build with transforms. In this chapter, we'll do a deep dive into the details of how they work.

Checking Out the Spec

Transforms are defined by the <u>CSS Transforms Module Level 2</u>[1] specification. At one point, two-dimensional and three-dimensional transforms were defined in separate specifications. As you move through the chapter, you'll notice some redundancy in function names.

How Transforms Affect Layout

Before we go too much further, there are some things you should know about how the _transform_ property affects layout. When you apply the _transform_ property to an element and its value is other than _none_, three things happen:

- the element becomes a containing block for child elements
- it establishes a new stacking context for the element and its children
- it imposes a local coordinate system within the element's bounding box

Let's look at these concepts individually.

transform **Creates a Containing Block**

When an element is positioned—that is, when the value of the _position_ property is something other _static_ —it's drawn relative to a containing block. A containing block is the closest positioned ancestor or, failing that, the root element (such as _html_ or _svg_) of a document.

In figure 7-4, the child rectangle has a _position_ value of _absolute_ . Its _right_ and _bottom_ properties are both set to _0_ . Its parent element has a _position_ value of _relative_ . Because the parent in this case is positioned, it becomes a containing block for the child. If the parent rectangle was not positioned, this child element would instead be drawn at the bottom right of the browser window.

[1.] https://drafts.csswg.org/css-transforms-2/

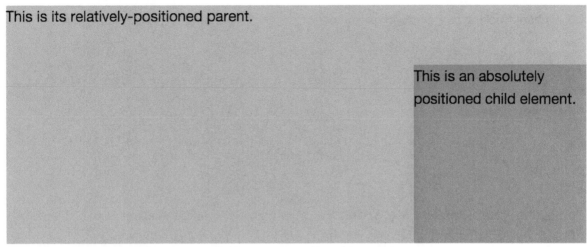

7-4. A child element with position: absolute inside a container with position: relative

Transforms work similarly. Setting the value of *transform* to something other than *none* turns the transformed element into a containing block. Positioned children of a transformed element are positioned relative to that element, as seen in figure 7-5.

7-5. A child element with position: absolute nested within an element with transform: skewX(-15deg)

In figure 7-5, the parent element *is not* positioned. The *transform* property is what's creating this containing block.

transform **Creates a New Stacking Context**

A transform also creates a new stacking context for the element it's applied to. As you may recall from Chapter 5, *Layouts*, elements within a stacking context are painted from back to front, as follows:

1   child-stacking contexts with a negative stack level (for example, positioned *z-index: -1*)

2   nonpositioned elements

3   child-stacking contexts with a stack level of *0* (for example, positioned and *z-index: 0;* or *z-index: auto;*)

4   child-stacking contexts with positive stack levels (for example, *z-index: 1*) sit at the top of the stack

Setting the value of *transform* to something other than *none* puts the element's stack level at *0* , and causes a transformed element to be stacked in front of nonpositioned elements. The *z-index* values of each child element will be relative to the parent. Let's update our example from Chapter 5 to see how this works:

```
<div style="position:relative;">
    <div id="a">
        <p><b>div#a</b></p>
    </div>

    <div id="b" style="transform: scale(2) translate(25%, 15%);">
        <p><b>div#b</b></p>
    </div>

    <div id="c" style="position:relative; z-index: 1">
        <p><b>div#c</b></p>
    </div>
    <div id="d" style="position:absolute; z-index: -1">
        <p><b>div#d</b></p>
    </div>
</div>
```

In this case (see figure 7-6), *div#d* sits at the bottom of the stack, and *div#a* sits above it. But *div#b* comes next because the *transform* property forces its *z-index* value to be *0* instead of *auto* . With *z-index: 1* , *div#c* sits at the top of the stack.

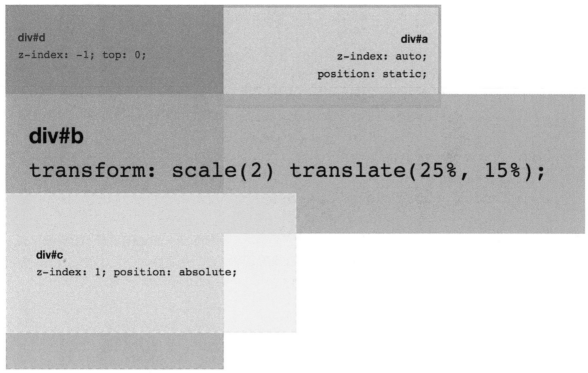

7-6. A stacking context with positioned and unpositioned elements with varying z-index values

Three-dimensional transforms add additional complexity. An element shifted along the Z-axis may render on a different plane than its container. Elements may also intersect with other elements across layers. Still, the basic rules of the stacking order apply.

Transformed elements may also overlap other elements on the page and prevent them from receiving mouse, touch, or pointer events. Applying *pointer-events: none* to the transformed element will solve this issue.[2]

Browsers apply transforms after elements have been sized and positioned. Unlike floated elements, transformed elements aren't removed from the normal flow.[3] Content and other elements won't wrap around transformed elements.

Because transforms are applied after the layout has been calculated, they don't affect document layout. Although transformed child elements may overflow the parent element's bounding box, they don't affect the position of other elements on the page. They also don't affect a the *HTMLElement.offsetLeft* or *HTMLElement.offsetTop* DOM properties of an element. Using these

---

[2] The *pointer-events* CSS property is distinct from the PointerEvents DOM event object.

[3] Document flow is described by the **Visual formatting model** section of the CSS2.1 specification (http://www.w3.org/TR/CSS21/visuren.html). Updates to this model are partly described by the **CSS Display Module Level 3** (http://dev.w3.org/csswg/css-display/).

properties to detect the rendered position of an element will give you inaccurate results.

Transforms do, however, affect client rectangle values and visual rendering of elements. To determine the rendered left and top positions of an element, use the `HTMLElement.getClientRects()` or `HTMLElement.getBoundingClientRect()` DOM methods (for example, `document.getElementById('#targetEl').getClientRects()`). Because they don't force the browser to calculate page layout, transforms typically perform better than properties such as `left` and `height` when animated.

`transform` Creates a Local Coordinate System

You may recall from geometry class that the Cartesian coordinate system is a way of specifying points in a plane. You may also recall that a plane is a flat, two-dimensional surface that extends infinitely along the horizontal and vertical axes. These axes are also known as the X-axis and Y-axis.

Point values along the X-axis increase as you move from left to right, and decrease from right to left. Y-axis point values increase as you move up, and decrease as you move down. The X and Y axes are perpendicular to each other. Where they cross is known as the *origin*, and the coordinates of its location are always (0,0), as illustrated in figure 7-7.

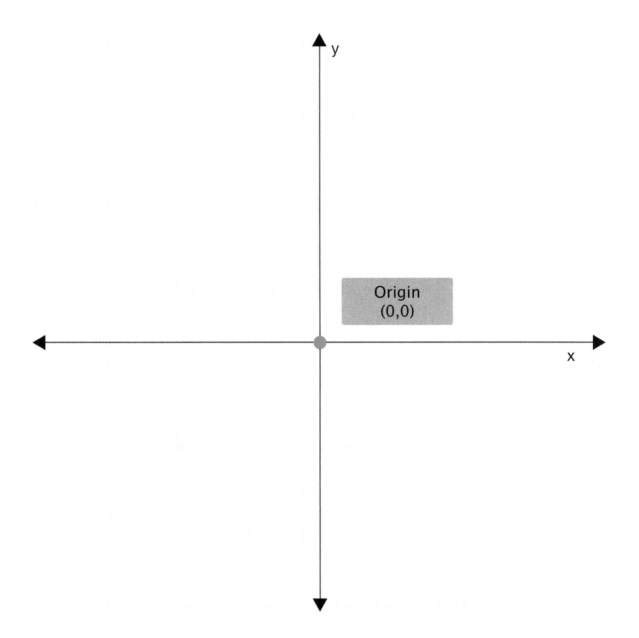

7-7. A two-dimensional coordinate system

In a three-dimensional coordinate system, there's also a Z-axis. This axis is perpendicular to both the X and Y axes, as well as the screen (see figure 7-8). The point at which the Z-axis crosses the X and Y axes is also known as the origin. Its coordinates are (0,0,0).

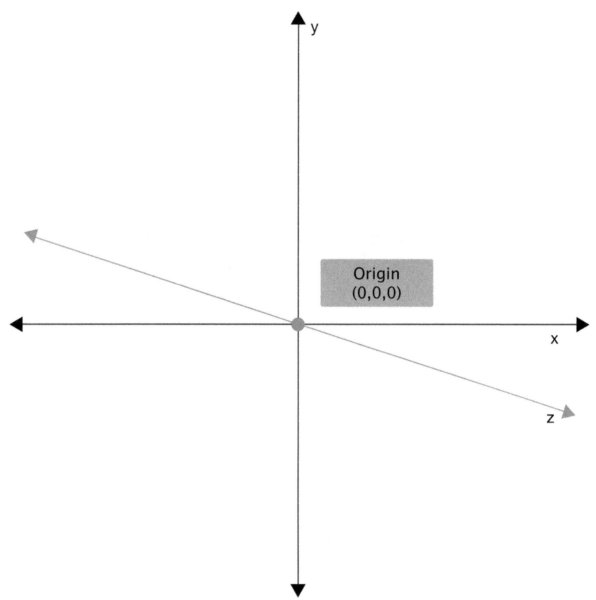

7-8. A three-dimensional coordinate system

A rendered HTML document is, essentially, a coordinate system. The top-left corner is the origin, with coordinates of (0,0) or (0,0,0). Values increase along the X-axis as you move right. Values increase along the Y-axis as you move down the screen or page. Z-axis values increase as elements move towards the viewer and decrease as they move away from the viewer.

Setting the value of `transform` to a value besides `none` adds a **local coordinate system** to the selected elements. The origin—point (0,0) or (0,0,0)—in this local coordinate system sits at the center of the element's bounding box. We can change the position of the origin, however, by using the `transform-origin` property. Points within the element's bounding box are then transformed relative to this local origin.

The `transform-origin` **Property**

The *transform-origin* property accepts up to three values, one for each of the X, Y, and Z positions—for example, *transform-origin: 300px 300px* for a 2D transformation, or *transform-origin: 0 0 200px* for a 3D transformation.

If one value is specified, the second value is assumed to be *center* , and the third value is assumed to be *0px* .

Both the X and Y coordinates may be percentages, lengths, or positioning keywords. Positioning keywords are *left* , *center* , *right* , *top* , and *bottom* . The Z position, however, must be a length. In other words, *transform-origin: left bottom 200px* works, but *transform-origin: left bottom 20%* doesn't.

Setting *transform-origin* moves the (0,0) point of the local coordinate system to a new location within the element's bounding box. This, of course, modifies the transformation, sometimes radically. Figure 7-9 shows a *transform-origin* point of *50% 50%* and one at *0px 0px* .

7-9. Rectangles with transform-origin values of 50% 50% (left) and 0 0 (right)

Now that you know a little more about how transforms affect document layout, let's dig into the transform functions. This is how we make the magic. Transforms let us rotate, flip, skew, and scale elements. When combined with animations and transitions, we can create sophisticated motion graphic effects.

Transforms can be grouped into two categories: 2D and 3D. Each group contains functions for rotating, skewing, scaling, and translating. 2D functions are concerned with transformations of points along the X and Y axes. 3D functions add the third dimension of depth and affect points along the Z-axis.

2D Transform Functions

There are four primary two-dimensional transform functions: `rotate`, `scale`, `skew`, and `translate`. Six other functions let us transform an element in a single dimension: `scaleX` and `scaleY`; `skewX` and `skewY`; and `translateX` and `translateY`.

`rotate()`

A rotation transform spins an element around its origin by the angle specified around the `transform-origin` point. Using `rotate()` tilts an element clockwise (positive angle values) or counter-clockwise (negative angle values). Its effect is much like a windmill or pinwheel, as seen in figure 7-10.

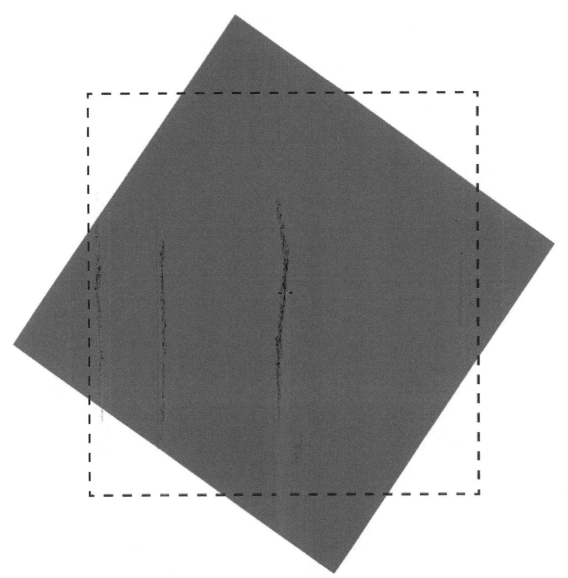

7-10. The purple box has been rotated 55 degrees from its start position, shown by the dotted line

The `rotate()` function accepts values in angle units. Angle units are defined by the <u>CSS Values and Units Module Level 3</u>[4]. These may be `deg` (degrees), `rad` (radians), `grad` (gradians), or `turn` units. One complete rotation is equal to `360deg`, `6.28rad`, `400grad`, or `1turn`.

Rotation values that exceed one rotation (say, `540deg` or `1.5turn`) are rendered according to their remaindered value, unless animated or transitioned. In other words, `540deg` is rendered the same as `180deg` (540 degrees minus 360 degrees) and `1.5turn` is rendered the same as `.5turn` (1.5 - 1). But a transition or animation from `0deg` to `540deg` or `1turn` to `1.5turn` will rotate the element one-and-a-half times.

---

[4] https://drafts.csswg.org/css-values-3/#angles

2D Scaling Functions: scale, scaleX, and scaleY

With scaling functions, we can increase or decrease the rendered size of an element in the X-dimension (*scaleX*), Y-dimension (*scaleY*), or both (*scale*). Scaling is illustrated in figure 7-11, where the border illustrates the original boundaries of the box, and the + marks its center point.

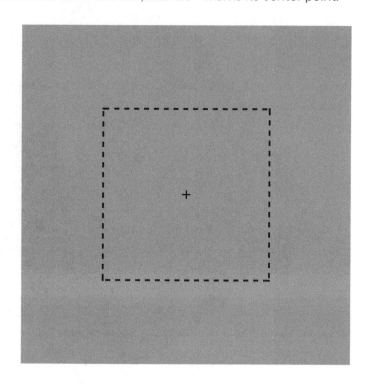

7-11. A box (left) is scaled by a factor of 2 (right)

Each scale function accepts a multiplier or factor as its argument. This multiplier can be just about any positive or negative number. Percentage values aren't supported. Positive multipliers greater than *1* increase the size of an element. For example, *scale(1.5)* increases the size of the element in the X and Y directions 1.5 times. Positive multipliers between *0* and *1* will reduce the size of an element.

Values less than *0* will also cause an element to scale up or down in size and create a reflection (flip) transform.

 Watch Your Scale

Using *scale(0)* will cause the element to disappear, because multiplying a number by zero results in a product of zero.

Using *scale(1)* creates an **identity transformation**, which means it's drawn to the screen as if no scaling transformation was applied. Using *scale(-1)* won't change the drawn size of an element, but the negative value will cause the element to be reflected. Even though the element doesn't appear transformed, it still triggers a new stacking context and containing block.

It's possible to scale the X and Y dimensions separately using the *scale* function. Just pass it two arguments: *scale(1.5, 2)* . The first argument scales the X-dimension; the second scales the Y-dimension. We could, for example, reflect an object along the X-axis alone using *scale(-1, 1)* . Passing a single argument scales both dimensions by the same factor.

2D Translation Functions: translateX, translateY, **and** translate

Translating an element offsets its painted position from its layout position by the specified distance. As with other transforms, translating an element doesn't change its *offsetLeft* or *offsetTop* positions. It does, however, affect where it's visually positioned on screen.

Each 2D translation function— *translateX* , *translateY* , and *translate* —accepts lengths or percentages for arguments. Length units include pixels (*px*), *em* , *rem* , and viewport units (*vw* and *vh*).

The *translateX* function changes the horizontal rendering position of an element. If an element is positioned 0px from the left, *transform: transitionX(50px)* shifts its rendered position 50px to the right of its start position. Similarly, *translateY* changes the vertical rendering position of an element. A transform of *transform: transitionY(50px)* offsets the element vertically by 50px.

With *translate()* , we can shift an element vertically and horizontally using a single function. It accepts up to two arguments: the X translation value, and the Y translation value. Figure 7-12shows the effect of an element with a *transform* value of *translate(120%, -50px)* , where the left green square is in the original position, and the right green square is translated 120% horizontally and -50px vertically from its containing element (the dashed border).

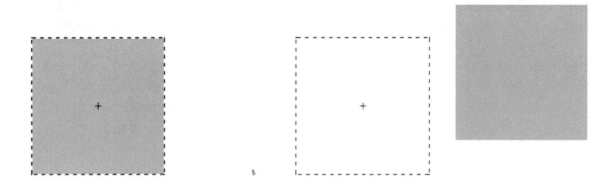

7-12. The effect of having an element with a transform value of translate(120%, -50px)

Passing a single argument to `translate` is the equivalent of using `translateX`; the Y translation value will be set to `0`. Using `translate()` is the more concise option. Applying `translate(100px, 200px)` is the equivalent of `translateX(100px) translateY(200px)`.

Positive translation values move an element to the right (for `translateX`) or downward (for `translateY`). Negative values move an element to the left (`translateX`) or upward (`translateY`).

Translations are particularly great for moving items left, right, up, or down. Updating the value of the `left`, `right`, `top`, and `bottom` properties forces the browser to recalculate layout information for the entire document. But transforms are calculated *after* the layout has been calculated. They affect where the elements *appear* on screen, but not their actual dimensions. Yes, it's weird to think about document layout and rendering as separate concepts, but in terms of browsers, they are.[5]

Transform Properties May Be Coming to a Browser near You

The latest version of the CSS Transforms specification adds `translate`, `rotate`, and `scale` *properties* to CSS. Transform properties work much like their corresponding transform functions, but values are space-separated instead of comma-separated. We could, for example, express `transform: rotate3d(1, 1, 1, 45deg)` using the `rotate` property: `rotate: 1 1 1`

[5.] Google's <u>Why Performance Matters</u> (https://developers.google.com/web/fundamentals/performance/why-performance-matters/) discusses some of the differences between layout or rendering, and painting or drawing.

`45deg` . Similarly, `translate: 15% 10% 300px` is visually the same as `transform: translate3d(15%, 10%, 300px)` and `scale: 1.5 1.5 3` is the same as `transform: scale3d(1.5, 1.5, 3)` . With these properties we can manage rotation, translation or scale transformations separately from other transformations.

At the time of writing, browser support for transform properties is still pretty sparse. Chrome and Samsung Internet support them out of the box. In Firefox versions 60 and later, support is hidden behind a flag; visit `about: config` and set `layout.css.individual-transform.enabled` to `true` .

skew, skewX, **and** skewY

Skew transformations shift the angles and distances between points while keeping them in the same plane. Skew transformations are also known as *shear transformations*, and they distort the shapes of elements, as seen in figure 7-13, where the dashed line represents the original bounding box of the element.

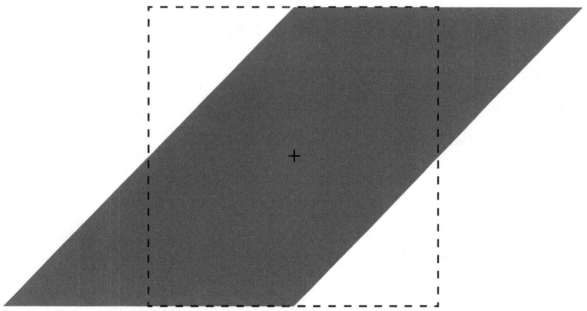

7-13. A rectangle is skewed 45 degrees along its X-dimension

The skew functions— `skew` , `skewX` , and `skewY` —accept most angle units as arguments. Degrees, gradians, and radians are valid angle units for the skew functions, while turn units, perhaps obviously, are not.

The `skewX` function shears an element in the X or horizontal direction (see figure 7-14). It accepts a single parameter, which again must be an angle unit. Positive values shift the element to the left, and negative values shift it towards the right.

7-14. The left image is not transformed, while the right image reveals the effect of transform: skewX(30deg)

Similarly, `skewY` shears an element in the Y or vertical direction. Figure 7-15 shows the effect of `transform: skewY(30deg)`. Points to the right of the origin are shifted downward with positive values. Negative values shift these points upward.

7-15. Again, the left image remains untransformed, and the right image is skewed vertically by 30 degrees

This brings us to the `skew` function. The `skew` function requires one argument, but accepts up to two. The first argument skews an element in the X direction, and the second skews it in the Y direction. If only one argument is provided, the second value is assumed to be zero, making it the equivalent of skewing in the X direction alone. In other words, `skew(45deg)` renders the same as `skewX(45deg)`.

Current Transform Matrix

So far, we've discussed transform functions separately, but they can also be combined. Want to scale and rotate an object? No problem: use a **transform list**. For example:

```css
.rotatescale {
    transform: rotate(45deg) scale(2);
}
```

This produces the results you see below.

7-16. The original element (left) and after a combined rotation and scaling transformation is applied (right)

Order matters when using transform functions. This is a point that's better shown than talked about, so let's look at an example to illustrate. The following CSS skews and rotates an element:

```css
.transformEl {
    transform: skew(10deg, 15deg) rotate(45deg);
}
```

It gives us the result you see below.

7-17. An element after a transformation of skew(10deg, 15deg) rotate(45deg)

What happens if you rotate an element first and then skew it?

```
.transformEl {
    transform:   rotate(45deg) skew(10deg, 15deg);
}
```

The effect, shown in figure 7-18, is quite different.

7-18. An element after it has been rotated and then skewed

Each of these transforms has a different *current transform matrix* created by the order of its transform functions. To fully understand why this is, we'll need to learn a little bit of *matrix multiplication*. This will also help us understand the `matrix` and `matrix3d` functions.

Matrix Multiplication and the Matrix Functions

A **matrix** is an array of numbers or expressions arranged in a rectangle of rows and columns. All transforms can be expressed using a 4×4 matrix:

$$\begin{bmatrix} m_{11} & m_{21} & m_{31} & m_{41} \\ m_{12} & m_{22} & m_{32} & m_{42} \\ m_{13} & m_{23} & m_{33} & m_{43} \\ m_{14} & m_{24} & m_{34} & m_{44} \end{bmatrix}$$

7-19. The 4×4 matrix for 3D transforms

This matrix corresponds to the `matrix3d` function, which accepts 16 arguments, one for each value of the 4×4 matrix. Two-dimensional transforms can also be expressed using a 3×3 matrix, seen in figure 7-20.

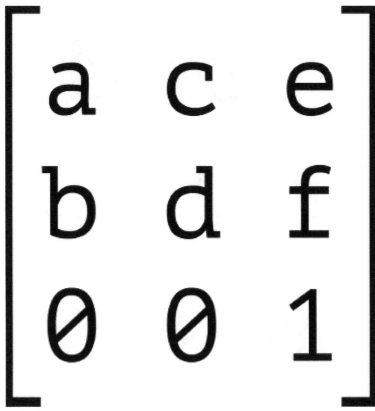

7-20. A 3×3 matrix used for 2D transforms

This 3×3 matrix corresponds to the `matrix` transform function. The `matrix()` function accepts six parameters, one each for values *a* through *f*.

Each transform function can be described using a matrix and the `matrix` or `matrix3d` functions. Figure 7-21 shows the 4×4 matrix for the `scale3d` function, where *sx*, *sy*, and *sz* are the scaling factors of the X, Y, and Z dimensions respectively.

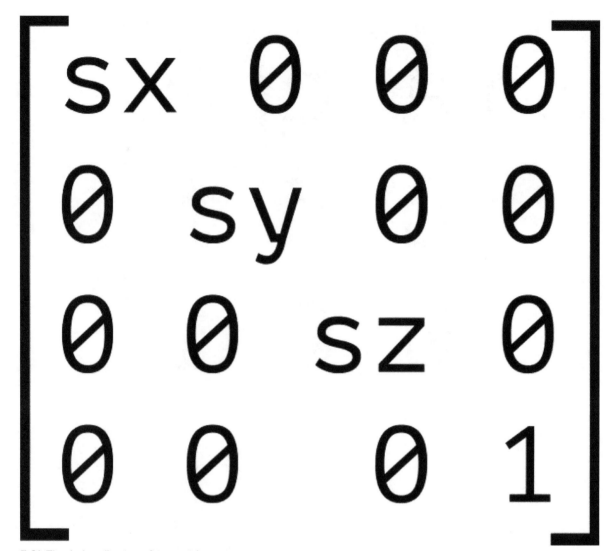

7-21. The 4×4 scaling transform matrix

When we combine transforms—such as `transform: scale(2) translate(30px, 50px)` —the browser multiplies the matrices for each function to create a new matrix. This new matrix is what's applied to the element.

But here's the thing about matrix multiplication: it isn't commutative. With simple values, the product of 3×2 is the same as 2×3. With matrices, however, the product of *A*×*B* is not necessarily the same as the product of *B*×*A*. Let's look at figure 7-22 as an example. We'll calculate the matrix product of `transform: scale(2) translate(30px, 50px)` .

$$\begin{bmatrix} 2 & 0 & 0 & 0 \\ 0 & 2 & 0 & 0 \\ 0 & 0 & 1 & 0 \\ 0 & 0 & 0 & 1 \end{bmatrix} \times \begin{bmatrix} 1 & 0 & 0 & 30 \\ 0 & 1 & 0 & 50 \\ 0 & 0 & 1 & 0 \\ 0 & 0 & 0 & 1 \end{bmatrix} = \begin{bmatrix} 2 & 0 & 0 & 60 \\ 0 & 2 & 0 & 100 \\ 0 & 0 & 1 & 0 \\ 0 & 0 & 0 & 1 \end{bmatrix}$$

7-22. The product of the matrices for scale(2) and translate(30px, 50px)

Our element has been scaled by a factor of two, and then translated 60px horizontally and 100px vertically. We can also express this product using the `matrix` function: `transform: matrix(2, 0, 0, 2, 60, 100)`. Now let's switch the order of these transforms—that is, `transform: translate(30px, 50px) scale(2)`. The results are shown in figure 7-23.

$$\begin{bmatrix} 1 & 0 & 0 & 30 \\ 0 & 1 & 0 & 50 \\ 0 & 0 & 1 & 0 \\ 0 & 0 & 0 & 1 \end{bmatrix} \times \begin{bmatrix} 2 & 0 & 0 & 0 \\ 0 & 2 & 0 & 0 \\ 0 & 0 & 1 & 0 \\ 0 & 0 & 0 & 1 \end{bmatrix} = \begin{bmatrix} 2 & 0 & 0 & 30 \\ 0 & 2 & 0 & 50 \\ 0 & 0 & 1 & 0 \\ 0 & 0 & 0 & 1 \end{bmatrix}$$

7-23. The product of the matrices for translate(30px, 50px) and scale(2)

Notice that our object is still scaled by a factor of two, but here it's translated by 30px horizontally and 50px vertically instead. Expressed using the `matrix` function, this is `transform: matrix(2, 0, 0, 2, 30, 50)`.

It's also worth noting that inherited transforms function similarly to transform lists. Each child transform is multiplied by any transform applied to its parent. For example, take the following code:

```
<div style="transform: skewX(25deg)">
    <p style="transform: rotate(-15deg)"></p>
</div>
```

This is rendered the same as the following:

```
<div>
```

```
    <p style="transform: skewX(25deg) rotate(-15deg)"></p>
  </div>
```

The current transform matrix of the `p` element will be the same in both cases. Though we've focused on 2D transforms so far, the above also applies to 3D transforms. The third dimension adds the illusion of depth. It also brings some additional complexity in the form of new functions and properties.

3D Transform Functions

There are nine functions for creating 3D transforms. Each of these functions modifies the Z-coordinates of an element and/or its children. Remember, Z-coordinates are points along the plane that sit perpendicular to the viewer. With the exception of `rotateZ()`, these functions create and change the illusion of depth on screen.

rotateX() and rotateY()

The `rotateX()` and `rotateY()` functions rotate an element around the X and Y axes respectively. Using `rotateX()` creates a somersault effect, causing an object to flip top-over-tail around a horizontal axis. With `rotateY()`, the effect is more like that of a spinning top, rotating around a vertical axis.

Like `rotate()`, both `rotateX()` and `rotateY()` accept an angle measurement as an argument. This angle can be expressed in degrees (`deg`), radians (`rad`), gradians (`grad`), or turn units. As mentioned earlier in the chapter, `rotateZ()` works the same way as `rotate()`. It's a relic from when 2D and 3D transforms were defined by separate specifications.

Positive angle values for `rotateX()` cause an element to tilt backwards, as shown in figure 7-24.

7-24. An element with transform: rotate(45deg) applied

Negative angle values for *rotateX()* do the opposite, causing the element to tilt forward:

7-25. An element with a negative rotation (transform: rotate(-45deg)) applied

Negative angles for *rotateY()* cause the element to tilt counter-clockwise. In figure 7-26, the element has had a rotation of -55 degrees around the Y-axis.

7-26. An element with transform: rotateY(-55deg) applied

Positive values tilt it clockwise, as shown in figure 7-27.

7-27. An element with transform: rotateY(55deg) applied

The containing element in figure 7-25, figiure 7-26, and figure 7-27 has a *perspective* value of *200px* . We'll discuss the *perspective* property later in this chapter. For now, it's enough to know that this property adds a sense of depth and exaggerates the effect of the three-dimensional rotation. Compare figure 7-28 to figure 7-27. Both have been rotated along the Y-axis by 55 degrees, but in figure 7-28 , the parent container has a *perspective* value of *none* . Our object looks more squished than rotated. Use *perspective* on a container element when creating a 3D transform.

7-28. An element with transform: rotateY(55deg), nested within a container with perspective:none

 Disappearing Elements

There's another facet to be aware of when working with 3D rotations. Rotating an element by ±90 degrees or ±270 degrees can sometimes cause it to disappear from the screen. Each element on a page has an infinitesimal thickness. By rotating it a quarter or three-quarters of a turn, we're looking at its infinitesimally thin side. It's kind of like looking at the edge of a sheet of paper that's perpendicular to your face. Adjusting the `perspective` and `perspective-origin` values of a parent element can prevent this behavior in some cases, but not all of them.

Rotating around Multiple Axes with `rotate3d()`

Sometimes, we want to rotate an object around more than one axis. Perhaps you want to rotate an element counter-clockwise and tilt it by 45 degrees, as in figure 7-29. This is what `rotate3d()` does.

7-29. Rotating around both the X and Y axes by 45 degrees

The `rotate3d()` function accepts four arguments. The first three make up an X, Y, Z direction vector, and each of these arguments should be a number. The fourth argument for `rotate3d()` should be an angle. The transformed object will be rotated by the angle around the direction vector defined by the first three arguments.

What those first three numbers *are* matters less than the ratio between them. For example, `transform: rotate3d(100,5,0,15deg);` and `transform: rotate3d(20,1,0,15deg);` have equivalent 3D matrices and produce the same effect.

That said, because of how the **rotate3d matrix is calculated**[6], something like `transform: rotate3d(1, 500, 0, 15deg);` won't produce a significantly different effect than `transform: rotate3d(1, 1, 0, 15deg);` .

Just about any non-zero value for any of the first three parameters will create a tilt along that

6. https://drafts.csswg.org/css-transforms-2/#Rotate3dDefined

axis. Zero values will prevent a tilt. As you may have guessed, `rotateX(45deg)` is the equivalent of `rotate3d(1, 0, 0, 45deg)` and `rotateY(25deg)` could also be written as `rotate3d(0, 1, 0, 25deg)`.

If the first three arguments are `0` (such as `transform: rotate3d(0, 0, 0, 45deg)`), the element won't be transformed. Using negative numbers for the X, Y, or Z vector arguments is valid; it will just negate the value of the angle. In other words, `rotate3d(-1, 0, 0, 45deg)` is equivalent to `rotate3d(1, 0, 0, -45deg)`.

Using `rotate3d()` rotates an element by the given angle along multiple axes at once. If you want to rotate an element by different angles around multiple axes, you should use `rotateX()`, `rotateY()`, and `rotate()` or `rotateZ()` separately.

The `perspective()` Function

The `perspective()` function controls the foreshortening of an object when one end is tilted towards the viewer. **Foreshortening** is a specific way of drawing perspective—that is, simulating three dimensions when you only have two dimensions. With foreshortening, the end of objects that are tilted towards the viewer appear larger, and the end furthest from the viewer appears smaller. It mimics the distortion that occurs when you view an object up close versus viewing it at a distance.

The more technical definition, pulled from the **CSS Transforms Module Level 2**[7], says that `perspective()` "specifies a perspective projection matrix." The definition continues:

> *This matrix scales points in X and Y based on their Z value, scaling points with positive Z values away from the origin, and those with negative Z values towards the origin. Points on the Z=0 plane are unchanged.*

In practice, this means that `perspective()` will have a visible effect only when some of an object's points have a non-zero Z-coordinate. Use it with another 3D function in a transform list (for example, `transform: perspective(400px) rotateX(45deg)`), or apply it to the child of a transformed parent.

The `perspective()` function accepts a single argument. This argument must be a length greater than zero. Negative values are invalid, and the transform won't be applied. Lower values create a

---

[7]. https://drafts.csswg.org/css-transforms-2/#funcdef-perspective

more exaggerated foreshortening effect, as you can see below. In this image, the value of our *transform* is *perspective(10px) rotate3d(1,1,1,-45deg)* .

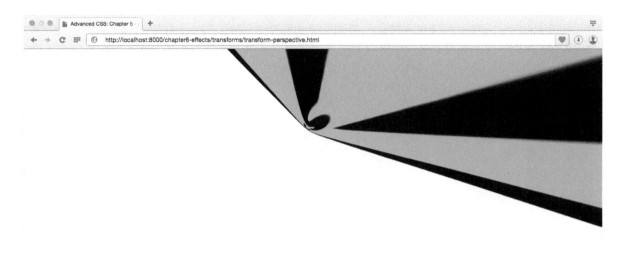

7-30. Exaggerated foreshortening

Higher values create a moderate amount of foreshortening. Figure 7-31 illustrates the impact of a higher perspective value. Its *transform* property value is *perspective(500px) rotate3d(1,1,1,-45deg)* .

7-31. An element with a transform value of perspective(500px) rotate3d(1,1,1,-45deg)

Order really matters when working with the *perspective()* function. A good rule of thumb is to list it first, as we've done in the examples here. You *can* list it elsewhere in the transform list (for example, *rotate3d(1,0,1,-45deg) perspective(100px)*), but the resulting current transform matrix doesn't create much of an effect.

There's also a point of diminishing returns with the *perspective()* function (and with the *perspective* property, as well). Increasing the argument's value beyond a certain threshold will create little difference in how the element and its children are painted to the screen.

 perspective() **versus** perspective

> A word of caution: the transforms specification defines both a *perspective()* function and a *perspective* property. Though both are used to calculate the perspective matrix, they differ in how they're used. The *perspective* property affects—and must be applied to—the containing element. It sets an imaginary distance between the viewer and the stage. The *perspective()* function, on the other hand, can be applied to elements as part of a *transform* list.

Translating Depth with `translateZ()` and `translate3d()`

Earlier in this chapter, we discussed how to translate an element horizontally or vertically using `translateX()` and `translateY()`. We can also, however, translate along the Z-axis. There are two functions that allow us to do this: `translateZ()` and `translate3d()`. We can combine them with transitions to create zoom effects, or mimic the feeling of moving through a chute.[8]

The `translateZ()` function accepts a single length parameter as its argument. Length units are the only valid units for this function. Remember that we're projecting three-dimensional coordinates into a two-dimensional space, so percentages don't make much sense. The `translateZ()` function shifts the object towards or away from the user by the specified length. Negative values shift the element or group away from the user, in effect shrinking it, as can be seen in figure 7-32.

[8.] The 2011 Beer Camp site (http://2011.beercamp.com/) has one of the more memorable examples of this technique.

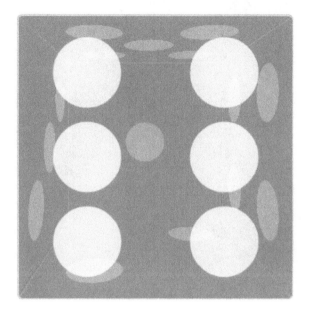

7-32. The effect of transform: translateZ(-150px)

Positive values shift the element towards the viewer, making it appear larger. Sometimes the effect is to fill the entire viewport, thereby engulfing the viewer, as seen in figure 7-33.

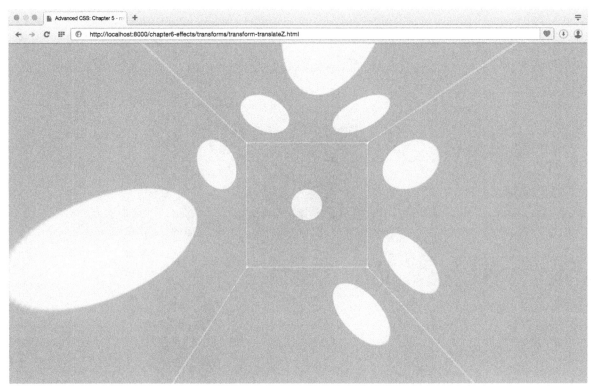

7-33. The effect of transform: translateZ(150px)

If the value of *translateZ()* is large enough, the element will disappear from view. It's actually moved behind the viewer in this imagined 3D space. Similarly, if the value of *translateZ()* is small enough, say *translateZ(-40000px)*, the element will disappear from view because it's now "too far" from the viewer and too small to draw on screen.

translate3d() is just a more concise way of translating in two or three directions at once. It accepts three arguments: one each for the X, Y, and Z directions. Translation values for the X and Y direction arguments may be lengths or percentages, but the Z-direction argument (the third argument) must be a length value. Keep in mind that *translateX(50%) translateY(10%) translateZ(100px)* is the equivalent of *translate3d(50%, 10%, 100px)*. Use *translate3d* when you want to translate more than one dimension but also want more concise code.

Scaling the Z-dimension: scaleZ() and scale3d()

We can also scale an object's Z-dimension using the *scaleZ()* and *scale3d()* functions. The *scaleZ()* function transforms points along the Z-axis alone, while *scale3d()* lets us scale all three dimensions at once. Scaling the Z-dimension changes the depth of an object, and in some combinations can be used to create zoom effects. Experiment with them and see.

The *scaleZ()* function accepts a number as its argument. As with *scaleX()* and *scaleY()*, positive values greater than *1* increase the size of the element's Z-dimension. Values between 0 and 1 decrease its size. Negative values between 0 and -1 decrease the element's size along the Z-dimension, while values less than -1 increase it. Because these values are negative, however, the element and its children will be inverted. In figure 7-34, the left die shows an element group with *transform: scaleZ(0.5)* applied. The box on the right has a transformation of *scaleZ(-0.5)* applied. Notice that the positions of the six face and one face have been swapped in the example with a negative scale.

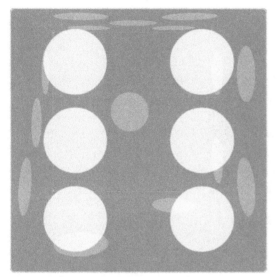
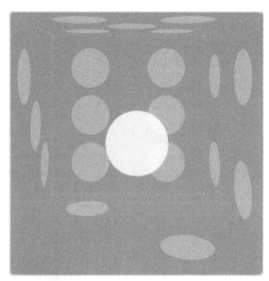

7-34. Element groups with transform: scaleZ(0.5) and transform: scaleZ(-0.5) styles

The *scale3d()* function accepts three arguments, and all three arguments are required in order for this function to work. The first argument scales the X dimension. The second argument scales its Y dimension, and the third argument scales the Z dimension. As with *translate3d()*, the *scale3d()* function is just a more concise way to write transforms that scale in multiple dimensions. Rather than using *scaleX(1.2) scaleY(5) scaleZ(2)*, for example, you could use *scale3d(1.2, 5, 2)*.

Transform functions are only part of what you need to create 3D transforms. You'll also need CSS properties that manage how objects are drawn in a simulated three-dimensional space. These properties directly affect the perception of depth and distance.

Creating Depth with the perspective Property

To make a 3D-transformed object look like it's sitting in a three-dimensional space, we need the *perspective* property. The *perspective* property adjusts the distance between the drawing plane and the viewer. We're still projecting three-dimensional coordinates into a two-dimensional space. But adding *perspective* to a containing element causes its children to have the appearance of being in a 3D space.

As with *transform* , *perspective* creates both a new containing block and a new stacking context when the value is something other than *none* . Along with the *perspective-origin* property, *perspective* is used to calculate the perspective matrix. We'll cover *perspective-origin* in the next section.[9]

Aside from the *none* keyword, *perspective* also accepts a length as its value. Values must be positive (for example, *200px* or *10em*). Percentages don't work. Neither do negative values such as *-20px* .

Smaller values for *perspective* increase the visual size of the element, as seen below, which has a *perspective* value of *500px* . Items that are closer to the viewer on the Z-axis appear larger than those further away.

7-35. Perspective value of 500px

[9.] Use a *-webkit-* prefix for *perspective* and *perspective-origin* to support users of Safari ≤ 8 and UC Browser (*-webkit-perspective* and *-webkit-perspective-origin*).

Larger values, on the other hand, make elements appear smaller. The container element in figure 7-36 has a `perspective` value of `2000px`. This is similar to how your eye perceives objects of varying distances.

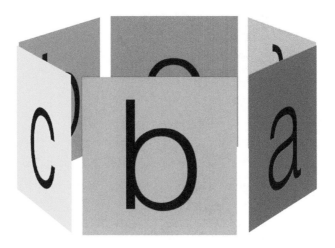

7-36. Perspective value of 2000px

Modifying the Point of View with `perspective-origin`

If you've studied how to draw in perspective, the `perspective-origin` property will feel like old hat. To draw in perspective, you first make a point on your page or canvas. This point is known as the **vanishing point**. It's the point in your drawing at which items will theoretically disappear from view.

Next, draw a shape of your choosing. We'll keep this example simple, and use a rectangle.

Step three is to draw a series of lines towards the vanishing point, as shown in figure 7-37 These lines, also known as **convergence lines**, serve as guides for drawing shapes that are sized appropriately given their perceived distance from the viewer.

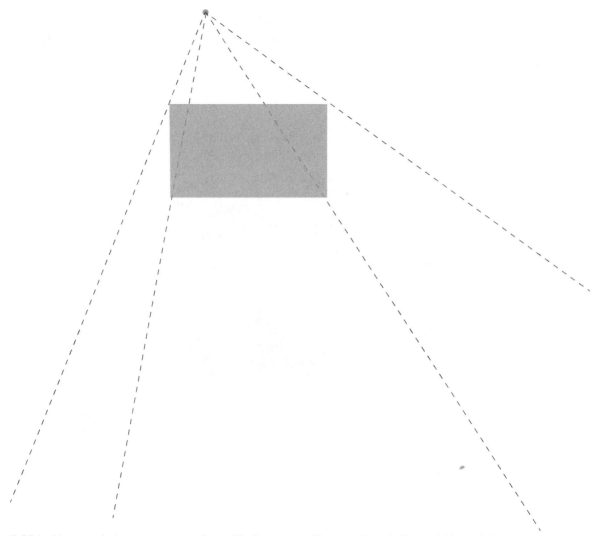

7-37. In this example, boxes appear smaller and further away as they get closer to the vanishing point

As you can see in figure 7-38, the rectangles that appear closer to the viewer are larger. Those that appear further away are smaller.

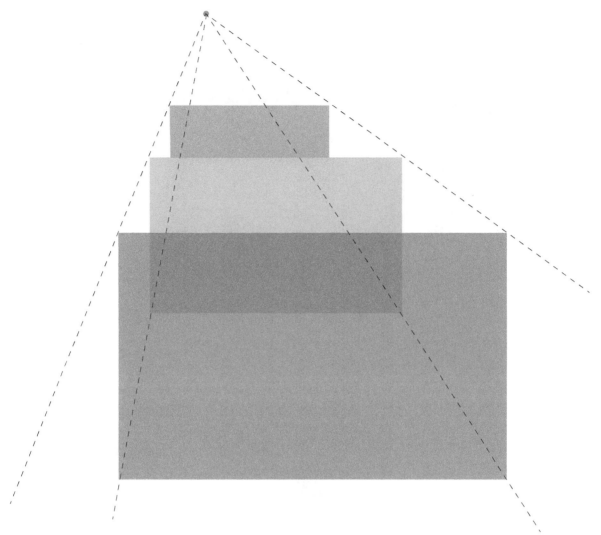

7-38. In this example, boxes appear smaller and further away as they get closer to the vanishing point

This is essentially how the `perspective-origin` property works. It sets the coordinates of the vanishing point for the stage. Negative Y values give the impression that the viewer is looking down at the stage, while positive ones imply looking up from below it. Negative X values mimic the effect of looking from the right of the stage. Positive X values mimic looking from its left. Figure 7-39 shows a containing element with a perspective-origin of `-50% -50%`.

7-39. A containing element with perspective-origin: -50% -50%

As with *transform-origin* , the initial value of *perspective-origin* is *50% 50%* —the center point of the containing element. Values for *perspective-origin* may be lengths or percentages.

Positioning keywords— *left* , *right* , *top* , *bottom* , and *center* —are also valid. The *center* keyword is the same as *50% 50%* . Both *bottom* and *right* compute to positions of *100%* along the vertical and horizontal positions respectively. The *top* and *left* keywords compute to vertical and horizontal positions of *0%* . In all cases, *perspective-origin* is an offset from the top-left corner of the container.

Preserving Three Dimensions with transform-style

As you work with 3D transforms, you may stumble across a scenario in which your transforms fail to work—or they work, but only for one element. This is caused by grouping property values[10]. Some combinations of CSS properties and values require the browser to flatten the representation of child elements before the property is applied. These include *opacity* when the value is less than *1* and *overflow* when the value is something other than *visible* .

Here's the counterintuitive part: *transform* and *perspective* also trigger this flattening when their value is something other than *none* . In effect, this means that child elements stack according to their source order if they have the same z-index value, regardless of the transform

[10] https://drafts.csswg.org/css-transforms-2/#grouping-property-values

applied. Consider the following source:

```html
<div class="wrapper">
    <figure>a</figure>
    <figure>f</figure>
</div>
```

And the following CSS:

```css
.wrapper {
    perspective: 2000px;
    perspective-origin: 50% -200px;
}
.wrapper figure {
    position: absolute;
    top: 0;
    width: 200px;
    height: 200px;
}
.wrapper figure:first-child {
    transform: rotateY(60deg) translateZ(191px);
    background: #3f51b5;
}
.wrapper figure:nth-child(2) {
    transform: rotateY(120deg) translateZ(191px);
    background: #8bc34a;
}
```

In this example, since we've applied `perspective: 1000px` to `.wrapper`, our `figure` elements are flattened. Since both elements also have the same calculated `z-index`, `.wrapper figure:nth-child(2)` will be the topmost element in the stack, as witnessed in figure 7-40. Note that `.wrapper figure:first-child` is still visible. It's just not the topmost element. Here the computed value of `transform-style` is `flat`.

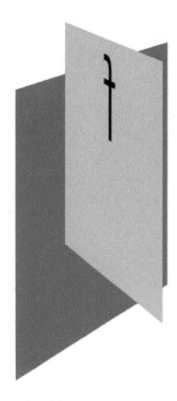

7-40. Elements with a transform-style value of flat

To work around this, we set the value of *transform-style* to *preserve-3d* . Let's update our CSS:

```css
.wrapper {
    perspective: 2000px;
    perspective-origin: 50% -200px;
    transform-style: preserve-3d;
}
.wrapper figure {
    position: absolute;
    top: 0;
    width: 200px;
    height: 200px;
}
.wrapper figure:first-child {
    transform: rotateY(60deg) translateZ(191px);
    background: #3f51b5;
}
.wrapper figure:nth-child(2) {
    transform: rotateY(120deg) translateZ(191px);
    background: #8bc34a;
}
```

Now `.wrapper figure:first-child` becomes the topmost element, as our `rotateY` functions suggest it should be in figure 7-41.

7-41. Elements with a transform-style value of preserve-3d

In the vast majority of cases, you should use `transform-style: preserve-3d`. Use `transform-style: flat` only when you want to collapse child elements into the same layer as their parent.[11]

Showing Both Faces with the `backface-visibility` Property

By default, the back face of an element is a mirror image of its front face. With stacked or overlapping elements, the reverse side is always visible to the viewer, regardless of which side sits at the top of the stack.

Sometimes, however, we don't want this back side to be visible. Let's return to the card metaphor

---

[11.] The WebKit team's demo <u>Transform Style</u> (https://www.webkit.org/blog-files/3d-transforms/transform-style.html) shows the effect of `transform-style: flat`. It's an old demo that was created for WebKit browsers, so you'll need to use a WebKit- or Blink-based browser such as Safari, Chrome, Opera, or Samsung Internet to view it.

mentioned in the introduction to this chapter. This time we'll use a playing card, seen in figure 7-42. With any card, we only want one side to be visible to the user at a time. To manage the visibility of an object's back side, we can use the `backface-visibility` property.

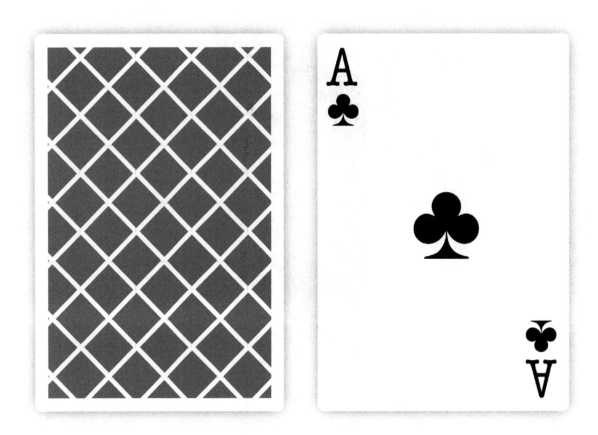

7-42. With cards, we only want to see one side at a time

The initial value of `backface-visibility` is `visible`. Rear faces will always be shown. But if we want to hide a visible back face, we can use `backface-visibility: hidden` instead.

Let's create our playing card. First our HTML:

```
<div class="card">
    <div class="side front">
        <div class="suit">&clubs;</div>
    </div>
    <div class="side back"></div>
</div>
```

In this markup, we've set up front and back sides for a *card* container. Here's our card CSS:[12]

```
.card {
    border: 1px solid #ccc;
    height: 300px;
    position: relative;
    transition: transform 1s linear;
    transform-style: preserve-3d;
    width: 240px;
}
```

The important part to notice here is *transform-style: preserve-3d*. Again, we'll need this property to prevent the flattening that occurs by default when we use the *transform* property. Now let's set up the CSS for the front and back sides of our cards:

```
/* Applies to both child div elements */
.side {
    height: inherit;
    left: 0;
    position: absolute;
    top: 0;
    width: inherit;
}
.front {
    transform: rotateY(180deg);
}
.back {
    background: rgba(204, 204, 204, 0.8);
}
.suit {
    line-height: 1;
    text-align: center;
    font-size: 300px;
}
```

Both sides are absolutely positioned, so they'll stack according to their source order. We've also flipped the *.front* sides around the Y-axis by 180 degrees. When it's all put together, your card should look a bit like the image in figure 7-43.

---

12. For broadest browser compatibility, make sure you include prefixed versions of *transition* and *transform-style*.

7-43. A see-through card with backface-visibility: visible (its initial value)

Both sides of the card are visible at the same time. Let's revise our CSS slightly. We'll add
backface-visibility: hidden to our *.side* ruleset:

```
.side {
    backface-visibility: hidden;
    height: inherit;
    left: 0;
    position: absolute;
```

```
    top: 0;
    width: inherit;
}
```

Now, *div.front* is hidden. If you see a gray box and no club symbol, it's working as expected.

 Prefixes

> Safari 12 and earlier versions require the *-webkit-* vendor prefix for the
> *backface-visibility* property.

The utility of *backface-visibility: hidden* becomes a little clearer when we flip *div.card*. Let's add a *.flipped* class to our CSS:

```
.flipped {
    transform: rotateY(180deg);
}
```

Now when we flip our card over (shown in figure 7-44), we see *div.front*, and only *div.front*.

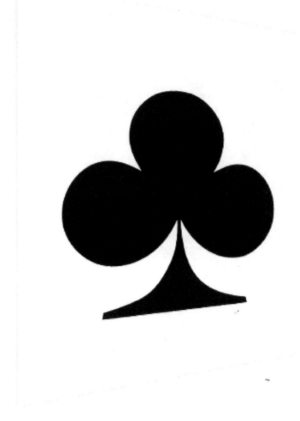

7-44. Flipping our card

Fiogure 7-45 shows two cards before being flipped. The card on the left has a `backface-visibility` value of `hidden`, while the one on the right has a value of `visible`.

7-45. Two cards prior to flipping

And in figure 7-46, we can see these same cards after the `flipped` class is added—that is, `<div class="card flipped">`.

7-46. The same cards after being rotated 180 degrees

Conclusion

Whew! That was a lot to take in. I hope after reading this chapter, you've learned how to:

- affect page layout and stacking order with transforms
- calculate the current transform matrix
- apply 2D transform functions that rotate, translate, and skew objects
- use 3D transforms to create the illusion of depth and dimension

In our next chapter, we'll look at conditional CSS, including `@supports`, newer `@media` features, and related JavaScript APIs.

Applying CSS Conditionally

Conditional CSS refers to CSS rules that are applied when a condition is met. A condition may be a CSS property and value combination, as with the `@supports` rule. A condition may test for a browser window condition such as width, as with the `@media` rule. Or a condition may be a device feature such as hover capability or pointer input, as with some newer features of `@media`. We'll discuss all of the above in this chapter.

Both `@media` and `@supports` are described by the CSS Conditional Rules Module Level 3 specification[1]. The `@media` rule—which you probably know as *media queries*—is fully defined by the Media Queries specification[2].

Media Queries and `@media`

The `@media` rule is actually a long-standing feature of CSS. Its syntax was originally defined by the CSS 2 specification[3] back in 1998. Building on the media types defined by HTML 4, `@media` enabled developers to serve different styles to different media types— `print` or `screen`, for example.

With the Media Queries Level 3 specification[4], the `@media` rule was extended to add support for media *features* in addition to media types. Media features include window or viewport width, screen orientation, and resolution. Media Queries Level 4 added media **interaction queries**, a way to apply different styles for pointer device quality—the fine-grained control of a mouse or stylus versus the coarseness of a finger. Media Queries Level 5[5] adds feature queries for `light-level`, and `scripting` along with user preference feature queries such as `prefers-reduced-motion` and `prefers-reduced-transparency`.

Alas, most of the media types defined by HTML4 are now obsolete. Only `all`, `screen`, `print`, and `speech` are currently defined by any specification. Of those, only `all`, `screen` and `print` have widespread browser support. We'll briefly discuss them in the examples that follow. As for media features, we'll focus on what's available in browsers today.

Media Query Syntax: The Basics

Media query syntax seems simple, but sometimes it's a bit counterintuitive. In its simplest form, a media query consists of a media type, used alone or in combination with a media condition—such as `width` or `orientation`. A simple, type-based media query for screens looks like this:

[1.] https://drafts.csswg.org/css-conditional-3/
[2.] https://drafts.csswg.org/mediaqueries-4/
[3.] https://www.w3.org/TR/1998/REC-CSS2-19980512/media.html#at-media-rule
[4.] https://www.w3.org/TR/css3-mediaqueries/
[5.] https://drafts.csswg.org/mediaqueries-5/

```
@media screen {
    /* Styles go here */
}
```

CSS style rules are nested within this *@media* ruleset. They'll only apply when the document is displayed on a screen, as opposed to being printed.

```
@media screen {
    body {
        font-size: 20px;
    }
}
```

In this example, the text size for this document will be *20px* when it's viewed on a desktop, laptop, tablet, mobile phone, or television.

 ## If No Media Type Is Specified

When no media type is specified, it's the same as using *all* .

We can apply CSS to one or more media types by separating each query with a comma. If the browser or device meets *any* condition in the list, the styles will be applied. For example, we could limit styles to screen and print media using the following:

```
@media screen, print {
    body {
        font-size: 16px;
    }
}
```

The real power of media queries, however, comes when you add a media feature query. **Media feature queries** interrogate the capabilities of the device or conditions of the viewport.

A media feature query consists of a property and a value, separated by a colon. The query *must* also be wrapped in parentheses. Here's an example:

```
@media (width: 30em) {
    nav li {
        display: inline-block;
    }
}
```

What we're doing is applying a new style to *nav li* only when the width of the viewport is equal to *30em* . Since *em* units are relative, using them for width and lengths makes sense for screens. Let's use the *and* keyword to make a more specific media query:

```
@media screen and (width: 30em) {
    nav li {
        display: inline-block;
    }
}
```

These styles will be used only when the output device is a screen and its width is *30em* . Notice here that the media type *is not* enclosed by parentheses, unlike our media feature *(width: 30em)* .

The query above has a small problem, however. If the viewport is wider than *30em* or narrower than *30em* —and not *exactly* *30em* —these styles won't be applied. What we need instead is a *range*.

Range Media Feature Queries and `min-` and `max-` Prefixes

A more flexible media query tests for a minimum or maximum viewport width. We can apply styles when the viewport is *at least* this wide, or *more than* that wide. Luckily for us, the Media Queries Level 3 specification defined the *min-* and *max-* prefixes for this purpose. These prefixes establish the lower or upper boundaries of a feature range.

Let's update our previous code:

```
@media (max-width: 30em) {
    nav li {
        display: block;
    }
}
```

In this example, *nav li* will have a *display:* property value of *block* from a viewport width of *0* , *up to and including* a maximum viewport width of *30em* .

We can also define a media query range using *min-* and *max-* , along with the *and* keyword. For example, if we wanted to switch from *display: block* to *display: flex* between *30em* and *100em* , we might do the following:

```
@media (min-width: 30em) and (max-width: 100em) {
    nav li {
        display: block;
    }
}
```

If both conditions are true—that is, the viewport width is at least *30em,* but not greater than *100em* —our styles will apply.

Not all media feature properties support ranges with `min-` and `max-` . The table below lists those that do, along with the type of value permitted for each.

Property	Description	Value type
`aspect-ratio`	The ratio of viewport `width` to `height`	ratio (such as `1024/768` or `16:9`)
`color`	Number of bits per color component of the device; `0` when the device is not a color device	integer
`color-index`	Minimum number of colors available on the device	integer
`height`	Height of the viewport or page box	length
`monochrome`	Number of bits per pixel in a monochrome frame buffer	integer
`resolution`[6]	Describes the pixel density of a device	resolution (`dpi`, `dpcm`, and `dppx`) units
`width`	Width of the viewport or page box	length

Future browsers may support comparison operators such as `>` and `<=` in addition to the `min` and `max` syntax for ranges. Instead of *@media (min-width: 30em) and (max-width: 100em)* , we could write this query as follows:

```
@media (width >= 30em) and (width <= 100em) {
    nav li {
        display: block;
    }
}
```

That's a little clearer than *@media (min-width: 30em) and (max-width: 100em)* . Unfortunately,

---

[6.] Safari doesn't yet support the `resolution` media feature. Instead, it still uses the non-standard, vendor-prefixed `-webkit-device-pixel-ratio` feature. For min/max ranges, use `-webkit-min-device-pixel-ratio` and `-webkit-max-device-pixel-ratio`.

this more compact syntax isn't yet supported by most browsers. Stick with *min-* and *max-* for now.

Discrete Media Feature Queries

There's a second type of media feature—the discrete type. **Discrete media features** are properties that accept one of a set, or a predefined list of values. In some cases, the set of values is a boolean—either *true* or *false.*

Discrete media features are properties for which a quantity makes little sense. Here's an example using the *orientation* property. The example adjusts the proportional height of a logo when in *portrait* mode:

```
@media screen and (orientation: portrait) {
    #logo {
        height: 10vh;
        width: auto;
    }
}
```

 Remember the Parentheses!

Notes are useful asides that are related—but not critical—to the topic at hand. Think of them as extra tidbits of information.

The *orientation* feature is an example of a discrete media feature. It has two supported values, *portrait* and *landscape* . Minimum and maximum values don't make much sense for these properties. The table below lists discrete media features that are currently available in major browsers.

Property	Description	Acceptable values
any-hover	Ability of *any* connected input mechanism to have a hover state as determined by the user agent	none, hover
hover	Ability of the *primary* input mechanism to have a hover state as determined by the user agent	none
any-pointer	Presence and accuracy of *any* pointing device available to the user	none, coarse, coarse
pointer	Presence and accuracy of the *primary* pointing device as determined by the user agent	none, coarse, coarse
grid	Whether the device is grid (such as a teletype terminal or phone with a single fixed font) or bitmap. Don't confuse this with CSS grid layout	Boolean[7]
orientation	Describes behavior for whatever is larger out of width or height. When the width is greater than height, the orientation is landscape. When the inverse is true, the orientation is portrait	portrait, landscape
scan	Which scanning process is used by the output display	interlace, progressive

Other discrete media features include `overflow-block` and `overflow-inline`, which describe the behavior of the device when content overflows in the block or inline direction (think billboards or slideshows). Eventually, we may also see support for `scripting` and `light-level` features, which test for JavaScript support and ambient light conditions.

One discrete feature query we can use now is `hover` (along with `any-hover`). The `hover` media feature query allows us to set different styles based on whether or not the primary input mechanism supports a `:hover` state. The `any-hover` feature works similarly, but applies to any input mechanism, not just the primary one. It's a discrete feature type, and has just two valid values:

- *none* : the device has no hover state, or has one that's inconvenient (for example, it's available after a long press)
- *hover* : the device has a hover state

---

[7] *Boolean* feature queries have an unusual syntax. You can use either 0 or 1 as a value, or just the feature itself. In the case of `grid`, this would be `@media (grid)` or `@media (grid: 1)`.

Consider the case of radio buttons and checkbox form controls on touch screens. Touch screen devices typically have an on-demand hover state, but may lack one completely. Adult-sized fingers are also fatter than the pointers of most mouse or trackpad inputs. For those devices, we might want to add more padding around the label, making it easier to tap:

```css
@media screen and (hover: on-demand) {
    input[type=checkbox] + label {
        padding: .5em;
    }
}
```

Another other media feature that's landed in browsers is the *pointer* media feature (and *any-pointer*). With *pointer* , we can query the presence and accuracy of a pointing device for the *primary* input mechanism. The *any-pointer* property, of course, tests the presence and accuracy of *any pointer* available as an input mechanism. Both media features accept one of the following values:

- *none* : the device's primary input mechanism is not a pointing device
- *coarse* : the primary input mechanism is a pointing device with limited accuracy
- *fine* : the device's primary input mechanism includes an accurate pointing device

Devices with pointing inputs include stylus-based screens or pads, touch screens, mice, and trackpads. Of those, touch screens are generally less accurate. Stylus inputs, on the other hand, are very accurate—but like touch screens, they lack a hover state. With that in mind, we might update our *hover* query from earlier so that we only add padding when the *pointer* is *coarse* :

```css
@media screen and (hover: none) and (pointer: coarse) {
    input[type=checkbox] + label {
        padding: .5em;
    }
}
```

To date, every major browser except Firefox supports *hover* / *any-hover* and *pointer* / *any-pointer* .

Improving Accessibility with `prefers-reduced-motion`

As mentioned in Chapter 6, *Transitions and Animations*, large-scale animations can create sensations of dizziness and nausea for people with vestibular disorders. Flickering animations can cause seizures for people with photosensitive epilepsy.

Seizures and dizziness don't make for a very good user experience. At the same time, animation can improve usability for users who aren't affected by vestibular disorders. As a way to balance improved usability for some while preventing debilitating conditions in others, WebKit proposed a *prefers-reduced-motion* feature query. It has two possible values: *no-preference* and *reduce*.

 Rationale

"Responsive Design for Motion[8]", a blog post from the WebKit team, explains the team's rationale for proposing the query, as well as how to use it.

With *prefers-reduced-motion*, we can provide an alternative animation or disable it altogether, as shown in the following example:

```
@media screen and (prefers-reduced-motion: reduce) {
    .wiggle {
        animation-play-state: paused;
    }
}
```

In this case, if the user's preference is to reduce motion, the *.wiggle* animation will be disabled.

When used without a value, *prefers-reduced-motion* is true. In other words, we could remove *reduce* from the above media query and it has an equivalent meaning:

```
@media screen and (prefers-reduced-motion) {
    .wiggle {
        animation-play-state: paused;
    }
}
```

So far, support for *prefers-reduced-motion* is limited to Safari. Until support is more widespread, adhere to WCAG guidelines for animations, and offer users the ability to disable them altogether.

Nesting @media Rules

It's also possible to nest *@media* rules. When might nesting media queries be useful? Here's one example:

---

8. https://webkit.org/blog/7551/responsive-design-for-motion/

```
@media screen {
    @media (min-width: 20em) {
        img {
            display: block;
            width: 100%;
            height: auto;
        }
    }

    @media (min-width: 40em) {
        img {
            display: inline-block;
            max-width: 300px;
        }
    }
}
```

In this example, we've grouped all our *screen* styles together, with sub-groups for particular viewport widths.

Working around Legacy Browser Support with `only`

As mentioned in the beginning of this chapter, *@media* has been around for a while. However, the syntax and grammar of *@media* has changed significantly from its original implementation. As the Media Queries Level 4 specification <u>explains</u>[9], the original error-handling behavior:

> would consume the characters of a media query up to the first non-alphanumeric character, and interpret that as a media type, ignoring the rest. For example, the media query *screen and (color)* would be truncated to just *screen*.

To avoid this, we can use the *only* keyword to hide media queries from browsers that support the older syntax. The *only* keyword must precede a media query, and affects the entire query:

```
@media only screen and (min-resolution: 1.5dppx) {
    /* Styles go here */
}
```

The *only* keyword tells the browser that these styles should be applied only when the following condition is met. The good news is that the older error-handling behavior is mostly an edge case

---

[9] https://www.w3.org/TR/mediaqueries-4/#mq-only

among browsers in use today. For most current browsers and current web users, using the *only* keyword is unnecessary. I've included it here for completeness.

Negating Media Queries

We can also negate a media query using the *not* keyword. The *not* keyword must come at the beginning of the query, before any media types or features. For example, to hide styles from *print* media, we might use the following:

```css
@media not print {
    body {
        background: url('paisley.png');
    }
}
```

If we wanted to specify low-resolution icons for lower-resolution devices instead, we might use this snippet:

```css
@media not print and (min-resolution: 1.5dppx) {
    .external {
        background: url('arrow-lowres.png');
    }
}
```

Notice here that *not* comes before and negates the *entire* media query. You can't insert *not* after an *and* clause. Arguments such as *@media not print and not (min-resolution: 2dppx)* or *@media screen and not (min-resolution: 2dppx)* violate the rules of media query grammar. However, you can use *not* at the beginning of each query in a media query list:

```css
@media not (hover: hover), not (pointer: coarse) {
    /* Styles go here */
}
```

Styles within this grouping rule would be applied when the device is without a hover state or when the pointing device has low accuracy.

Other Ways to Use Media Queries

Thus far, we've talked about *@media* blocks within stylesheets, but this isn't the only way to use media types and queries. We can also use them with *@import*, or the *media* attribute. For example, to import a stylesheet *typography.css* when the document is viewed on screen or printed, we could use the following CSS:

```
@import url(typography.css) screen, print;
```

But we can also add a media feature query to an *@import* rule. In the following example, we're serving the *hi-res-icons.css* stylesheet only when the device has a minimum resolution of *1.5dppx* or *96dpi* :

```
@import url(hi-res-icons.css) (min-resolution: 1.5dppx), (min-resolution: 96dpi);
```

 ## HTTP/1.1

For browsers and servers using HTTP/1.1, *@import* adds an additional HTTP request and blocks other assets from downloading. Use it with care!

Another way to use queries is with the *media* attribute, which can be used with the *style* , *link* , *video* , and *source* elements. In the following example, we'll only apply these linked styles if the device width is 480px wide or less:

```
<link rel="stylesheet" href="styles.css" type="text/css" media="screen and (max-width: 480px)">
```

 ### Performance Considerations

In every browser tested, the stylesheet will be requested and downloaded, even when the media query doesn't apply. However, linked assets within that stylesheet (for example, background images defined with *url()*) won't be.

 ### Precedence

If your linked stylesheets also contain media queries, these will take precedence over the value of the *media* attribute.

We can also use the *media* attribute with the *source* element to serve different files for different window widths and device resolutions. What follows is an example using the *source* element and *media* attribute with the *picture* element:

```
<picture>
    <source srcset="image-wide.jpg" media="(min-width: 1024px)">
```

```
    <source srcset="image-med.jpg" media="(min-width: 680px)">
    <img src="image-narrow.jpg" alt="Adequate description of the image contents.">
</picture>
```

 Browser Support

Neither Internet Explorer 11 nor Microsoft Edge 12 support the `picture` element. To add support for those browsers, use a polyfill such as Scott Jehl's Picturefill[10].

Content-driven Media Queries

A current common practice when using media queries is to set `min-width` and `max-width` *breakpoints* based on popular device sizes. A **breakpoint** is the width or height that triggers a media query and its resulting layout changes. Raise your hand if you've ever written CSS that resembles this:

```
@media screen and (max-width: 320px) {
    ⋮
}
@media screen (min-width: 320px) and (max-width: 480px) {
    ⋮
}
@media screen (min-width: 481px) and (max-width: 768px) {
    ⋮
}
@media screen (min-width: 769px) {
    ⋮
}
```

These work for a large number of users. But device screen widths are more varied than this. Rather than focus on the most popular devices and screen sizes, use a content-centric approach.

 Don't Use `device-width` **with Media Queries**

Avoid using `device-width` (including `min` / `max`) altogether for media queries. High DPI devices in particular may have a device width that doesn't match its actual pixel capability.

A content-centric approach to media queries sets breakpoints based on the point at which the

---

10. https://github.com/scottjehl/picturefill

layout starts to show its weaknesses. One strategy is to start small, which is also known as a **mobile-first** approach. As Bryan Reiger <u>puts it</u>[11], "the absence of support for `@media` queries is in fact the first media query."

You can do a lot to create a flexible, responsive layout *before* adding media queries. Then as you increase the viewport width or height, add styles that take advantage of the additional real estate. For example, how wide is the browser window when lines of text become too long to read? That can be the point at which your layout switches from a single-column layout (figure 8-1) to a two-column layout (figure 8-2).

---

[11] https://www.slideshare.net/bryanrieger/rethinking-the-mobile-web-by-yiibu

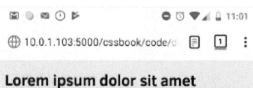

8-1. A document viewed in a narrow mobile browser

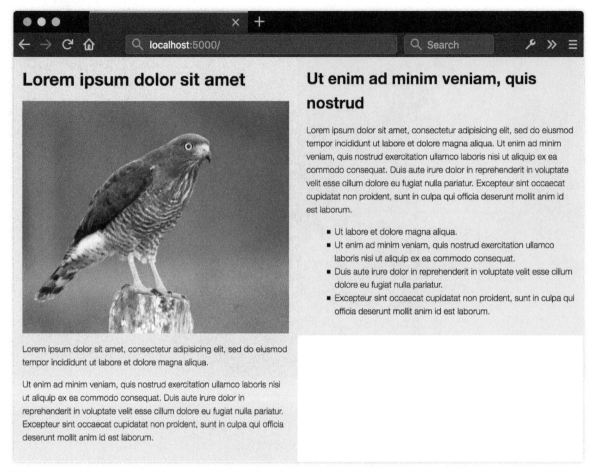

8-2. A document viewed in a wider, laptop-sized browser

There are two advantages to this approach. First, your site will still work on older mobile browsers that lack support for media queries. The second reason is more important: this approach prepares your site for a wider range of screen widths and resolutions.

Using Media Queries with JavaScript

Media queries also have a JavaScript API, better known as `matchMedia()`. If you're not versed in JavaScript, don't worry. We'll keep the examples short so that they're easier to understand. The API for media queries is actually defined by a different specification, the <u>CSSOM View Module</u>[12]. It's not CSS, strictly speaking, but since it's closely related to `@media`, we'll cover it.

The `matchMedia()` method is a property of the `window` object. That means we can refer to it using `window.matchMedia()` or just `matchMedia()`. The former is clearer, since it indicates that this is a native JavaScript method, but the latter saves a few keystrokes. I'm a lazy typist, so I'll

---

[12] https://drafts.csswg.org/cssom-view/

use *matchMedia()* in the examples that follow.

Use *matchMedia()* to test whether a particular media condition is met. The function accepts a single argument, which must be a valid media query.

Why use a media query with JavaScript, rather than CSS? Perhaps you'd like to display a set of images in a grid on larger screens, but trigger a slide show on small screens. Maybe you want to swap the *src* value of a *video* element based on the screen size or resolution. These are cases for using *matchMedia()* .

Here's a simple example of *matchMedia* in action. This code checks whether the viewport width is greater than or equal to *45em* :

```
var isWideScreen = matchMedia("(min-width: 45em)");
console.log(isWideScreen.matches); // Logs true or false to console
```

Using *matchMedia()* creates a *MediaQueryList* object. Here, that object is stored in the *isWideScreen* variable. Every *MediaQueryList* object contains two properties:

- *media* : returns the media query argument that was passed to *matchMedia()*
- *matches* : returns *true* if the condition is met and *false* otherwise

Since we want to know whether it's true that the browser window is at least *45em* wide, we need to examine the *matches* property.

MediaQueryList.matches will return *false* when either:

- the condition isn't met at the time *matchMedia()* is invoked
- the syntax of the media query is invalid
- the browser doesn't support the feature query

Otherwise, its value will be *true* .

Here's another example of using *matchMedia* . We'll update the source of a *video* element based on the size of the current viewport and resolution:

```
if(matchMedia("(max-width: 480px) and (max-resolution: 1dppx)") {
    document.querySelector('video').src = 'smallvideo.mp4';
}
```

If the condition doesn't match—or the browser doesn't support the *resolution* feature query—the value of *src* won't be changed.

Error Checking with `not all`

Typically, the value of the *media* property will be the media query we've tested. But maybe you forgot to include the parentheses around your feature query (a syntax error). Or perhaps the query uses a *pointer* feature query, but the browser is yet to support it. In both of those cases, the browser will return a *not all* value. This is media query speak for "this doesn't apply to any media condition."

In cases where the media query is a list—that is, when it contains multiple conditions—the value of *matchMedia().media* will also contain multiple values. If part of that query list is invalid or unsupported, its value will be *not all* . Here's an example:

```
var mq = matchMedia("(hover: none), (max-width: 25em)");
```

In browsers lacking support for the *hover: none* media feature query, the value of *mq.media* will be *not all, (max-width: 25em)* . In browsers that do support it, the value of *mq.media* will be *(hover: none), (max-width: 25em)* . Let's look at another example:

```
var mq = matchMedia("min-resolution: 1.5dppx, (max-width: 25em)");
```

In this example, the value of *mq.media* will also be *not all, (max-width: 25em)* . In this case, however, it's because our first feature query uses the wrong syntax. Remember that media feature queries need to be enclosed in parentheses. The argument should be *matchMedia("(min-resolution: 1.5dppx), (max-width: 25em)");* instead.

Listening for Media Changes

Media conditions aren't necessarily static. Conditions can change when the user resizes the browser, or toggles between portrait and landscape mode. Luckily, our specification authors thought of that, and added a means by which we can monitor and respond to changes in our document's environment: the *addListener()* method. The *addListener()* method accepts a function—what's known as a **callback function**—as its argument.

Let's add a class name when our document enters landscape orientation. The first step is to create a *MediaQueryList* object using *matchMedia* and a media query:

```
var isLandscape = matchMedia("(orientation: landscape)");
```

Step two is to define our callback function. Our `MediaQueryList` object will be passed to this callback function as its sole argument:

```
var toggleClass = function (mediaquery) {
    if (mediaquery.matches) {
      document.body.classList.add('widescreen');
    } else {
      document.body.classList.remove('widescreen');
    }
}
```

Media query events aren't very smart. They're fired any time the value of `MediaQueryList.matches` changes, regardless of whether or not the condition is `true`. This means we need to examine the value of `MediaQueryList.matches` or `MediaQueryList.media` for our `MediaQueryList` object. In this case, if the value of `mediaquery.matches` is `true`, we'll add a class name to our `body` element. Otherwise, we'll remove it.

Finally, let's add this event listener to our `MediaQueryList` object with `addListener`:

```
isLandscape.addListener( toggleClass );
```

To remove a listener, use `removeListener` as shown:

```
isLandscape.removeListener( toggleClass );
```

In early versions of the CSSOM View specification, `addListener` and `removeListener` were supposed to be separate mechanisms, removed from the DOM event queue. This changed in the Level 4 specification. Eventually, we'll be able to use the standard `addEventListener` and `removeEventListener` DOM methods to listen for a `change` event. Our examples from before could then be rewritten like so:

```
// Add a listener
isLandscape.addEventListener('change', toggleClass);

// Remove the listener
isLandscape.removeEventListener('change', toggleClass);
'change'
```

At the time of writing, Safari and Microsoft Edge haven't yet implemented this change. They still support `addListener` / `removeListener` exclusively. In other browsers, *addListener* / *removeListener* are just aliases of *addEventListener* / *removeEventListener* . Use *addListener* and *removeListener* until Safari and Microsoft Edge support the newer specification.

Testing for Property Support with @supports

With *@supports* , we can add CSS rules based on whether the browser supports a particular property and value. "And value" is key. Some CSS properties and values have been redefined or expanded since CSS2.1. Using *@supports* lets us test for those changes. Like *@media* , *@supports* consists of two parts: the CSS at-rule, and a DOM-based API for use with JavaScript.

Why might we use *@supports* ? Here's a scenario: as <u>originally specified</u>[13], *display* allowed four possible values: *block* , *inline* , *list-item* , and *none* . Later specifications added *table-** values, *flex* , and *grid* . With *@supports* , we can define CSS rules that will be applied only when the browser supports *display: grid* :

```
@supports (display: grid) {
    .gallery {
        display: grid;
        grid-template-columns: repeat(4, auto);
    }
}
```

To define a condition, wrap the property and value you'd like to test in a set of parentheses as shown. Both portions are required; a condition such as *@supports (hyphens)* won't work as a test.

To combine conditions, use the *and* keyword. For example, if you wanted to apply styles when both the *text-decoration-color* and *text-decoration-style* are supported, you could use the following:

```
@supports (text-decoration-color: #c09) and (text-decoration-style: double) {
    .title {
        font-style: normal;
        text-decoration: underline double #f60;
    }
}
```

The *@supports* syntax also allows disjunctions using the *or* keyword. Disjunctions are especially useful for testing vendor-prefixed property support. Let's revisit our *display: flex*

---

13. https://www.w3.org/TR/CSS1/#display

example. Older versions of WebKit-based browsers require a vendor prefix for Flexbox support. We can augment our *@supports* condition to take that into account:

```css
@supports (display: flex) or (display: -webkit-flex) {
    nav ul {
        display: -webkit-flex;
        display: flex;
    }
}
```

Finally, we can also define a collection of styles if a condition isn't supported by using the *not* keyword:

```css
@supports not (display: grid) {
    nav {
        display: flex;
    }
}
```

The *not* keyword can only be used to negate one condition at a time. In other words, *@supports not (text-decoration-color: #c09) and (text-decoration-style: double)* is not valid. But you *can* combine two tests into a single condition by using an outer set of parentheses: *@supports not ((text-decoration-color: #c09) and (text-decoration-style: double))* .

At the time of writing, the *not* keyword has limited utility. Browsers that lack support for features you'd test also lack support for *@supports* . For example, Internet Explorer 11 doesn't support *display: grid* . But since it also lacks support for *@supports* , it would ignore our *nav {display: flex;}* rule.

In most cases, we can leverage CSS error handling and the cascade instead. CSS ignores rules that it can't parse, and the last-defined rule wins. Instead of using *@supports not (display: grid)* , as shown above, we could instead use the following:

```css
nav {
    display: flex; /* Browsers that support Flexbox, but not Grid, will use this line. */
    display: grid; /* Browsers that support Grid will use this one. */
}
```

Using error handling and the cascade often works enough that you can forgo using *@supports* altogether.

CSS.supports **DOM API**

Along with the *@supports* rule comes a scriptable API: *CSS.supports()* . Think of it as a CSS-only version of [Modernizr](https://modernizr.com/)[14]. *CSS.supports()* always returns a boolean (*true* or *false*) value depending on whether or not the browser supports that property and value combination.

CSS.supports() accepts a parentheses-wrapped CSS declaration as its argument. For example:

```
CSS.supports('(text-decoration: underline wavy #e91e63)');
```

If the browser supports this syntax for *text-decoration* , *CSS.supports* will return *true* . Otherwise, it will return *false* .

We can also test multiple conditions using conjunctions (*and* keyword) or disjunctions (*or* keyword). *CSS.supports* also allows negation using the *not* keyword. For example, we can test whether a browser supports *display: -webkit-flex* or *display: flex* using the following:

```
CSS.supports('(display: -webkit-flex) or (display: flex)');
```

Most browsers treat parentheses as optional when testing a *single* property and value combination. Microsoft Edge, to date, doesn't.

When testing support for multiple conditions, each one *must* be wrapped in parentheses, as we've done here. Failing to do so means that *CSS.supports()* may return a false negative.

For the broadest compatibility, always wrap your condition arguments in parentheses.

Understanding the Cascade for @supports **and** @media

Using *@supports* or *@media* doesn't increase the specificity or importance of a rule. Normal cascade rules apply, meaning that any styles defined after an *@supports* or *@media* block will override rules within the block. Consider the following CSS:

```
@supports (text-decoration: underline wavy #c09) {
    .title {
        font-style: normal;
        text-decoration: underline wavy #c09;
    }
```

---

[14]. https://modernizr.com/

```
    }
  .title {
      font-style: italic;
  }
```

All elements with a `title` class will be both italicized and underlined. The subsequent `font-style: italic;` line overrides the `font-style: normal;`. That's not what we want here. Instead, we need to flip the order of our rulesets as shown, so that `font-style: normal` takes precedence over `font-style: italic`:

```
  .title {
      font-style: italic;
  }
  @supports (text-decoration: underline wavy #c09) {
      .title {
          font-style: normal;
          text-decoration: underline wavy #c09;
      }
  }
```

It's best to use these features progressively. Define your base styles—the styles that every one of your targeted browsers can handle. Then use `@supports` or `@media` to override and supplement those styles in browsers that can handle newer features.

Conclusion

Both `@media` and `@supports` are powerful and flexible ways to progressively enhance your CSS and serve a range of devices. Now that this chapter is complete, you should know how to use:

- `@media` to create flexible layouts for a range of devices and inputs
- `window.matchMedia()` and the `addListener` / `removeListener` methods to call JavaScript based on a media query
- `@supports` and the `CSS.supports()` to progressively enhance documents

There's an area of CSS that's a little more experimental than what we've discussed in this chapter: using CSS with SVG. SVG, or Scalable Vector Graphics, use markup to describe how images should be rendered on-screen. Because they're markup, we can use many CSS properties with SVG elements, or express SVG attributes using CSS properties. We dig into the details in the next chapter.

Using CSS with SVG

Chapter

9

So far, we've talked about using CSS with HTML, but we can also use CSS with SVG, or *Scalable Vector Graphics*. SVG is a markup format for describing flat, two-dimensional images. Because it's a markup language, it has a Document Object Model, and can be used with CSS.

By using CSS with SVG, we can change the appearance of SVG based on user interaction. Or we can use the same SVG document in multiple places, and show or hide portions of it based on the width of the viewport.

Some of what we'll discuss here has limited browser support at the time of writing. That may change by the time this book arrives in your hands.

Before we go any further, however, let's talk about what SVG is and why you should use it.

Vector Images versus Raster Images

Most of the images currently used on the Web are raster images, also known as bitmap images. **Raster images** are made up of pixels on a fixed grid, with a set number of pixels per inch. JPEG, WebP, GIF, and PNG are all examples of raster image formats.

Raster images are *resolution dependent*. A 96dpi PNG image will look great on a device with a 96dpi display resolution. When viewed on a 144dpi display, however, that same image will appear fuzzy or pixelated. Raster images also have fixed dimensions and look best at their original size. Scaling a 150 x 150px image up to 300 x 300px will distort it.

Vector images, on the other hand, use primitive shapes and mathematical expressions to construct the image. Instead of pixels on a grid, vector image formats describe the shapes that make up an image and their placement within the document's coordinate system. As a result, vector images are resolution *independent*, and retain their quality regardless of display resolution or display dimensions.

Resolution independence is the biggest advantage of SVG. We can scale images up or down with no loss of quality. The same image will look great on both high and low DPI (dots-per-inch) devices. That said, SVG is poorly suited to the amount of color data required for photographs. It's best for drawings and shapes. Use it in place of PNG and GIF images, or custom fonts for logos, charts, and icons.

Another advantage of SVG is that it was designed to be used with other web languages. We can create, modify, and manipulate SVG images with JavaScript. Or, as we'll see in this chapter, we can style and animate SVG using CSS.

Associating CSS with SVG Documents

Using CSS with SVG is a lot like using it with HTML. We can apply CSS using the *style* attribute of an SVG element; group CSS within a document using the *style* element; or link to an external stylesheet. The pros and cons of each method are the same as when using CSS with HTML.

Using the style Attribute

Here's a simple SVG document where the code creates a black circle, as shown in figure 9-1:

```
<svg version="1.1" xmlns="http://www.w3.org/2000/svg" viewBox="0 0 200 200"
↪enable-background="new 0 0 200 200">
    <circle cx="101.3" cy="96.8" r="79.6"/>
</svg>
```

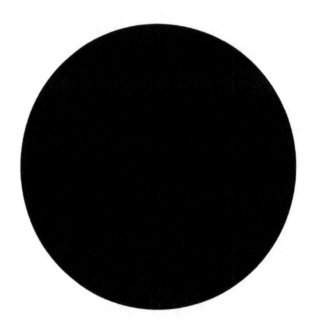

9-1. A circle in SVG

Let's give our circle a pink fill using CSS and the *style* attribute, the result of which can be seen in figure 9-2:

```
<svg version="1.1" xmlns="http://www.w3.org/2000/svg" viewBox="0 0 200 200"
↪enable-background="new 0 0 200 200">
```

```
        <circle cx="101.3" cy="96.8" r="79.6" style="fill: #f9f" />
    </svg>
```

9-2. Using the style attribute to add a fill color

Here's one difference between using CSS with HTML and using it with SVG: property names. Many of the CSS properties that we use with HTML documents aren't compatible with SVG, and vice versa. We'll come back to this point later in the chapter.

Using the *style* attribute isn't the best way to use CSS, of course. Doing so limits the reusability of those styles. Instead, we should use embedded or linked CSS.

Embedding CSS in SVG Documents

A better approach to using CSS with SVG is to embed it using the *style* element like this:

```
<svg version="1.1" xmlns="http://www.w3.org/2000/svg" viewBox="0 0
 200 200" enable-background="new 0 0 200 200">
    <style type="text/css">
        circle {
            fill: #0c0;
        }
```

```
    </style>
    <circle cx="101.3" cy="96.8" r="79.6" />
</svg>
```

Embedding CSS in an SVG document lets us reuse those styles for multiple elements within the same document, but it prevents that CSS from being shared across multiple documents. That's probably acceptable for logos and icons, but if you're creating a library of chart styles, use an external CSS file instead.

Linking from SVG to an External CSS File

As with HTML, linking to an external CSS file makes it possible to share styles across several SVG documents. To link an external CSS file, add `<? xml-stylesheet ?>` to the beginning of your SVG file:

```
<?xml version="1.0" encoding="utf-8"?>
<?xml-stylesheet href="style.css" type="text/css"?>
<svg version="1.1" xmlns="http://www.w3.org/2000/svg" viewBox="0 0
↳ 200 200" enable-background="new 0 0 200 200">
    <circle cx="101.3" cy="96.8" r="79.6" />
</svg>
```

Using the `<link>` Element

Alternatively, use the XHTML `link` element. Just be sure to add the namespace attribute `xmlns=http://www.w3.org/1999/xhtml` to your tag:

```
<defs>
    <link href="style.css" type="text/css" rel="stylesheet"
↳ xmlns="http://www.w3.org/1999/xhtml"/>
</defs>
```

The `link` element isn't an SVG element. It belongs to HTML and XHTML. Under the rules of XML, though, we can borrow elements and their behavior from other XML dialects such as XHTML. To do this, however, we have to add the `xmlns` namespace attribute to the `link` tag.

Using `@import`

We can also link to an external stylesheet by using `@import` inside `<style>` and `</style>` tags:

```
<style type="text/css">
@import('style.css');
</style>
```

Limitations of Externally-linked CSS

Linking from SVG files to external assets, including CSS file, doesn't work with the `img` element. It's a security limitation of the `img` element that's baked into most browsers.

If you're using the `img` element to serve SVG images, you'll need to do either of these two things:

1 Use the `style` element within your SVG document.

2 Use the `object` or `iframe` elements to embed your SVG file.[1] Using `object` or `iframe` also makes the SVG document tree available to the parent document's document tree, which means that we can use JavaScript to interact with it (for example, `document.querySelector('object').contentDocument`).

Inline SVG and External Assets

Inline SVG has a similar limitation in Firefox and Safari. In those browsers, external CSS files won't load. We can, however, link to the CSS for our SVG document from the `head` of our HTML document:

```
<head>
    ⋮
    <link href="svg.css" type="text/css" rel="stylesheet" />
</head>
```

We can also use the `style` element instead.

SVG elements within HTML documents become part of the HTML document tree. Rather than manage SVG-related CSS and HTML-related CSS separately, you may also wish to group the CSS for your SVG document with the CSS of its parent.

[1.] Craig Buckler's piece "How to Add Scalable Vector Graphics to Your Web Page" (https://www.sitepoint.com/add-svg-to-web-page/) discusses these methods in detail.

SVG images created with software such as Sketch, Inkscape, or Illustrator can also be edited using a standard text editor to add CSS. In most cases, doing so won't affect your ability to modify the image with that drawing application, but the application may remove your CSS or otherwise change your markup when you edit and re-save it.

Differences between SVG and HTML

While SVG and HTML are both markup languages, there are two significant differences between them that affect how they work with CSS:

1 SVG doesn't adhere to the CSS box model

2 SVG lacks a positioning scheme

SVG Doesn't Adhere to the CSS Box Model

As pointed out in Chapter 5, *Layouts*, when used with HTML, CSS layout follows the rules of the CSS box model. SVG, on the other hand, uses coordinates for layout. It adheres to what may be best understood as a "shape model."

SVG shapes aren't limited to rectangular boxes. As a result, most box-model-related properties are inapplicable to SVG elements. You can't, for instance, change the `padding` or `margin` of an SVG element. You can't use the `box-sizing`, `box-shadow`, `outline`, or `border-*` properties. Grid layout, floats, and Flexbox also don't work.

You can, however, use CSS to set or change a range of SVG properties and attribute values. The full list is outlined in the <u>SVG specification</u>[2]. We'll discuss a few of them in this chapter, within the context of specific techniques.

SVG Lacks a Positioning Scheme

When CSS is used with HTML, element boxes can:

- exist within a normal flow
- be removed from normal flow with the `float` property
- be removed from normal flow with the `position` property

The CSS specification refers to these as *positioning schemes*. Positioning schemes don't exist in SVG. The `position` property has no effect on SVG elements. Neither do properties such as `top`,

---

[2] https://www.w3.org/TR/SVG/propidx.html

left and *bottom* , which depend on elements being positioned. You also can't float elements within an SVG document.

Instead, SVG uses a coordinate system for element placement. To create a *circle* , for example, you need to set its center point coordinates using the *cx* and *cy* attributes, and set a radius length using the *r* attribute. A polygon consists of a series of point coordinates and line segments drawn between them. In other words, you can define where an element will be drawn to the SVG canvas, but you can't "position" them in the CSS sense of the word.

Related to positioning schemes, SVG also lacks the idea of *z-index* and stacking contexts.[3] SVG elements are stacked according to their source order. Those that appear later in the document sit towards the top of the stack. If you want to change the stacking order of SVG elements, you'll need to move them around in the source or use JavaScript to reorder them in the DOM tree.

In fact, most CSS 2.1 properties don't apply to SVG documents. Exceptions include animations and transforms, *display* , *overflow* , *visibility* , and a few font and text-related properties. Instead, you'll have to use <u>SVG-specific styling properties with SVG documents</u>[4]. Most of these properties can also be expressed as SVG element attributes.

Styling SVG Elements

Here's a simple example of how to style SVG elements using CSS. First our SVG document, which is a stand-alone file:

```
<?xml version="1.0" encoding="utf-8"?>
<?xml-stylesheet href="styles.css" type="text/css" ?>
<svg version="1.1" xmlns="http://www.w3.org/2000/svg" xmlns:xlink=
↪"http://www.w3.org/1999/xlink" x="0px" y="0px" viewBox="0 0 497
↪ 184" enable-background="new 0 0 497 184" xml:space="preserve">
    <polygon id="star" points="77,23.7 98.2,66.6 145.5,66.5 111.2,
↪106.9,119.3,154 77,131.8 34.7,154 42.8,106.9 8.5,67.5 55.8,
↪66.6 "/>
    <circle id="circle" cx="245" cy="88.9" r="67.5"/>
</svg>
```

This markup creates the image shown below.

[3.] The <u>SVG 2 specification</u> (https://svgwg.org/svg2-draft/) *does* define behavior for *z-index* and stacking contexts in SVG documents, but most browsers don't yet support that part of the spec.
[4.] https://www.w3.org/TR/SVG/propidx.html

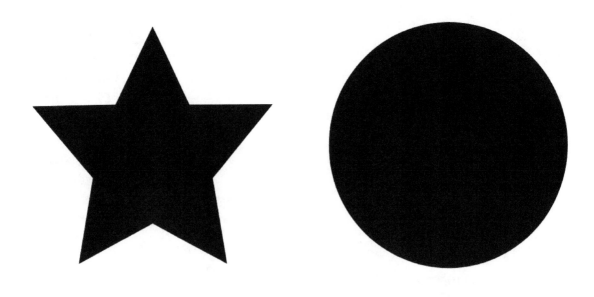

9-3. A simple circle and star SVG image

As has been mentioned, we can't use most CSS properties with SVG documents. But we can use CSS to change an element's color. Let's make our star yellow:

```
#star {
    fill: rgb(255,185,0);
}
```

You'll often see the *fill* attribute used with SVG tags—for example, *<circle fill="rgb(255,185,0)" cx="3" cy="10" r="100">* —but it's also a property that can be used with CSS.

We can also use CSS to adjust an element's *stroke* , which is the outline of an SVG shape. A shape's stroke exists, even if no *stroke* properties are set. Let's give our circle a dark-blue, dashed border that's 10px wide. We'll also set its *fill* property to *cornflowerblue* :

```
circle {
    fill: cornflowerblue;
    stroke: darkblue;
    stroke-width: 10;
    stroke-dasharray: 10, 15;
}
```

```
    stroke-linecap: round;
}
```

Together this gives us the result below.

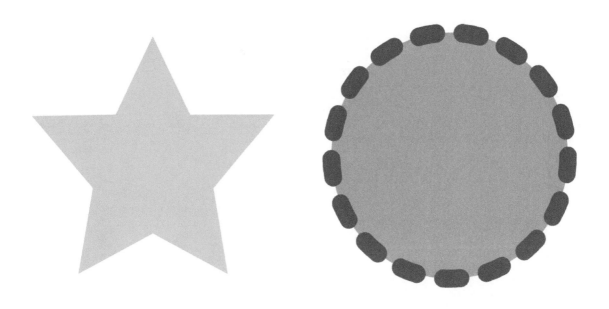

9-4. A simple circle and star SVG image

Not every SVG attribute is available via CSS—at least not in every browser. Most browsers support using CSS to change text, font, stroke, clipping, filter, gradient, color, and painting properties,[5] as defined by the SVG 1.1 specification.

Support for, say, setting *x* and *y* values via CSS is another matter. Many of the details are still being hashed out as part of the SVG 2.0 specification process. One day, we may be able to use CSS to set the definition of a *path* element:

```
path {
    d: "M27,167 C72,128 169,-21 267,68 C365,157 123,264 224,373 C291, 445 373, 401 471,239";
}
```

Alas, to date, only Chrome supports anything like this. It also uses the outdated *path* function

---

[5] Just a reminder that the complete list is available in the **Property Index** (https://www.w3.org/TR/SVG/propidx.html) appendix of the SVG specification.

syntax (that is, *d: path(…)*). Until this becomes more widely supported, use SVG attributes for path definitions and shape placement.

Animating and Transitioning SVG CSS Properties

Using CSS with SVG becomes more interesting when we add transitions and animations to the mix. The process is just like animating HTML elements with CSS, but with SVG-specific properties. Let's create a twinkling star effect using the following SVG document:

```
<svg version="1.1" xmlns="http://www.w3.org/2000/svg" x="0px"
  y="0px" viewBox="0 0 497 184" xml:space="preserve">
    <defs>
        <link href="twinkle.css" type="text/css" rel="stylesheet"
  xmlns="http://www.w3.org/1999/xhtml"/>
    </defs>
    <polygon class="star" points="77,23.7 98.2,66.6 145.5,66.5 111.2
  ,106.9 119.3,154 77,131.8 34.7,154 42.8,106.9 8.5,67.5
  55.8,66.6 "/>
    <polygon class="star twinkle" points="77,23.7 98.2,66.6 145.5,
  66.5 111.2,106.9 119.3,154 77,131.8 34.7,154 42.8,106.9
  8.5,67.5 55.8,66.6 "/>
</svg>
```

Our document contains two star-shaped polygon elements, each with a class name of *star* . To create the twinkling effect, we'll animate the first one. Here's our CSS:

```
@keyframes twinkle {
    from {
        fill-opacity: .4;
    }
    to {
        fill-opacity: 0;
        transform: scale(2);
    }
}
.star {
    fill: rgb(255,195,0);
    transform-origin: 50% 50%;
}
.twinkle {
    animation: twinkle 1.5s infinite forwards ease-in;
}
```

Here we've used the SVG-specific property *fill-opacity* . As with CSS, if the value of an SVG styling property can be interpolated, it can also be animated or transitioned. You can see two different points of the animation in figure 9-5.

9-5. States of our pulsing star animation

Let's look at another example. This time we'll create a drawing effect by transitioning the *stroke-dasharray* property. Here's our SVG document:

```
<svg version="1.1" xmlns="http://www.w3.org/2000/svg"
↪xmlns:xlink="http://www.w3.org/1999/xlink" x="0px" y="0px"
    viewBox="0 0 200 200" enable-background="new 0 0 200 200">
    <circle fill="transparent" stroke-width="16" cx="101.3"
↪ cy="96.8" r="79.6"/>
</svg>
```

The *stroke-dasharray* property accepts a comma-separated list of length or percentage values that creates a dashed pattern. Odd-numbered values determine the dash length. Even-numbered values determine the gap length. A *stroke-dasharray* value of *5, 10* means that the stroke will be 5px long with a gap of 10px between each dash. A value of *5, 5, 10* alternates 5pc and 10px dash lengths with 5px gaps in between.

We can use *stroke-dasharray* to create a drawing effect by starting with a zero dash length and a large gap, and ending with a large dash length and a dash gap of zero. Then we'll transition between the two. Here's what our CSS looks like:

```
circle {
```

```
    transition: stroke-dasharray 1s ease-in;
    fill: transparent;
    stroke-dasharray: 0, 500;
}
.animate {
    stroke-dasharray: 500, 0;
}
```

At the beginning of the transition, our stroke is invisible because the dash length is `0` and our gap is `500`. But when we add the *animate* class to our circle, we shift the dash length to `500` and eliminate the gap. The effect is a bit like drawing a circle with a pair of compasses. Why 500? It's the smallest value that worked to create this particular effect.

An Animated Path Future

Remember our example of defining a path via CSS from the previous section? In future browsers, we'll be able to animate or transition those values too:

```
path {
    d: "M27,167 C72,128 169,-21 267,68 C365,157 123,264 224,373 C291, 445 373, 401 471,239";
    transition: d 1s ease-in-out;
}
.straighten {
    d: "M27,167 C72,128 169,-21 267,68 C365,157 123,264 224,373 C291,445 373, 401 471,239";
}
"M27,167 C72,128 169,-21 267,68 C365,157 123,264 224,373 C291,445 373, 401 471,239"
```

Unfortunately, support for animating path definitions is limited to Blink-based browsers such as Chrome. For now, we need to use JavaScript to animate path definitions. GreenSock[6] and its MorphSVGPlugin is the leading JavaScript library for animating SVG shapes. SVG.js[7] and the svg.pathmorphing.js plugin is another option.

Using SVG with Media Queries

With HTML documents, we might show, hide, or rearrange parts of the page based on the conditions of the viewport. If the browser window is 480px wide, for example, we might shift our navigation from a horizontal one to a vertical, collapsible list. We can do something similar with media queries and SVG documents. Consider a logo, such as that of the fictitious Hexagon Web Design & Development:

[6.] https://greensock.com/
[7.] http://svgjs.com/

9-6. A very real logo for a fictitious company

Without media queries, this SVG logo would simply stretch or shrink to fit the viewport or its container. But with media queries, we can do more clever things.

Let's distinguish between the HTML document viewport and the SVG document viewport. When SVG is inline, the HTML viewport and the SVG viewport are one and the same. The SVG document behaves like any other HTML element. On the other hand, when an SVG document is linked—as with the `object` or `img` elements—we're dealing with the SVG document viewport.

Media queries work in both cases, but when the SVG document is linked, its viewport is independent of its HTML document. In that case, the size of the browser window doesn't determine the size of the SVG viewport. Instead, the viewport size is determined by the dimensions of the `object` , `iframe` , or `img` element. Take the (abridged) SVG document that follows as an example:[8]

```
<svg version="1.1" id="HexagonLogo" xmlns="http://www.w3.org/2000/
↪svg" xmlns:xlink="http://www.w3.org/1999/xlink" x="0px" y="0px"
↪ viewBox="0 0 555 174" xml:space="preserve">
    <defs>
        <style type="text/css">
        /* CSS goes here */
        </style>
    </defs>
    <g id="hex">
        <polygon id="hexagonbg" points="55.2,162 10,86.5 55.2,11
↪ 145.5,11 190.7,86.5 145.5,162  "/>
```

8. A full demonstration of this technique, including the complete source of this SVG document, is available in the code archive.

```
        <path id="letterH" fill="#FFFFFF" d="M58,35.5h33v35.2h18.
↪4V35.5 h33.2v103.4h-33.2v-38.3H91v38.3H58V35.5z M77.5,126.5V87.
↪3h45.6v39.2h4V47.9h-4v35.6H77.5V47.9h-4v78.6H77.5z"/>
    </g>

    <g id="word-mark">
        <g id="hexagon-word">
            ...
        </g>
        <g id="web-design-and-dev">
            ...
        </g>
    </g>
</svg>
```

In smaller viewports, let's show just the H in a hexagon symbol:

```
@media (max-width: 20em) {
    [id=word-mark] {
        display: none;
    }
}
```

Now, whenever our SVG's container is less than or equal to *20em* , only the symbol portion of our logo will be visible:

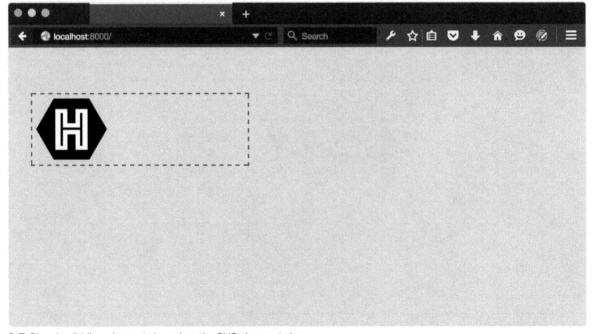

9-7. Showing/hiding elements based on the SVG viewport size

To trigger this view from the HTML document, set the width of the SVG container:

```
<object data="hexlogo.svg" type="image/svg+xml" style="width: 20em;"></object>
```

As you may have noticed from looking at figure 9-7, our SVG image retains its intrinsic dimensions even though part of it has been hidden. This, unfortunately, is a limitation of SVG. To fix it, we need to change the `viewBox` attribute of the SVG document, but only when the viewport is below a certain size. This is a great use case for `matchMedia`.[9]

The `viewBox` attribute, as its name suggests, determines the viewable area of an SVG element. By adjusting it, we can determine which part of an SVG image fills the viewport. What follows is an example using `matchMedia` and a media query to update the `viewBox` attribute:

```
<script type="text/javascript">
var svg, originalViewBox, max20em, mq, updateViewBox;

svg = document.querySelector('svg');

/* Store the original value in a variable */
originalViewBox = svg.getAttribute('viewBox');

/* Define our media query and media query object */
mq  = matchMedia("(max-width: 20em)");

/* Define the handler */
updateViewBox = function(){
    if (mq.matches) {
        /* Change the viewBox dimensions to show the hexagon */
        svg.setAttribute('viewBox', "0 0 200 174");
    } else {
        svg.setAttribute('viewBox', originalViewBox);
    }
}

/* Fire on document load */
// WebKit/Blink browsers
svg.onload = updateViewBox;

// Firefox & IE
svg.addEventListener('SVGLoad', updateViewBox, true);

/* Fire if the media condition changes */
mq.addListener(updateViewBox);
```

---

[9] `matchMedia` is discussed in Chapter 8, _Applying CSS Conditionally_.

```
</script>
```

 Browsers and SVGLoad

Browsers are a little bit of a mess when it comes to handling the *SVGLoad* event. In my tests, *addEventListener* worked most consistently with Firefox. For best results in Chrome and Safari, use the *onLoad* event attribute. Microsoft Edge also works best with *onLoad* , but only when used as an attribute of the *<svg>* tag. In other words, *<svg onLoad="updateViewBox">* .

Now, whenever the SVG container is *20em* or less, the value of *viewBox* will be *"0 0 200 174"* . When it exceeds *20em* , *viewBox* will be restored to its initial value:

9-8. Adjusting the viewBox attribute based on the viewport's width

More on Creating Interactive SVG Documents

For a fuller primer on creating interactive SVG documents, read the "Dynamic SVG and JavaScript[10]" chapter of *An SVG Primer for Today's Browsers* from the W3C.

Since this technique uses either the *onLoad* event attribute or the *SVGLoad* event, it's a good idea to embed our CSS and JavaScript within the SVG file. When CSS is external, the *SVGLoad* event may fire before its associated CSS finishes loading.

Using Media Queries with background-size

SVG documents and media queries aren't limited to foreground images. We can also resize the SVG viewport using the CSS *background-size* property. All of the latest major browsers support this technique, but older browser versions don't. Be careful when using this technique in production.

We'll start with this SVG document:

```
<?xml version="1.0" encoding="utf-8"?>
<svg version="1.1" id="Layer_1" xmlns="http://www.w3.org/2000/svg"
↪ xmlns:xlink="http://www.w3.org/1999/xlink" x="0px" y="0px"
↪ viewBox="-20 -20 250 250" xml:space="preserve">
    <style type="text/css">
      circle {
            stroke: #000;
            stroke-width: 30;
            fill: #009688;
      }
      @media (width: 100px) {
          circle {
              fill: #673ab7;
          }
      }
      @media (width: 300px) {
          circle {
              fill: #ffc107;
          }
      }
    </style>
    </defs>
    <circle cx="100" cy="100" r="100" />
    <circle cx="100" cy="100" r="50" />
```

10. https://www.w3.org/Graphics/SVG/IG/resources/svgprimer.html#JavaScript

```
</svg>
```

This is a simple case. Our `circle` elements will get a new `fill` color at specific viewport widths. When the viewport is 20px wide, the fill will be teal. When it's 300px wide, it will be yellow.

To make this work, we have to use our SVG image as a background image and set the selector's `background-size` property. In this case, we'll use our image as a background for the body `element` and for `li` elements. Figure 9-9 shows the results:

```
body, li {
    background: url(../images/circles.svg);
}
body {
    background-color: #9c27b0;
    background-size: 300px auto;
}
li {
    background-size: 20px auto;
    background-repeat: no-repeat;
    background-position: left 3px;
    padding-left: 25px;
}
```

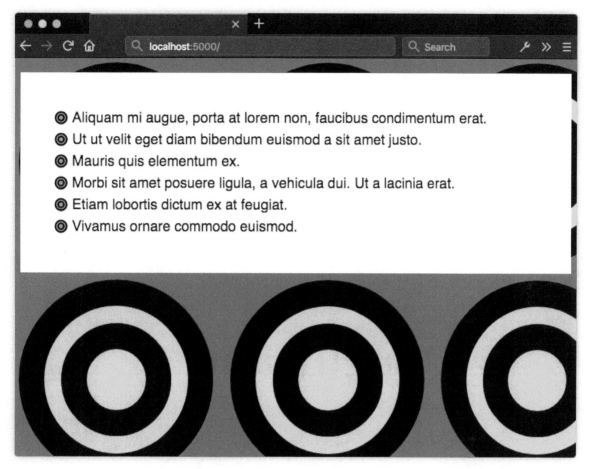

9-9. Manipulating the SVG viewport with the CSS background-size property

Conclusion

Using SVG with CSS gives us more possibilities for flexible and adaptive documents. Upon completing this chapter, you should now know how to:

- use CSS to style SVG elements
- animate SVG properties
- employ CSS media queries and the `matchMedia` API to show and hide portions of an SVG document.

Conclusion

In this book, we've covered some of the finer points and broad strokes of CSS. In some ways, we've only scratched the surface.

With the CSS Working Group's switch to modularized specifications and shorter browser release cycles, new CSS features are created and implemented much more quickly. Attempting to keep up and stay ahead of the curve can leave your head spinning. Indeed, there are a few specifications and features that we've barely mentioned in this book.

So what's on the horizon?

CSS Shapes

Web page layouts have historically been limited to rectangles of varying sizes—and sometimes circles with the help of *border-radius* . With <u>CSS Shapes</u>[1], however, we'll soon be able to flow content into and around complex, non-rectangular shapes.

Let's look at a simple example using a floated element and some accompanying text:

```
<div class="shape"></div>
<p class="content">Integer venenatis, nisi sed congue ...</p>
```

And we'll use the following CSS:

```
.content {
    width: 600px;
}
.shape {
    background: purple;
    shape-outside: polygon(0 0, 100% 40%, 100% 100%, 80% 100%);
    clip-path: polygon(0 0, 100% 40%, 100% 100%, 80% 100%);
    float: left;
    width: 300px;
    height: 300px;
    margin: 20px;
}
```

The *shape-outside* property determines how other elements in the document will flow around *.shape* . To start with, in order to make elements actually flow around *.shape* at all, we've added *float: left* :

---

[1]. https://www.w3.org/TR/css-shapes/

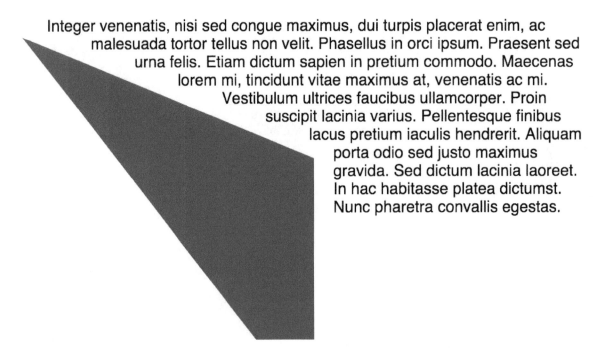

10-1. Using shape-outside without a clip path

However, the background color of `.shape` doesn't follow the edges of the polygon created with `shape-outside`. For that, we need to set a `clip-path` value equal to that of `shape-outside`. That gives us the layout shown below.

Integer venenatis, nisi sed congue maximus, dui turpis placerat enim, ac malesuada tortor tellus non velit. Phasellus in orci ipsum. Praesent sed urna felis. Etiam dictum sapien in pretium commodo. Maecenas lorem mi, tincidunt vitae maximus at, venenatis ac mi. Vestibulum ultrices faucibus ullamcorper. Proin suscipit lacinia varius. Pellentesque finibus lacus pretium iaculis hendrerit. Aliquam porta odio sed justo maximus gravida. Sed dictum lacinia laoreet. In hac habitasse platea dictumst. Nunc pharetra convallis egestas.

10-2. Using shape-outside in combination with the clip-path property to create layouts that go beyond boxes

Firefox 62+, Chrome 37+ and Safari 10.1+ all support CSS shapes by default. In Microsoft Edge, it's still under consideration. It's fine to use it with progressive enhancement. Just be sure to include an alternative layout for browsers that lack support.

Perhaps surprisingly, the `clip-path` property isn't defined by the CSS Shapes specification. Instead, it's outlined in the <u>CSS Masking Module Level 1</u>[2]. All current major browsers support the use of `clip-path` with SVG documents. All except Microsoft Edge support the use of `clip-path` with HTML elements as well. Safari ≤ 12 and Chrome versions 24–54 require a `-webkit-` vendor prefix (for example, `-webkit-clip-path`).

CSS Masking

Masking is another CSS feature that's coming to browsers. It may be familiar to you if you've ever worked with graphics editors such as Photoshop, Acorn, or GIMP. It's an effect created when one layer hides—*masks*—portions of another layer, as illustrated below.

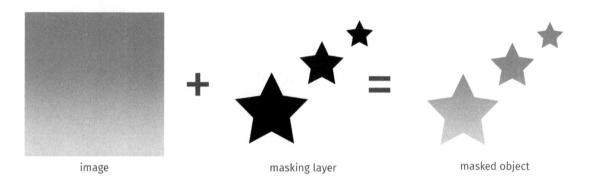

image   masking layer   masked object

10-3. Masking merges two layers into a single masked object

Let's look at an example. We'll add a mask to the paragraph:

---

2. https://www.w3.org/TR/css-masking/

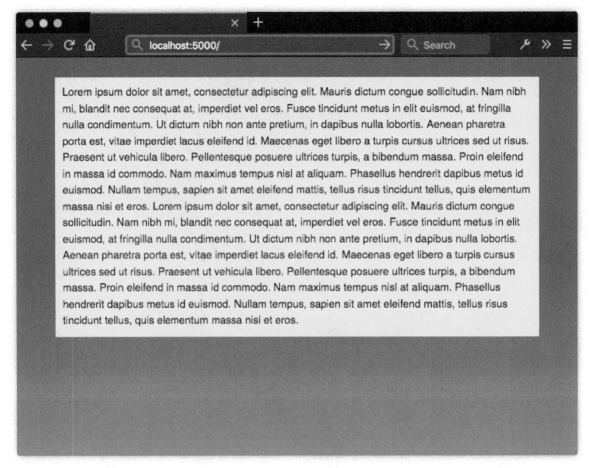

10-4. Our paragraph before adding a mask

In CSS, masks are created using the *mask-** family of properties. To create a mask, use *mask-image* . Its value should be a *url()* or a CSS image such as *linear-gradient* or *radial-gradient* .

We'll use an image named *octagon.svg* to illustrate. Since this is a scalable vector image, we'll also set the size of the mask using *mask-size* . The *mask-size* property works much like the *background-size* property and accepts the same values:

```
p {
    background: yellow;
    color: #000;

    /* For WebKit and Blink browsers. */
    -webkit-mask-image: url(octagon.svg);
    -webkit-mask-size: auto 100%;
```

```
    /* For browsers that support the unprefixed properties. */
    mask-image: url(octagon.svg);
    mask-size: auto 100%;
}
```

Figure 10-5 shows the result. Notice that the visible parts of the paragraph fall *within* the octagon shape. Other areas of the paragraph are hidden from view.

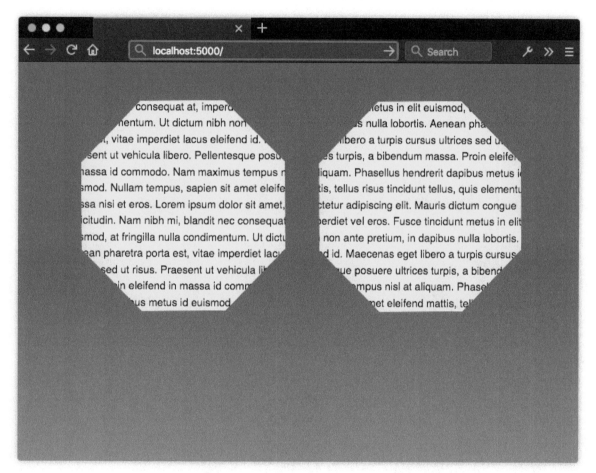

10-5. Our paragraph after adding a mask, and adjusting its size

We can also combine the lines above using the `mask` shorthand property:

```
p {
    background: yellow;
    color: #000;

    /* For WebKit and Blink browsers. */
    -webkit-mask: url(octagon.svg) / auto 100%;
```

```
    /* For browsers that support the unprefixed properties. */
    mask: url(octagon.svg) / auto 100%;
}
```

Although the `clip-path` property of the CSS Masking specification is widely supported, support for other properties is less robust. Firefox (version 53 and later) is furthest along. It supports all of the properties defined by the specification.

Chrome, Safari, and Samsung Internet support most masking properties. They do, however, lack support for `mask-composite`, and all `mask-*` properties still require a `-webkit-` vendor prefix. Microsoft Edge 18+ doesn't yet support the `mask-box-*` properties.

The Mozilla Developer Network has a more detailed overview of _`mask` and related properties_[3].

Scroll Snap

As the web platform grows, it has also gained features that mimic native applications. One such feature is the CSS Scroll Snap Module[4]. **Scroll snap** lets developers define the distance an interface should travel during a scroll action. You might use it to build slide shows or paged interfaces—features that currently require JavaScript and expensive DOM operations.

Scroll snap as a feature has undergone a good deal of change. An earlier, 2013 version of the specification—called Scroll Snap *Points* at the time—defined a coordinates-and-pixels-based approach to specifying scroll distance. This version of the specification was implemented in Microsoft Edge, Internet Explorer 11, and Firefox.

Chrome 69+ and Safari 11+ implement the latest version of the specification, which uses a box alignment model. That's what we'll focus on in this section.

 Watch Out for Tutorials That Cover the Old Spec

Many of the scroll snap tutorials currently floating around the web are based on the earlier CSS Scroll Snap *Points* specification. The presence of the word "points" in the title is one sign that the tutorial may rely on the old specification. A more reliable indicator, however, is the presence of the `scroll-snap-points-x` or `scroll-snap-points-y` properties.

---

3. https://developer.mozilla.org/en-US/docs/Web/CSS/mask
4. https://drafts.csswg.org/css-scroll-snap-1/

Since scroll snap is really well-suited to slide show layouts, that's what we'll build. Here's our markup:

```
<div class="slideshow">
  <img src="avocado-and-bacon-salad.jpg" alt="avocado and bacon salad">
  <img src="salad-eggs-and-scallops.jpg" alt="salad topped with hard boiled eggs, seared scallops">
  <img src="seafood-and-noodles.jpg" alt="seafood stew over noodles">
  <img src="grilled-salmon-and-side-salad.jpg" alt="grilled salmon steak, avocado and side salad">
  <img src="avocado-toast-with-egg.jpg" alt="avocado toast with egg">
</div>
```

That's all we need. We don't need to have an outer wrapping element with an inner sliding container. We also don't need any JavaScript.

Now for our CSS:

```
* {
    box-sizing: border-box;
}
html, body {
    padding: 0;
    margin: 0;
}
.slideshow {
    scroll-snap-type: x mandatory; /* Indicates scroll axis and behavior */
    overflow-x: auto;              /* Should be either scroll or auto */
    display: flex;
    height: 100vh;
}
.slideshow img {
    width: 100vw;
    height: 100vh;
    scroll-snap-align: center;
}
```

Adding `scroll-snap-type` to `.slideshow` creates a scroll container. The value for this property, `x mandatory`, describes the direction in which we'd like to scroll, and the *scroll snap strictness*. In this case, the `mandatory` value tells the browser that it *must* snap to a snap position when there's no active scroll operation. Using `display: flex` just ensures that all of our images stack horizontally.

The other property we need is `scroll-snap-align`. This property indicates how to align each image's scroll snap area within the scroll container's snap port. It accepts three values: `start`, `end`, and `center`. In this case, we've used `center`, which means that each image will be centered within the viewport:

10-6. How scroll-snap-align: center aligns images within a scroll container, in Chrome 70 for Android

For a more comprehensive look at Scroll Snap, read "Well-Controlled Scrolling with CSS Scroll Snap[5]" from the Google Web Fundamentals guide.

Blend Modes and CSS Filters

Visual effects is another area of CSS with some interesting activity. Aside from transforms, there are two specifications to keep an eye on: Compositing and Blending Level 1[6] and Filter Effects Module Level 1[7].

Blend modes make it possible to blend background colors and images using effects commonly found in graphics software such as Photoshop. Defined modes include `multiply`, `screen`, `overlay`, and `color-dodge`. We can use these blend modes to combine layered elements and backgrounds.

---

5. https://developers.google.com/web/updates/2018/07/css-scroll-snap
6. https://drafts.fxtf.org/compositing-1/
7. https://www.w3.org/TR/filter-effects/

10-7. The original background image (left) is modified (right) using background-blend-mode: multiply

Here we've used the `background-blend-mode` property to give the background photograph a purplish tint. For `background-blend-mode` to work, you'll have to set one or more background images *or* a background image and a background color. To create the background effect in figure 10-7, you'd use the following CSS:

```css
.blend {
    background: orchid url(images/snail.jpg);
    background-blend-mode: multiply;
}
```

Current versions of Chrome, Firefox, Safari, and Opera support the `background-blend-mode` as well as the `mix-blend-mode` property. Safari, however, lacks support for the `hue`, `saturation`, `luminosity`, and `color` filters. Neither Microsoft Edge nor Internet Explorer support this property yet.

Blend modes affect how the layers within a stacking context may be visually combined. CSS Filters, on the other hand, alter the rendering of layers *without* combining them. With CSS Filters, we can blur objects, change them from color to grayscale or sepia tone, modify their hue, or invert their colors. Each CSS filter is a function, and we can use them alone or in a filter list.

10-8. The effect of filter: blur(10px) grayscale(1)

If we want to blur an image and make it grayscale, as in figure 10-8, we can use the following CSS:

```
img {
    filter: blur(10px) grayscale(1);
}
```

Full support for filters is available without a prefix in Firefox 35+. Firefox versions 3.6–34 only support the `url()` function for filters. Chrome 18+, Opera 15+, and Safari 6+ also support filters with a `-webkit-` prefix. Microsoft Edge supports most filter functions, but doesn't yet support the use of external images as filters. Filter effects can also be animated, unlike blend modes.

How to Follow Changes and Additions to CSS

Keeping track of all this can be overwhelming. Just when you think you're up to date on everything, you find a new spec that you didn't know existed, or an existing spec changes in a significant way. Because specifications and implementations are often in flux, keeping up with changes to CSS can be tough. But it is possible.

The World Wide Web Consortium manages a list of <u>current specifications and their status</u>[8]. One of the best ways to become a CSS expert is to carefully read specifications. Specifications explain how features are *supposed* to work, and can help you understand what may be going wrong in your CSS.

If you'd like to track the development and discussion of CSS specifications, try the CSS Working Group's GitHub repository. It contains <u>current drafts</u>[9] of specifications, and a list of <u>issues</u>[10] that

---

[8.] https://www.w3.org/Style/CSS/
[9.] ttps://github.com/w3c/csswg-drafts

developers, browser vendors, and specification editors are working through. The CSS Working Group also has a <u>Twitter account</u>[11] if you'd just like to keep up with developments without getting into the proverbial weeds.

Tracking Browser Support

There are also several resources for tracking browser support for CSS features. <u>Can I Use</u>[12] is perhaps the leader in this space. It tracks support for a range of CSS, HTML, SVG, and JavaScript features in every major browser across several versions.

Most browser vendors also provide their own feature-tracking dashboards. <u>Chrome Status</u>[13] and <u>Microsoft Edge's Platform Status</u>[14] are great ways to keep up with the CSS features currently supported in Chrome and Edge. You can track Firefox's progress with the <u>Firefox Platform Status</u>[15] dashboard. And while Safari doesn't have its own dashboard, its feature set tracks pretty closely to what's found on the <u>WebKit Feature Status</u>[16] page.

Most browser vendors also contribute support data to the robust documentation of the <u>Mozilla Developer Network</u>[17].

Documentation and Tutorials

The Mozilla Developer Network is an amazing resource for web development more generally. It's <u>CSS Reference</u>[18] is perhaps the best on the Web. Almost every property is documented, and each property's page includes examples of use, details whether it's experimental or production-ready, and links to the relevant specification.

For general CSS tricks, tips, and techniques, <u>CSS-Tricks</u>[19] is an excellent resource. The site includes tutorials on CSS and other front-end development topics.

SitePoint.com, too, has a treasure trove of CSS-related material. Its <u>HTML and CSS</u>[20] channel

---

10. https://github.com/w3c/csswg-drafts/issues
11. https://twitter.com/csswg
12. https://caniuse.com/
13. https://www.chromestatus.com/features
14. https://developer.microsoft.com/en-us/microsoft-edge/platform/status/
15. "https://platform-status.mozilla.org/
16. https://webkit.org/status/
17. https://developer.mozilla.org/
18. https://developer.mozilla.org/en-US/docs/Web/CSS
19. https://css-tricks.com
20. https://www.sitepoint.com/html-css/

has lots of CSS tutorials, including topics such as Grid, CSS optimization, authoring tools, and progressive enhancement. If you need help, you can always ask a question in the <u>SitePoint Forums</u>[21].

And that's how this book ends. Of course, reading this book isn't sufficient for becoming a true CSS master. The best way to achieve mastery is by putting knowledge into practice. My hope is that you've come away with a better understanding of a range of CSS topics, including specificity, layout, and project architecture. These topics provide a solid foundation on your journey to mastering CSS.

[21.] https://www.sitepoint.com/community/c/html-css